SUCH MELODIOUS RACKET

Such Melodious Racket

THE LOST HISTORY OF JAZZ

IN CANADA, 1914 – 1949

MARK MILLER

THE MERCURY PRESS

The publisher gratefully acknowledges the financial assistance of the Canada Council for
the Arts and the Ontario Arts Council.

Cover design by Gordon Robertson
Edited by Beverley Daurio
Composition and page design by Task

Printed and bound in Canada by Metropole Litho
Printed on acid-free paper
First Edition
1 2 3 4 5   01 00 99 98 97

Canadian Cataloguing in Publication

Miller, Mark, 1951-
Such melodious racket : the lost history of jazz in Canada, 1914-1949
Includes bibliographical references and index.
ISBN 1-55128-046-9
1. Jazz - Canada - History and criticism. I. Title.
ML3509.C3M649 1997   781.65'0971   C97-932038-0

Represented in Canada by the Literary Press Group
Distributed in Canada by General Distribution Services

The Mercury Press
2569 Dundas Street West
Toronto, Ontario
CANADA M6P 1X7

TABLE OF CONTENTS

Advertisements, *Montreal Star*, 24 Jan 1920.

PREFACE

The research and writing of *Such Melodious Racket: The Lost History of Jazz in Canada, 1914-1949* is music historiography as a form of archeology — that is, an effort first to discover and retrieve the surviving details and then to piece them together in a way that illuminates the introduction, dissemination and early development of jazz in this country, from the Canadian debut in 1914 of an early and important New Orleans ensemble, the Creole Band, to the US debut 35 years later of the Montreal pianist Oscar Peterson.

Consider the evidence that remains in 1997. Few are the musicians still living whose careers date back any farther than 1930. Few, too, are the jazz, or even jazz-related recordings made in Canada in the years before 1950; in many cases those 78s extant are rarities, single copies held in private or archival collections. This is especially significant in view of the central role that recordings have played in legitimizing a musician's place in the history of jazz, which vaunts the oft-recorded journeyman over the little-recorded genius.

Some of the venues where the music itself was performed in Canada before 1950 still stand. The Patricia and Regent hotels continue to do business on Vancouver's East Hastings Street, although what was the commercial heart of the city when Jelly Roll Morton strolled its sidewalks in 1919 and 1920 has long since become Canada's most notorious skid row. And the Palais Royale — castle to Canada's King of Swing, Bert Niosi, during the 1930s and 1940s — remains in good repair on Toronto's Lakeshore Boulevard, a modest landmark for commuters en route to and from Burlington, Hamilton and points west and south.

On the other hand, the legendary nightspots of Montreal's St. Antoine district, centre of the city's black community during the first half of the 20th century, have been demolished. Rockhead's Paradise and the Café St. Michel are now empty lots across from Molson Centre, the new home of the Montreal Canadiens, at the corner of Mountain and St. Antoine — surprisingly small lots in fact, in view of the mythology that surrounds the two clubs. And a nearby hotel, the Chateau Champlain, towers over the site of the former Alberta Lounge, where Oscar Peterson led his first trio in the late 1940s. Gone, too, among many other halls and haunts, are the Palace Pier in Toronto — the name survives as a condominium project overlooking Lake Ontario not far from the Palais Royale — and the Gerrish Street Hall in Halifax.

Bricks and mortar — or wood and nails as the case may be — do not in any event yield very much information about the musicians who pioneered jazz in Canada. The research for *Such Melodious Racket* began instead with the newspapers of the time. There, in the small print — particularly in the centimetre-high lettering of entertainment and classified ads in Canadian dailies — this story took skeletal shape.

Such sources offer the "who," "when" and "where" of early jazz activity in Canada — a name (be it of a musician or a band), as well as a venue and a date. Rarely, alas, do they supply the "what" or the "why" — either the nature of the music played or the aspirations of the musicians who played it. That any background should exist at all about George Paris, a pioneer among Canadian jazz musicians, is entirely a function of his celebrity in another field entirely — sports.

There is some flesh to be found for the bones in the autobiographies or biographies of American musicians like Morton and Eddie Condon and in letters written to the Chicago *Defender* by black performers travelling in Canada. Other details may be gleaned from news items in the trade publications *Billboard, Down Beat, Metronome, Orchestra World* and *Variety*, from reports submitted by locals of the American Federation of Musicians to the union's monthly publication, *The International Musician*, and, finally, from articles in the scattered issues that survive of three short-lived Toronto periodicals devoted to the Canadian jazz and dance-band scene, *Ad Lib* (1944-7), *Prom* (1946) and *Jazz Panorama* (1946-7).

There are also many photographs, some of them clear originals and some of them murky copies made from yellowing newspapers, to put faces to the names. Generally speaking, an image's historical value, rather than its graphic potential, has been the determining factor in whether or not it appears in the pages that follow.

And although there aren't many Canadian voices left to speak for the

1920s, there are more for the 1930s and more again for the 1940s. The text of *Such Melodious Racket* swells with this slowly growing chorus of memories.

The research and writing of history is an ongoing, evolutionary process. Each new investigation confirms, contradicts, clarifies or corrects the work that has preceded it. So it is that *Such Melodious Racket* inevitably modifies in some of these same ways various assertions made in my first book, *Jazz in Canada: Fourteen Lives* (1982), and in John Gilmore's *Swinging in Paradise: The Story of Jazz in Montreal* (1988) and *Who's Who of Jazz in Montreal: Ragtime to 1970* (1989), each of which touches generally, or locally, on the same period.

As the first national history of jazz in Canada, *Such Melodious Racket* is a relatively late addition to jazz literature. Similar studies have long since been undertaken in Great Britain, the major European countries, Australia and the former Soviet Union, each new effort furthering an understanding of the development of jazz internationally, both in relation to and independent of its US origins.

That this has not been as pressing an issue in Canada is in itself revealing. The country's self-image has been so profoundly shaped throughout the 20th century by the immediate and dominant influence of American popular culture, that Canadians might well conclude by default — if they have given any thought to the matter at all — that the country has had no substantive jazz history of its own. Not, at least, prior to the emergence of Oscar Peterson.

While Canada's proximity to the United States meant that American jazz musicians made their way here before they made their way anywhere else, their Canadian sojourns have generally passed unremarked in jazz historiography, as if "Canada," far from being another country, was simply the next stop after Bellingham, Bismarck or Buffalo.

Figuratively speaking, *Such Melodious Racket* draws the 49th parallel through the history of jazz.

These same early visitors, figures as legendary as Jelly Roll Morton and as obscure as L.B. Morgan, helped to establish a jazz tradition in Canada before 1920. In turn, Canadians have played jazz virtually from the outset of its arrival. Yet their existence has also escaped the notice of history, which has accorded them a place only on the occasion of their success in the United

9

States and then often without acknowledging their country of origin, effectively rendering them Americans by omission.

It was Duke Ellington who, after making more than 200 appearances in Canada during his long and exhalted career as a composer and bandleader, discerned a truism that has been largely absent from any discussion of the country's place in the jazz tradition. Ever the gracious guest, he wrote in 1973, "I am well aware that a problem of communication exists between Canada with its twenty-one million people and us, the big neighbour to the south, with our two hundred and three million. Canada has a character and spirit of its own, which we should recognize and never take for granted."[1]

A character and spirit of its own, yes. And in jazz, a history.

Such Melodious Racket celebrates that history.

ACKNOWLEDGEMENTS

Such Melodious Racket: The Lost History of Jazz in Canada, 1914-1949 draws on both oral history and archival research. Many musicians were interviewed between 1992 and 1997 expressly for this project, and others between 1976 and 1992 in connection with my earlier books about jazz in Canada. These individuals are listed with my gratitude in the Appendix; I thank them for their candour and courtesy in face of questions that in some cases took them back more than 60 years.

In matters of archival research, I must first acknowledge the work of Lawrence Gushee, whose investigations into the history of the Creole Band and the early career of Jelly Roll Morton (see bibliography) provided me with starting points for *Such Melodious Racket*, as well as a standard of scholarship to which I might aspire. Dr. Gushee has been a helpful and interested correspondent throughout the progress of the book.

My thanks also to Archie Alleyne, Jack Litchfield, Eugene Miller and Bruce Vermazen for sharing their unpublished research into black jazz in Toronto, the Compo ledgers, "hot dance" bands and the Six Brown Brothers, respectively.

Thanks — for research assistance and/or professional courtesies rendered — are due as well to a variety of collectors, musicians, journalists, kindred spirits and helpful souls spanning four countries.

In Canada — Glen Acorn, Q.C., Bucky Adams, Pat Armstrong (B.C. Sports Hall of Fame & Museum), Stewart Barnett (Vancouver Musicians' Association), Colin Bray, Ross Brethour, Alain Brunet (*La Presse*, Montreal), Lucinda Chodan (Montreal *Gazette*), Clyde Clark, Beverly Cline, Melvin Crump, Roy Forbes, Paul Grosney, Jack Harrison, Paul Hoeffler, Selwyn Jacob, Sheila Marshall, Alan Matheson, Duart Maclean, Kathleen McMorrow (Music Library, University of Toronto), Bill Munson, Maureen Nevins (Music Division, National Library of Canada), John Norris (*Coda*), Ted O'Reilly (CJRT-FM), Art Pilkington, Peter Power (Atlantic Federation of Musicians), Jack Sadler, Joe Showler, Frank Sklove, Michael Snow, Sheldon Taylor, Hart Wheeler, Lloyd Williams and Phil Williams.

In the United States — Paul de Barros, Jim Gallert, Grace Holden, Stan Kuwik, Floyd Levin, Mike Montgomery, Phil Pospychala, Sherrie Tucker and Sheila Vaughan.

In England — Bill Shortt and Laurie Wright. In Australia — Mike Sutcliffe.

Special thanks, for research assistance above and beyond the call of duty, to Nancy Marrelli and Nathalie Hodgson (Concordia University Archives, Montreal), Rita Ness (Metro Toronto Reference Library), Richard Green and Gilles St. Laurent (Music Division, National Library of Canada), Charlotte A. Kolczynski and Metro Voloshin (Boston Public Library), Bruce Boyd Raeburn and Alma D. Williams (Hogan Jazz Archive, Tulane University, New Orleans) and Bozy White (International Association of Jazz Record Collectors' Bruce Davidson Lending Library).

On a personal note, I am grateful to the many friends and colleagues whose expressions of interest and gestures of support have encouraged and sustained my work on *Such Melodious Racket* — James Adams, Salem Alaton, Keith Alcock, Jack Batten, Jack Chambers, Geoff Chapman, Marc Chenard, Lucinda Chodan, Monika Croydon, Ken Drucker, Robin Elliott, Roy Forbes, Raymond Gervais, Richard Green, Paul Hoeffler, Elaine Knapp, Andrea Koziol, David Lancashire, Andrea LeBorgne, David Lee, Jack and Margaret Litchfield, Katie Malloch, Ruth Miller, Eugene Miller, Alan Matheson, Bill Munson, Lorne Nehring, John Norris, Ted O'Reilly, Paul Reynolds, Jack Sadler, Thomas Socknat, Craig Story, Ron Sweetman, Sherrie Tucker, Patricia Wardrop, Kevin Whitehead, Richard Whyte and Robert Witmer.

On the editorial side, I extend my sincerest appreciation to Bev and Don Daurio of The Mercury Press for their willingness to accept *Such Melodious Racket* on its own terms, and further to Bev Daurio, as my editor, first for her quick and sympathetic grasp of my aspirations as well as my difficulties in undertaking such a book, and then for her great care in seeing it into print.

My thanks also to Jack Chambers, Ken Drucker, Anne Forte, Paul Hoeffler, David Lancashire, Jack Litchfield, Sherrie Tucker, Patricia Wardrop and Richard Whyte for their comments on various parts of the manuscript as the writing progressed.

And a word, finally, for the unknown Saskatoon *Star* reviewer who, in a 1918 review of Minnie Burke and her Four Kings of Jazzcopation, turned the phrase that gives this book its title.

The research and writing of *Such Melodious Racket* was supported in part by the Toronto Arts Council's Grants to Writers program (1992) and the Canada Council's Arts Awards Service (1993).

Mark Miller, July 1997

INTRODUCTION

Now, for the second set, we have a surprise for everybody, something which we couldn't advertise because we ourselves didn't know it was going to happen. Up in Canada there's been a very wonderful piano player and all the bands that have travelled through Canada have heard him and raved about him. Today, he flew to New York to hear our concert, and I saw him in the audience, and I prevailed upon him to join our group. I think he's very wonderful and something you ought to hear because we think he's going to be one of the giants of jazz. From Canada — it's his first appearance in the United States — Oscar Peterson...

Norman Granz, Carnegie Hall, New York, September 18, 1949[1]

The Canadian dollar may have been devalued, but the talent the country is exporting these days certainly is on the upgrade. A Montreal citizen, Oscar Peterson, stopped the Norman Granz Jazz at the Philharmonic concert dead cold in its tracks here last month.

Michael Levin, *Down Beat*, October 21, 1949[2]

Oscar Peterson's nationality is crucial to any assessment of his career... it explains why Oscar's formative years as a musician went unremarked, so that when he finally appeared in the United States, he burst upon the American jazz scene with the impact of a new planet.

Richard Palmer, *Oscar Peterson*, 1984[3]

When Oscar Peterson stepped onstage at Carnegie Hall in New York on the night of September 18, 1949, he established a Canadian presence in jazz that this most-American-of-music had not seen before.

Canadian jazz musicians had been working in the United States since the 1920s. Some, like the influential arranger Gil Evans (1912-88, of Toronto), were taken there as children and effectively grew up as Americans. Others, among them Peterson's fellow Montrealer, trumpeter Maynard Ferguson, left Canada as professional musicians.

None, however, had Peterson's immediate impact. None would have his enduring success.

Jazz in 1949 was closing out the sixth decade in its evolution as America's great gift to the world of music. There remain many unanswered questions surrounding its origins but the consensus of historical interpretation, in brief, points to the confluence in New Orleans of several musical traditions brought together over time by a variety of local social, economic and cultural factors.[4]

In the beginning a music unique to African-Americans, jazz synthesized the expressive and extemporaneous qualities of blues, spirituals and work songs, the rhythmic vivacity of ragtime and the instrumentation and sheer presence of brass bands into a startling new sound. The same principles of synthesis have remained a constant to jazz ever since, renewing it several times over in the course of the 20th century.

The original elements of jazz revealed their sources clearly. Blues, spirituals and work songs echoed the melodies, cross rhythms and call-and-response patterns of West African music, an aural tradition carried to America under the duress of slavery. Ragtime and band music, on the other hand, reflected the more composerly notions of the European cultures that now dominated the New World.

Each of these elements was present to one degree or another in the musical life of New Orleans by the late 1800s. New Orleans itself was the most European of US cities, with its French heritage and Spanish influence. At the same time, it had both a large black population and an affluent community of Creoles of Color, the latter of black and French or Spanish ancestry.

The distinction between blacks and Creoles of Color is particularly important to the history of jazz. The Creoles of Color identified themselves with their European culture and aspired in most of their endeavours, including music, to its ideals. In 1894, however, Louisiana passed a law that, for the express purpose of segregating blacks from whites, defined any person with African ancestry — no matter how far removed — as black.

Creoles of Color saw their social and economic standing decline on all fronts. Musically, the Creoles, with their formal training and "proper" instrumental technique in the European manner, found themselves working of necessity in the company of black players who had come by their skills — no less than their instruments, which were often relics from the Civil and Spanish-American wars — rather more haphazardly. Each group of musicians was affected by the traditions, methods and interests of the other; the resulting exchange, accommodation and eventual melding of ideas were formative steps in the development of jazz.

New Orleans offered its Creole and black musicians a variety of employment opportunities. As both a Gulf of Mexico seaport, and a major centre of commerce to the US south, the Crescent City boasted a large red-light district, Storyville, named for the politician who spearheaded the legalization of prostitution within its boundaries in 1897. Pianists worked in the smaller Storyville brothels, and ensembles performed at the larger establishments — until civic authorities closed down "The District" in 1917.

Brass players, meanwhile, were heard throughout the city, playing for funeral processions, parades, picnics and dances. Charles (Buddy) Bolden (1833-1931) is one of the few bandsmen known by name from this early period; by reputation a cornetist of great power, he is often identified as the "first" jazz musician on the basis of his activities during the years around 1900,[5] although such a designation is usually qualified by the recollections of his contemporaries to the effect that he was a blues player whose improvisational fluency, by the standard of later jazz soloists, was limited.

New Orleans musicians started to carry this transitional form of jazz to the rest of the United States before 1910. Cornetist Ernest Coycault and bassist Bill Johnson visited Los Angeles in 1908; pianist Jelly Roll Morton began moving around the country in vaudeville at about the same time. And, as will be seen in *Such Melodious Racket*, Johnson's Creole Band brought the new music to Canada in 1914.

As jazz continued its gradual evolution through the 1910s and into the

1920s, many of its proponents participated in the general migration of southern blacks to the newly industrialized north. Morton settled in Chicago in 1914 for three years before moving to the west coast. Cornetist Freddie Keppard of the Creole Band was living in the Windy City by 1917, as was soprano saxophonist and clarinetist Sidney Bechet, albeit briefly. A second important New Orleans cornetist, Joe (King) Oliver, arrived in Chicago early in 1919. Oliver in turn summoned a third, Louis Armstrong, in the summer of 1922. The presence of these and other New Orleans musicians, some of them white, naturally inspired a younger generation of local players, virtually all of them white — notably cornetist Bix Beiderbecke and clarinetist Benny Goodman, who began to make their own mark on jazz in the mid-1920s.

Sidney Bechet and Louis Armstrong soon emerged as the first great soloists from what had been essentially an ensemble music. Jazz in its original form thrived on the casual polyphony created by some combination of clarinet, cornet (later trumpet) and trombone atop the vigorous rhythms of, variously, piano, guitar or banjo, tuba or string bass, and drums. The effect was carefree and self-involved: emotions were openly and often gutterally expressed, humour and novelty happily indulged.

If early jazz was unwritten music, though, and thus allowed some latitude for variation in renditions of the blues, rags and popular songs that made up its repertoire, it was not yet fully improvised in the sense that jazz has come to be understood as improvised — that is, conceived afresh at each new performance. As often as not, the content of an "improvisation" was worked out over time from a common body of melodic ideas and embellishments, personalized with the player's own signature "licks" and then repeated more or less verbatim from one night to the next. By the mid-1920s, however, Armstrong and Bechet — both virtuoso instrumentalists — were departing freely from memory in their solos and playing with increasing independence from their fellow musicians.[6]

Their example — Armstrong's with Oliver's Creole Jazz Band, the Fletcher Henderson Orchestra in New York and his own Hot Fives and Sevens, Bechet's in a miscellany of recorded settings — both electrified and revolutionized jazz, establishing the pivotal role that soloists would play alongside the great bandleaders, composers and arrangers as the music moved from the New Orleans and Chicago styles of the 1920s through swing during the 1930s and on to bebop in the 1940s.

The history of jazz cannot, of course, be reduced to a single, continuous line of development. A variety of external factors have influenced and even altered its course, among them the interest taken in jazz by a powerful US entertainment industry quick to identify the enormous potential market for these audacious new sounds. Thus a musical form that had developed according to its own logic for the previous 25 years was suddenly subject to new and largely commercial considerations, giving rise in the early 1920s to such variants as pretentious "symphonic" jazz and jaunty "hot dance" music, each moderating in some way the vivacious rhythmic, melodic and emotional qualities of jazz in its original form.

As the core traditions of jazz continued to evolve through the 20th century, they would have both pure and popular manifestations. The latter — precisely because of their broader dissemination — were often more readily heard in Canada than the former, and had a significant effect on the way in which jazz would develop in this country.

Canada shares with the United States many common elements of culture, including language, technological sophistication, democratic principles of government and general affluence. It also differs in several respects, not least in matters of demography.

Though marginally the larger country, Canada has but a tenth the population of the United States, based for the most part in cities and towns near the border that divides the two countries. The black population of Canada has been proportionately even smaller, and the relationship between blacks and whites has been far less a defining issue in Canadian history.

(It has been an issue nonetheless: although visiting black American musicians and entertainers are quoted favourably at several points in *Such Melodious Racket* on the subject of the racial tolerance that they found in Canada during the 1920s, their comments must be read comparatively against the background of their experiences at home, especially in the US south.

These remarks should not be taken as evidence that racism was absent from Canadian society.)

For its size and underpopulation, Canada is a country of local and regional rather than national perspectives. Typically, the early history of jazz in Canada is a history of jazz in the major cities, each an insular "scene" with only tenuous of links to the others. The connections that were so important to early American jazz history between New Orleans and Chicago, Chicago and New York, and later Kansas City and New York, had few if any parallels in Canada, where musicians generally limited themselves to their own regions. Those of a mind to advance their careers looked to the United States as often as they looked elsewhere in Canada.

Musicians in Montreal and Toronto, for example, were more likely to know about jazz in New York, Chicago or Los Angeles than in each others' cities — let alone in Vancouver, more than 4000 kilometres away. Indeed, the flow of recordings from the United States and the strength of US radio in Canada, not to mention the availability of publications like *Down Beat* and *Metronome*, kept Canadian musicians and fans alike fully abreast of the American scene. Jazz in Canada, meanwhile, had no comparable means of promulgating itself, either nationally or internationally, which made the American influence that much more indomitable.

Only a few jazz recordings were made in Canada during the 1920s, virtually none in the 1930s, and a few more beginning in the mid-1940s, among them Oscar Peterson's first efforts. Private (or commercial) radio initially offered jazz some exposure (including a broadcast by a black quartet, Gumps Jazz Hounds, on Edmonton station CJCA at the remarkably early date of October 1922) but private radio was also generally local radio. Network radio, on the other hand, first organized in Canada by the Canadian National Railway in 1923, offered the country's jazz musicians very limited exposure — when it offered them any exposure at all.

The CNR was followed as a national broadcaster by the Canadian Radio Broadcasting Commission in 1932, and the CRBC by the Canadian Broad-casting Corporation in 1936. To these organizations, the last two publicly owned, fell the task of giving Canadians a voice on airways that were dominated by the powerful US networks — CBS, NBC, Mutual and, in time, ABC. American programming, which included jazz and dance music, could be heard in Canada either directly from nearby US cities or selectively by relay on private Canadian stations and, in some instances, on the Canadian network of the day. In other words, even Canadian broadcast content could be of US origin.

Jazz was most often presented nationally on the CBC in the context of variety shows. The young Robert Farnon, later an inestimably influential arranger and conductor in London studios, contributed the occasional jazzy cornet solo to *The Happy Gang* from Toronto, while Oscar Peterson was featured on such shows as *Recipe Tunes* and *Light Up and Listen* from Montreal. Programs devoted exclusively to jazz were rare, however, and not often broadcast outside their originating region; the Ray Norris Quintet's *Serenade in Rhythm* and Bob Smith's long-running record show *Hot Air*, for two, were heard from Vancouver during the 1940s only in western Canada.

Bert Niosi, Canada's King of Swing, nevertheless had both national and regional series throughout the decade, and Oscar Peterson was eventually heard on his own cross-country broadcasts — 15-minute spots weekly during the summers of 1946 and 1947. So it was that Niosi and Peterson, who also toured and recorded during the late 1940s, became the first musicians to transcend the regionalism of the Canadian jazz scene. Niosi, now nearing 40, appeared content with his achievement. Not so Peterson, a generation younger; his move to the international stage was as inevitable as it would be dramatic.

In the years since his Carnegie Hall debut in 1949, Oscar Peterson has enjoyed undiminished celebrity as a recording and touring artist. His discography exceeded 130 albums under his own name alone by the mid-1990s and his concert itinerary has taken him from his home in Montreal — later Toronto, and still later nearby Mississauga — to halls throughout the world. Few jazz musicians, whatever their country of origin, could claim greater popularity.

Jazz in Canada, meanwhile, flourished rather more modestly for many years, the country's musicians generally following at a cautious distance the lead of their American contemporaries through bebop and its variant styles in the 1950s, the avant-garde of the 1960s and fusion jazz of the 1970s. Significantly, two Canadians who have been in the forefront of the music's continuing evolution, the Montreal-born pianist Paul Bley and the Toronto-born trumpeter Kenny Wheeler, left Canada in the early 1950s, Bley for the United States and Wheeler for England.

In the 1980s and 1990s, finally, Canada caught up with the world. The country's festivals, led by events in Montreal and Vancouver, have become justly renowned for their vision and integrity, while several Canadians have made impressive strides on the world stage, among them the veterans Ed Bickert, Oliver Jones, Peter Leitch and Rob McConnell — the last with his big band, the Boss Brass — and the younger Seamus Blake, Jane Bunnett, D.D. Jackson, Diana Krall and Renee Rosnes. Many others are waiting in the wings.

It is against this rising international profile that *Such Melodious Racket* returns to the early years and forgotten musicians of jazz in Canada; there can be no better time to illuminate the past than that moment when the future seems brightest.

TIME LINE

1914 — The Creole Band's first Canadian tour (Chapter 1)

1916 — The Creole Band returns (1)

1917 — Morgan Brothers' Syncopated Jaz Band at Cabaret Garden in
Calgary (3); the Tennessee Ten's first Canadian tour (2); George
Paris forms band for Patricia Cabaret in Vancouver (4)

1918 — Westmount Jazz Band at Victoria Hall in Montreal (4)

1919 — Jelly Roll Morton arrives in Vancouver (5); Original Winnipeg
Jazz Babies tour western Canada (4)

1920 — Yerkes' Blue Bird Orchestra records in Montreal (3); Millard
Thomas and Famous Chicago Jazz Band in first season at Princess
Theatre in Quebec City (6)

1921 — Jelly Roll Morton leaves Vancouver (5)

1922 — Shirley Oliver and Gumps Jazz Hounds on CJCA in Edmonton
(7); Melody Kings record in Montreal (9)

1924 — Charles (Bass) Foster at Star Theatre in St. John's (8); Guy
Lombardo and Royal Canadians record in Richmond, Indiana
(9); Millard Thomas and Famous Chicago Novelty Orchestra
record in Montreal (6); and New Princes' Toronto Band records
in London (9)

1925 — Carroll Dickerson's *Charleston Revue* tours western Canada (8);
Smiling Billy Steward's Alabama Jazz Band at the Zenith Café in
Saskatoon (10); Gilbert Watson records in Montreal (9)

1926 — Dave Caplan's "Toronto-Band from Canada" records in Berlin
(9)

1927 — Orange Blossoms at Casa Loma in Toronto (10); Chocolate
Dandies at Silver Slipper in Toronto (10)

1929 — Alphonso Trent's 12 Black Aces in southern Ontario (10)

1931 — Noel Allen forms Harlem Aces in Toronto (12); Myron Sutton
and Canadian Ambassadors at Gatineau Country Club in
Aylmer, Quebec (11)

1933 — Bert Niosi stars 17-year association with Palais Royale in Toronto (13)

1935 — Ollie Wagner's Knights of Harlem tour western Canada (12); Rex Battle's Maple Leaf Orchestra at Bob-Lo Island, Detroit River (13)

1936 — Bert Niosi proclaimed Canada's King of Swing (13); Irving Laing at Auditorium, Montreal (13)

1937 — Sandy De Santis at Palomar Ballroom in Vancouver, challenges Niosi's title (13)

1938 — Trump Davidson Orchestra tours Britain with Ray Noble (13); Onyx Club opens in Toronto (14)

1939 — Ollie Wagner reorganizes Knights of Harlem in Winnipeg (12)

1941 — Ray Norris' *Serenade in Rhythm* on air from CBC Vancouver (14)

1943 — Chris Gage leads first band at Silver Dell in Regina (15)

1944 — Cy McLean Orchestra opens at Club Top Hat in Toronto (12)

1945 — Oscar Peterson begins recording career in Montreal (15); Maynard Ferguson leads first orchestra at Verdun Pavilion (13); Bert Niosi Orchestra tours western Canada (13)

1946 — Oscar Peterson tours western Canada (15); Queen City Jazz Band active in Toronto (14)

1947 — Louis Metcalf's International Band starts two-and-a-half year engagement at Café St. Michel in Montreal (14); Bert Niosi Septet records in Montreal (13); Oscar Peterson Trio begins two-year engagement at Alberta Lounge in Montreal (15)

1948 — Moe Koffman records for Main Stem in Buffalo (14)

1949 — Oscar Peterson makes US debut at Carnegie Hall, New York (15)

CHAPTER ONE

The Creole Band

The history of jazz in Canada begins in Winnipeg on a Monday afternoon in 1914.

Some time after 2:30 p.m. on September 21, six black musicians took to the stage of the Pantages Theatre at the downtown corner of Market Street and Main in this thriving railway town, the gateway to Canada's west. In what was effectively their vaudeville debut, the performers appeared in the work clothes of field hands on a southern US plantation and, in the words of the Winnipeg *Tribune* the following day, "[played] some weird instruments in a wonderful way."[1]

The act was advertised in the Winnipeg newspapers as the New Orleans Creole Ragtime Band and listed in the US trade paper *Variety* as Creole's Band. It is known to history as the Original Creole Orchestra, the first group of New Orleans musicians to take the new music known as jazz well beyond the US south. Back home in the Crescent City, a teenaged Louis Armstrong had only recently been released from the waifs' home where he received his first cornet lessons; in Washington, DC, Edward Kennedy (Duke) Ellington, now in high school, was giving thought to his first piano piece, *Soda Fountain Rag*.

The youngest of the Creole Band's six men, Freddie Keppard, 25, stood as its dominant figure, one of New Orleans' cornet "Kings" in a line of succession that began with Buddy Bolden and would soon include Louis Armstrong. The pioneering string bassist Bill Johnson, 42, was the band's senior member, its leader and its manager. Clarinetist George Baquet, who had been the great Sidney Bechet's first teacher in New Orleans, was also on hand for this tour. Violinist and saxophonist James Palao, trombonist Edward Vincent and guitarist Norwood Williams completed the sextet.

Organized by Johnson just a few months earlier in Los Angeles, the Creole Band had come to the attention of the enterprising theatrical promoter Alexander Pantages in August when it played for a prize fight, drawing notice

Creole Band, 1914. From left, back row: Edward Vincent, Freddie Keppard, George Baquet, Bill Johnson. Front row: Dink Johnson, James Palao, Norwood Williams.
[Al Rose Collection, Hogan Jazz Archive, Tulane University, New Orleans]

in the local press for its raucous, ringside performance between rounds.[2] In a matter of weeks, it added the singer, dancer and comedian H. Morgan Prince and then joined the more than 60 acts that toured, five to a bill, on Pantages' circuit of theatres in the western United States and Canada.

Following an initial week in Winnipeg, the Creole Band and its four fellow acts proceeded by train west across the prairies to the smaller cities of Edmonton and Calgary; some 2200 kilometres from Los Angeles and 3300 kilometres from New Orleans, the troupe found itself travelling in an early autumn storm that covered southern Alberta with more than 100 centimetres of snow. The tour moved on to Spokane and Seattle, returned to Canada in November for engagements in Vancouver and Victoria, then continued with stops in Tacoma, Portland, San Francisco, Oakland, Los Angeles and San Diego, before winding up in Salt Lake City in early January 1915.

In each city the Creole Band played downbill to Frances Clare ("The dainty darling of vaudeville") and Guy Rawson, who presented the musical sketch "Yesterdays." The Great Harrahs, a roller-skating duo, were also on the bill, as were the "Irish Chatterbox" Arthur Whitlaw — a monologuist — and McConnell & Niemeyer, a song-and-dance team.

The Creole Band's initial Canadian appearances came at a time when the country was fully caught up in the excitement of a world war declared — and joined — only weeks before against Germany. By the time the band returned to Canada in November, the first contingent of soldiers had departed for advanced training in England. Headlines on Canadian newspapers in the fall of 1914 mirrored the country's preoccupation with events on French soil several thousand kilometres away.

According to brief reports in those same newspapers, the Creole Band was generally received with enthusiasm, although the similarity of the comments from the various cities in which the band appeared would suggest that reviewers were guided in their initial responses by publicity material supplied by the Pantages chain. Even so, the notices offer several clues as to the nature of the performance.

According to G. Ten Wright of the Edmonton *Bulletin*, "The big hit of the day was secured by the Creole Orchestra. Here half a dozen culle'd gentlemen play slide trombone, cornet, clarinet, violin, mandolin and bass viol. Another [H. Morgan Prince], dressed as everyone is taught to believe Old Black Joe looked, sings the song of that name. Both it and 'My Old Kentucky Home' proved most melodious and the applause was prolonged and sincere."[3]

Wright's counterpart at the *Journal* was less sympathetic: "The Creole band, which was given tumultuous applause, made a lot of noise, but that was all it was."[4]

Wright reaffirmed the act's success later in the week. "What might be styled the real hit of the show comes [third on the bill] in the form of the original New Orleans Creole orchestra. The curtain rises on a barn yard scene in Virginia with five [sic] dusky lads from the south playing a 'rag' on their various instruments."[5]

Word of its sensational performances appears to have preceded the Creole Band to Calgary, where it was the only act other than the dainty darling herself to be listed by name in local newspaper ads. Carl Quiller of the *Herald*, however, was ambivalent in his comments. "The New Orleans Creole musicians provide music of a rather noisy kind on a wide variety of instruments," he wrote at the end of his review. "Ragtime and old plantation melodies constitute their repertoire." Quiller took greater interest in the audience's lusty rendition of *It's a Long Way to Tipperary*, sung at the close of the opening-day matinee in honour of the fighting men overseas.[6]

Whatever the critical line, though, the Creole Band proved a popular success at each new stop. After only six weeks on the circuit, it would be touted by the Vancouver *Sun* as the "famous New Orleans Creole troupe." Its music, however, continued to defy description. The *Sun*, for example, previewed the act quaintly as "a splendid orchestra and glee club."[7]

If the word "jazz" does not appear in any references to the Creole Band at this time, Freddie Keppard, Bill Johnson *et al.* were no less jazz musicians. To the extent that the term was in general use at all by 1914, it apparently had sexual rather than musical connotations. Soon enough, "jazz" (and its variants "jass" or "jaz") would be used to describe the first bands to arrive in Chicago from New Orleans, notably those of the white musicians Tom Brown and Johnny Stein. But it was not until early 1917, when some of Stein's former musicians — now in New York — made their first recordings as the Original Dixieland Jass (or Jazz) Band, that the word came to identify a national musical craze and, soon enough, an international musical revolution.

The 20-minute vaudeville act that the Creole Band presented on Pantages stages very likely differed from the rougher, prototypical "jazz" performances it had offered so recently around Los Angeles. For one thing, the band's drummer there, Bill Johnson's younger brother Oliver (also known as "Dink"), did not participate in its Pantages tours, whether by personal choice or in view of the clamour that he would have added to what was already spirited by vaudeville standards. Keppard alone was reportedly loud enough that patrons in the first few rows of a theatre often sought refuge further back.[8]

Moreover, the Creole Band appears to have been groomed for its new audiences. In a preview of the Winnipeg engagement, the *Tribune* describes the act as "the latest specialty from the Pantages production department."[9] Certainly the presence of H. Morgan Prince's "Old Black Joe" character is inconsistent with a New Orleans band and, like the plantation setting of the skit, reflected the limited and demeaning range of images that black performers could present in vaudeville at the time — images that were born in the mock emulation of blacks offered by white minstrelsy during the mid-19th century[10] and then sustained, and inadvertently legitimized, by black minstrelsy beginning in the 1870s.

Nevertheless, the distinction between the Creole Band's "rags" and what in less than three years would be called "jazz" — if in fact there was a distinction at all — would only have been a matter of rhythmic evolution. At that, the cigar-chewing Johnson was already known to play string bass in a vigorous pizzicato style,[11] signalling the music's transition from the proper 2/4 strut of ragtime to the forward 4/4 swing of jazz. Keppard, meanwhile, was described as "the greatest hot trumpeter in existence" by fellow New Orleans Creole Jelly Roll Morton, who had made his acquaintance as early as 1907. "There was no end to his ideas," Morton enthused, "he could play one chorus eight or ten different ways."[12]

The significance of the Creole Band's five weeks in western Canada in 1914 is largely symbolic. That the first band to take New Orleans jazz widely afield would in fact have played Winnipeg and four other Canadian cities *before* it appeared in Chicago (where it opened in February 1915 at the Grand Theater) is no more than a quirk of history.

At this early date, live performance was the sole means of carrying jazz beyond the major urban US centres. Recordings enjoyed increasing popularity but were restricted to classical, popular and novelty repertoires until the first Original Dixieland Jazz Band titles, *Livery Stable Blues* and *Dixieland Jass Band One-Step*, were issued in the United States in March 1917 and in Canada two months later.[13] Radio, which would play such an important role in the dissemination of popular music of all descriptions in later decades, had reached only an experimental stage by 1914. The era's other means of circulating music, scores and piano rolls, played a significant role in the rise of ragtime, which prefigured jazz, but could not begin to capture the spontaneity of jazz itself.

If there was virtually no precedent in Canada for the Creole Band's boisterous improvisations,[14] there were nevertheless several Canadians, most of them white, who had composed piano rags and cakewalks in the style popularized by such black American composers as Scott Joplin and James Scott.

A Rag Time Spasm, 1899. Sheet music, cover page.
[Dorothy Farqharson Collection, Mills Memorial Library, McMaster University, Hamilton, Ontario]

The earliest Canadian titles known to reflect the ragtime craze, W. H. (William) Hodgins' *A Rag Time Spasm* and G. A. Adams' *The Cake Winner*, were both issued in Toronto in 1899; they followed by two years the first published rag in the United States, *The Mississippi Rag*, and were coincident with the appearance of Joplin's initial efforts in the idiom, *Original Rags* and *Maple Leaf Rag*.

The black Canadian composer Nathaniel Dett (1882-1943, of the Niagara Falls, Ontario, area) completed *After The Cakewalk — March Cakewalk* in 1900, at which point, according to some accounts, he was still a Canadian resident, and the distinguished white American ragtime composer Joseph F. Lamb wrote his early *Walper House Rag* (1903) while living in Berlin (later Kitchener), Ontario.

Jean-Baptiste Lafrenière, a theatre pianist in Montreal, and Charles Wellinger, who was similarly employed in Hamilton, Ontario, each completed piano rags among a variety of other compositions. Lafrenière's *Raggity Rag* and *Balloon Rag* were published in 1907 and 1911, respectively. Wellinger's *That Captivating Rag* appeared in 1914, and his *Intermission Rag* in 1916.

A younger theatre musician in Montreal, the pianist Harry Thomas (1890-1941, from Bristol, England), saw his *Rag Tags Rag* published in 1909.

With his mentor, the Strand Theatre's diminutive Willie Eckstein (1888–1963, of Montreal), Thomas subsequently wrote *Perpetual Rag* and *Delirious Rag*, recording both pieces as piano rolls in New York late in 1916.

Eckstein, Thomas and another, still younger Eckstein protégé, Vera Guilaroff (1902–1976, from London), were expert in the flourishing "novelty" rag style of the late 1910s and recorded frequently during the 1920s; their extravagant interpretive liberties, including extemporization in the classical tradition, in some respects parallelled — but cannot be taken for — jazz.

The Creole Band returned to Canadian Time — as vaudeville artists described their travels north of the border — during the summer of 1916. In the interim, the New Orleans musicians had made their New York debut in December 1915 and toured from January to May 1916 in *Town Topics*, a revue that at one point starred Sophie Tucker.

Louis Delisle ("Big Eye" Louis Nelson) and Freddie Keppard, circa 1916.
[Hogan Jazz Archive, Tulane University, New Orleans]

Back on the Pantages circuit in Canada as of mid-July, with clarinetist Louis Delisle (also known as "Big Eye" Louis Nelson) replacing George Baquet, the band again fulfilled week-long engagements in Winnipeg, Edmonton and Calgary. It also appeared for one night at the Orpheum Theatre in the small town of Lethbridge, Alberta, en route to Great Falls, Montana. After several other US stops, the band returned in September to Vancouver and Victoria.

For this tour, it took second billing to Jesse Lasky's Society Buds, a troupe of young women who performed a "musical comedietta." The show also featured the acrobats Welsh, Mealy and Montrose, a French-Canadian slack-wire artist named Kirtelli and an impressionist, Claudia Coleman.

In the main, notice taken in the local press again followed the lead suggested by the Pantages publicity department, which had offered "wild and untamed music" as the catchphrase of the tour. On occasion, however, local critics took some initiative of their own. "The music is weird, reminding one of an old circus band," noted a reviewer from the Manitoba *Free Press*.[15] "The selections are well rendered, even though a trifle weird at times," echoed his counterpart from the Vancouver *Sun*, attributing the unusual sound to the combination of instruments involved.[16]

The instrumentation was also noted in a remarkably perceptive review that appeared in the Victoria *Daily Colonist*. "Johnson's Creole Band was billed to play wild, untamed music and did not fail. To begin with, the musicians have a combination possibly without precedent in the musical world. Nobody but six negro eccentric players could shatter so many rules of a well-integrated band and make it so enticing to an audience. The cornet, clarinet, violin, guitar, trombone and double bass are played by individuals with seemingly absolute indifference to what the other man was doing but they always managed to arrive at appointed places in full accord."[17]

A musicologist in 1916 might have described the Creole Band's music in more precise, if less charitable terms, but there can be no doubt that this was jazz as the world would soon know it.

CHAPTER TWO
Canadian Time

The Creole Band continued to travel until 1918 but did not return to Canada. By then, however, several other jazz-oriented, song-and-dance acts were appearing on Pantages, Orpheum, Keith and independent stages across North America. The most successful was the Tennessee Ten, which toured the Orpheum circuit in western Canada in 1917 and 1919. Unlike the Creole Band, the Ten also played in central Canada, making three appearances in Toronto between 1918 and 1921 and single stops in Montreal and Hamilton in 1921.

The Tennessee Ten performed under the direction of U.S. (Ulysses) "Slow Kid" Thompson, a dancer and comedian noted for his acrobatic skill. Florence Mills was one of the troupe's two singers from 1917 to 1921 before taking the leading roles in the revues *Shuffle Along* and *Plantation Revue* that would make her one of the most celebrated black performers of the 1920s.[1]

The turnover among the Ten's seven musicians, meanwhile, appears to have been high. Composite personnel during the period in which the troupe travelled on Canadian Time included several men who would soon appear in New York or Chicago on some of the earliest black jazz recordings of the 1920s: cornetists Thomas Morris and Gus Aiken, clarinetists Horace Eubanks and Jimmy O'Bryant, banjo player James Turner, bassist Ed Garland and drummers Curtis Mosby and Paul Barbarin, the latter a member of the Ten during its engagements in October 1921 at Shea's Theatre in Toronto and the Lyric in Hamilton.[2]

Like the Creole Band before it, the Tennessee Ten made its Canadian debut — November 5, 1917 — in Winnipeg. Publicity material for this first northern tour, which also included week-long engagements in Calgary and Vancouver, promised the troupe in "Ethiopian songs, dances and antics, introducing their Famous Jazz Band..." And, again like the Creole Band, the Ten appeared in a rural setting, performing before a painted backdrop of a log cabin "interior," complete with door, window, fireplace and portraits of George Washington and Abraham Lincoln.

A review in the Winnipeg *Tribune* at the outset of the Ten's second round of western Canadian stops in August 1919 detailed the proceedings: "After a little preliminary around-the-old-cabin-door stuff the act comes to its raison d'etre, the dissemination of thirty-second degree jazz [i.e., of the highest level, probably an allusion to the Masonic order]. Jazz[,] as she is performed by the people who invented it[,] and a real dancer[,] make the act. The reception accorded the Ten was a near knockout. The applause kept up until all the Ten could do was say they didn't have anything else to put on."[3]

The response was no less effusive in Victoria, where the Tennessee Ten appeared en route from Calgary to Vancouver. A reporter for the Victoria *Daily Times* described "a scene almost unprecedented in Victoria... an overwhelming chorus of whistles, catcalls and loud applause continued for ten minutes as the audience strove to obtain an encore." The Ten, according to the *Times* review, "contributed a number of plantation songs and 'buck' dances, finishing up with a jazz band exposition. The dancing director in his endeavor to secure the maximum of noise from each instrumentalist, adopted

Tennessee Ten, *Hamilton Spectator*, 8 Oct 1921.

poses and threw somersaults which kept the audience in a continual roar of laughter and elicited the tremendous ovation which followed the act."[4]

The jazz musicians were in fact presented as comics whose "business" lay in their efforts, under Thompson's direction, to tune up. Finally — as Thompson told historians Jean and Marshall Stearns, many years later — "the band would hit a terrible chord and I would do a front somersault as if I was surprised out of my skin."[5]

As often as not, jazz in vaudeville was played in precisely this manner — for laughs. Far from being a nascent folk or art form, it was musical slapstick, a novelty, a riot of unseemly sounds that departed from — in fact, defied — the written note. Indeed, the more unseemly the sounds, the better. In promotion, practice and perception, this was a recurring theme whenever jazz was presented on the theatrical stage, as it would be in Canada well into the 1930s.

In Toronto, the Vernon Five, forgotten to history but touted at the time as "expert exponents of the new music known as jazz," performed at Shea's Theatre in late 1917. According to the *Globe*'s septuagenarian critic E.R. Parkhurst, the (presumably) white quintet of saxophones, xylophone, piano and drums "succeeded at times in making a diabolical noise, thus justifying their claims to [being] a 'Jazz' company."[6]

Four months later, another white act, Minnie Burke and her Four Kings of Jazzcopation, split a week between the Empire Theatre in Saskatoon and the Regina Theatre in Regina. Local reactions reflected the sometimes perplexing first impressions that the new music made. "Minnie Burke affords Saskatoon its first glimpse of a simon pure jazz band in action," reported the *Star* with some enthusiasm. "Her 'Four Jazz Kings' are freek [sic] musicians and make such melodious racket while Miss Burke, who calls herself 'The Skyrocket of Vaudeville,' breezes all over the stage, stepping to the lively syncopation of the piano–cornet–clarionet–drums barrage in the rear."[7]

Burke was greeted rather more cautiously in Regina. "For the first time, Regina theatre patrons have an opportunity of hearing and seeing 'jazz,'" noted the *Leader*. "Exactly what 'jazz' is, no one seems to really know except that it gives musicians an opportunity of performing all kind of weird gymnastic stunts while playing...".[8]

The *Leader* followed helpfully in April with a syndicated Saturday feature, "Music in the Home," that posed the question "What is a jazz band?" The column pointed to the saxophone as the music's defining element. "Do you know how it can sob, whine, wheeze and yelp?... It is not the violin, piano; or even the drums or banjo that make jazz so different. It is the saxaphone [sic] — the most curious, whimsical and humorously sad of all instruments."[9]

In these early years, in fact, "jazz" was synonymous with any broad musical interpretation, no matter what the material. The Tennessee Five Jazz Band that toured the Pantages circuit in 1918 with four dancers in *Cabaret De Luxe* included Rachmaninoff's *Prelude* and Dvorak's *Humoresque* in its act. "R.J." (Rhynd Jamieson), the theatre and music critic for the Vancouver *Sun*, was not impressed, huffing that "the aggressive chap who fiddles should not fool with such numbers."[10]

Typically, "jazz" was interchangeable with "novelty," "syncopation" (or "syncopated"), "pep" and "ginger," each referring to one or another perceived quality of the music in question, whether its exaggeration, its vivacity or its energy. By later standards — those, for example, that would call into question the authenticity of even the Original Dixieland Jazz Band on the basis of its stiff syncopation and lack of true improvisation — some of the music described in these terms may not have been jazz at all.

Vaudeville clearly played a role of mixed significance in the dissemination of jazz to Canadians, no less than to Americans in the many US centres that lay off the New Orleans/Mississippi River/Chicago axis. Inasmuch as vaudeville was a mainstream, if generally low-brow entertainment, its jazz acts reached a broad cross-section of the population. Consider the Creole Band's Canadian itinerary in 1914 and 1916: five weeks on each tour, six days of shows every week, and two or three shows per day — at least 60 and perhaps as many as 90 performances altogether, as well as street parades at each stop. How many thousands of Canadians — indeed how many *tens* of thousands — would have first heard jazz in this manner, knowingly or not?

At the same time, jazz was presented in terms that were unflattering —

as an energetic novelty based on racial stereotypes rooted in minstrelsy —
and in some respects misleading. Despite the fact that jazz is a music clearly
of urban origin, the Creole Band, the Tennessee Ten and others like
Robinson's Syncopators in the early 1920s were depicted as rustics. Moreover, many of vaudeville's so-called jazz acts had tenuous ties at best to the
tradition epitomized by Freddie Keppard, Bill Johnson, George Bacquet, Ed
Garland, Paul Barbarin and their fellow Creole Band and Tennessee Ten
members.

Other vaudeville performers, though not expressly jazz artists by nature,
helped to establish a general context for the new music's growing popularity.
Some were singers, including Sophie Tucker (The Last of the Red Hot
Mamas) and Blossom Seeley. Others were instrumental ensembles, among
them the black Musical Spillers and a highly successful and influential white
Canadian act, Ottawa's Six Brown Brothers. All were skilled entertainers who
put their particular novelty across with great panache.

Tucker and Blossom Seeley — the latter appearing in *Seeley's Syncopated
Studio* with cornetist Ray Lopez and others — parlayed mock-black vocal
styles into star billing on the Orpheum circuit for many years, preceding the
arrival of jazz in the mid-1910s and then capitalizing on its popularity in the
early 1920s. Minnie Burke, meanwhile, continued to tour until 1919, latterly
joined on Canadian Time by Eva Shirley, Ruth Roye, Aunt Jemima and her
Eight Syncopating Bakers and Mme Zenda — the last travelling with her
Famous Psychic Jazz Band, which promised to play "any melody called for
by thought transference."[11]

The Musical Spillers performed at the Bennett Theatre in Ottawa as early as
mid-April 1907 and made many other Canadian appearances through the
1910s and into the 1920s. Led by the Virginian-born multi-instrumentalist
William Neymeyer Spiller, this black ensemble — initially a trio — played
"the most itching ragtime"[12] on saxophones and xylophones. By 1911 the
Spillers comprised three men and three women handling a wide range of
band and orchestra instruments; their Canadian appearances included a week

in 1911 on a bill with humorist Will Rogers at Shea's Theatre in Toronto (where, according to E.R. Parkhurst of the *Globe*, their program included a "ragtime malformation" of the "Miserere" from *Il Trovatore*[13]) and another in 1913 with comedian W.C. Fields at the Orpheum in Montreal. William Spiller subsequently expanded the ensemble to as many as 13 players, women always present among them, his musicians over the years including the trumpeters Crickett Smith, Russell Smith (no relation), Leora Meoux (later the wife of noted New York pianist and bandleader Fletcher Henderson) and Rex Stewart. For all of their vaudeville success, though, the Spillers — like so many black artists active in this transitional period between ragtime and jazz — went unrecorded.

The Six Brown Brothers were sons of Allie (Allan) Brown, a bandmaster and orchestra conductor and cornet soloist who worked in Ottawa, Lindsay, Toronto, Woodstock and Detroit.[14] Some or all of Tom, Fred, Vern, William and Alex and Percy performed together as a boys band in Lindsay and Toronto under Tom's leadership during the late 1890s.

Tom Brown, circa 1921.
[Courtesy Lawrence Gushee]

Tom (1881?-1950, not to be confused with the pioneering New Orleans trombonist of the same name) was the first of the Browns to move to the United States, travelling in turn with the Guy Brothers Minstrels and the Ringling Brothers Circus during the early 1900s. His brothers followed one by one and in 1909, Tom, Fred, Alex and Vern were working as the Five Brown Brothers in US vaudeville with one Billy Markwith as the fifth; the group was invariably completed by one or more non-Browns as all of the brothers save Tom came and went during its 25-year history.[15] Initially, the

Browns — like the Musical Spillers — used a variety of instruments, reserving their saxophone feature as a finale. In 1911 they added a sixth member, and by 1914 they were playing saxophones exclusively.

The Browns appeared at Shea's Theatre, Toronto, in 1911 with the Gertrude Hoffman Revue and enjoyed an early and successful homecoming at Ottawa's Russell Theatre (where, coincidentally, Allie Brown was now the orchestra leader) in 1913 with Primrose and Dockstader's Minstrels. "If their performance was a delight from a musical point of view," reported the Ottawa *Citizen*, "it was none the less deliciously funny, for anything more delicately absurd and at the same time ludicrously farcical than their chicken music can scarcely be imagined."[16]

After a trip to England in 1914, the Browns starred on Broadway in *Chin Chin* (1914), *Jack O'Lantern* (1917) and *Tip Top* (1920), as well as a production of *The Bunch and Judy* (1922). They later travelled in the United States and Canada with the female impersonator Julian Eltinge in *The Black and White Revue of 1924*.

Tom, who appeared in blackface throughout the Browns' history, was responsible for much of their comedy, achieved through his ability to create humorous effects on a saxophone. In 1925, during a Six Brown Brothers tour of Australia, he explained the evolution of the act. "I began as a black-faced corner-man with lots of patter. But I would arrive at a town and the stage manager would come to me and say, 'That joke is old. So-and-so told it here weeks ago.' Then we went and paid highly for others to write our humor, and after a fortnight or so we would find other performers had stolen it and were using it. So I cut out the talking altogether and got the humor another way."[17]

Such was the Browns' success that a second sextet, Tom Brown's Clown Band, was established to accompany the touring version of *Chin Chin* when the brothers moved on to *Jack O' Lantern*. Moreover, at least two other saxophone bands were using the "Brown" name and format circa 1920, one led by Billy Markwith and the other by C. L. Brown (no relation). It may well have been one of these two units that appeared in western Canada under the name "Tom Brown's Saxophone Six" in January 1919. As described in the Regina *Leader*, the act — "The Unfair Court" — came with a

Six Brown Brothers, undated. Tom Brown in blackface; others unidentified.
[Courtesy Bruce Vermazen]

modestly theatrical premise that initially found five of the six musicians in a courtroom setting — "three of them as pretty tough characters, one as the sheriff and one as a magistrate. Tom Brown [sic] wanders into court with a wheelbarrow load of saxophones [i.e., the loot] and the music begins."[18]

After a hiatus in the mid–1920s when Tom Brown toured on his own in vaudeville with the Merry Minstrel Orchestra, the "Original" Six Brown

Brothers returned to the stage in 1927 and played RKO (Radio–Keith–Or-pheum) stages in the United States and Canada for another two years. The "Original" Browns who appeared in 1929 at Loew's Theatre in Toronto were in fact Tom, Fred, Vern, I.J. Carpenter and at least one of Allie Brown's grandsons, Tom Jr., and possibly a second — Allan Brown.[19]

Unlike the Musical Spillers, the Browns recorded on several occasions. Some 35 novelties, rags, blues, pop songs, classical pieces and excerpts from their Broadway shows were issued altogether,[20] the earliest recorded in 1911 (by the Brown Brothers Saxophone Quintette) for Columbia, the majority between 1914 and 1920 for Victor, and several in 1919 and 1920 for Emerson. The most popular of the Victor releases, including *That Moaning Saxophone Rag* (1914) and *Bull Frog Blues* (1916), composed by Tom Brown in collaboration with Brown "brothers" Harry Cook and Guy Shrigley, respec-tively, helped to identify the saxophone's potential in popular music. Indeed, the instrument's first virtuoso in jazz, Sidney Bechet, was just one musician intrigued by the group — in particular by its recording of *Bull Frog Blues*. Although the tune's novelty lay in the croak of the sextet's bass saxophone, Bechet found something else to his liking and soon purchased his first soprano saxophone.[21]

Two of the pieces recorded by the Six Brown Brothers, *Walkin' the Dog* and *Darktown Strutters' Ball*, were written by another Canadian-born vaudeville star, the black singer, monologuist and mimic Shelton Brooks (1886-1975, of Amherstburg, Ontario). Brooks, who also composed Sophie Tucker's theme song, *Some of These Days*, began his career in Detroit as a ragtime pianist and toured the Pantages circuit with a succession of partners during the 1910s and 1920s. He introduced *Darktown Strutters' Ball* while travelling in 1917 with Clarence Bowen as The Two Dark Spots of Joy. He subsequently worked with the singer and snare drummer Ollie Powers and, billed as the Jazz Hounds, with clarinetist Horace George. The latter failed to impress a reviewer from the *World* during a stop in March 1920 at the Orpheum in Vancouver. George, the writer sniffed, "plays what is described as jazz on the clarionet. It certainly isn't music."[22]

Two other black songwriters and entertainers, singer Noble Sissle and pianist Eubie Blake, appeared as the Dixie Duo at the Dominion Theatre in Ottawa in June 1920 and at Shea's in Toronto and the Lyric in Hamilton during the month of September. Their recording career was just recently underway and their first major stage success in New York, the revue *Shuffle Along*, was only a few months off. For the moment, though, they were on their uppers. Hamilton, according to a letter Blake sent to his wife Avis, was "a good place to come and die when you feel like dying alone... I suppose you can tell when I am in a slow burg. I write often." It was the pianist's third letter home in four days.[23]

SHELTON BROOKS

Shelton Brooks, circa 1910. Detail from cover of sheet music for Brooks' *It's Awf'ly Hard to Say Goodbye to Someone You Love*, Sunlight Music Co. Inc., Grand Opera House, Chicago, 1911. [Courtesy Mike Montgomery]

Notwithstanding the Dixie Duo's experiences, two-man song-and-comedy teams were among the most widely travelled of black American acts on Canadian Time — Shelton Brooks and his various partners, for example, as well as Green & Pugh, Anderson & Goines and Harrington & Mills. A sixth, Austin & Bailey (as of 1919, Austin & Delaney), was particularly successful, performing into the 1920s on the Pantages circuit as bell hops in *Syncopated Hotel*, latterly accompanied at the piano by Austin's wife, Lovie, a pioneering figure among women in jazz.

Austin & Bailey, the Dixie Duo, and the rest — like the Creole Band and the Tennessee Ten before them — were invariably just one of four or five acts on an otherwise white bill. Several large, all-black troupes also performed regularly in Canada during the 1910s and early 1920s, including Harvey's Greater Minstrels and the Famous Georgia Minstrels. Established in the late 1800s and now carrying some 40 performers each, the two companies were self-contained shows that appeared for two or three nights at independent theatres in major cities. Touring productions of *Holiday in*

Dixieland and *In Old Kentucky* operated in similar fashion, often appearing in small Canadian communities; the latter show, for example, was seen in Fernie, Cranbrook, Nelson and Grand Forks, British Columbia, during November 1919. The musicians involved — 18 in the case of the Georgia Minstrels — gave street parades at each new stop, weather permitting, and played for dances that often concluded lengthier engagements.

Vaudeville artists, be they teams or troupes, black or white, generally travelled on Canadian Time by rail; many an opening show was lost to a train's late arrival. On one such trip in 1919, Anderson & Goines were stranded for 36 hours between Fort William and Winnipeg when their CNR train derailed and plunged down a 50-foot embankment. Five cars were destroyed by fire.

"The whole show was on the train," the entertainers reported in a letter to the Chicago *Defender*. "There was a little comedy in the whole affair, for while unloading the express car some one [sic] discovered that there was a lot of wet goods [liquor] aboard, heading for some place. Some one rolled a ten-gallon keg of Mighty Good Stuff down the hill into the bushes... Result: the happiest and most cheerful bunch that I have seen in many a moon."[24]

The *Defender*'s correspondents referred as often to the comparatively less restrictive (or less stringently enforced) laws governing the consumption of alcohol in Canada — "the land of Scotch and other liquor," as Cliff Green of Green & Pugh put it, writing from Saint John, NB, in 1919[25] — as they remarked on the country's cold winter weather. Indeed, the one very likely made the other bearable.

Many black artists also found some momentary comfort in the milder degree of discrimination they encountered north of the border, although the *Defender*'s correspondents still made a point of mentioning the Canadian hotels and boarding houses known to welcome black entertainers. Smith House at 54 Hughson Street in Hamilton was one, early in 1918; the home of Mrs. Willis Foster at 966 Main, not far from Vancouver's East Hastings Street theatres, was another, in the summer of 1919. By inference, the rest of the Canadian hospitality industry, reflecting Canadian society more generally, was not quite as reliably accommodating toward its black American visitors.

Nevertheless, members of Harvey's Greater Minstrels could take an afternoon off in Saskatoon, during a three-day engagement in August 1919 at the Empire Theatre, to play baseball at Cairns Fields against a white team of local all-stars. The game drew notice the following day on the sports page of the Saskatoon *Star*, the report written in the manner of a theatrical review: "The Minstrels presented a classy aggregation but played in a loose style which caused three costly errors. The comedy features of the pastime were provided by the Minstrels and the catcher in particular [concert band director Levy Payne] kept the crowd in an excellent humor."[26]

The locals prevailed 6–4 in five innings.

One unusual sight in Saskatoon was followed just a week later by another — the arrival of six white Canadian musicians who called themselves the Original Winnipeg Jazz Babies. Teenagers all, the OWJB were on the road for the summer. Already a hit in their hometown, and in Regina, they made their Saskatoon debut August 21 at Butler-Byers Hall.

No longer was vaudeville the only place where Canadians could hear jazz; no longer were touring Americans the only musicians playing it.

CHAPTER THREE
Dance-O-Mania

Nearly 750,000 Canadians, from a population of about 8 million, served in uniform during the five years, 1914–18, of the Great War. Almost 60,000 died on the battlefields of Belgium and France — Ypres, Mont Sorrel, The Somme, Vimy Ridge, Hill 70, Passchendaele, Amiens...

Against this backdrop of dramatic events overseas, and a succession of crises at home culminating in an influenza epidemic responsible for at least 70,000 deaths over the winter of 1918-19, the advent and practise of a jaunty new music called jazz was scarcely a matter of great consequence or grave concern. Yet the tumult of the times made all the more effective an entertainment whose exaggeration and spirit broke with the grim focus and chafing discipline of the country's war effort and offered a release for the emotional swings that followed news of battle, advance, setback, stalemate, and finally, as of the November 1918 armistice, victory.

On the vaudeville stage, jazz was a diversion among diversions, an explosive 15 or 20 minutes of music, dance, song and comedy that competed for an audience's favour with all manner of variety performers and, latterly, with photoplays and cartoons. In the dance hall and the cabaret, however, jazz was the primary attraction. Moreover, it was a participatory entertainment in which dancers took an active role and were given a "stage" of their own — the dance floor — on which to play it. And play it they did, stepping lively to the Turkey Trot, the Grizzly Bear and the Bunny Hug.

Canadians first danced to "jazz bands" in 1917. There are no figures of legend comparable to Freddie Keppard and Bill Johnson of the Creole Band among the Americans who introduced the new music to the country's dance halls and cabarets. But by the time that the Tennessee Ten had made its first tour on Canadian Time late in 1917, several obscure US bands — some that remain wholly unidentified save by some generic description — had played residencies in Canadian cities. Local musicians followed suit in short order.

Jazz initially arrived in Montreal from the two largest nearby US cities,

New York and Boston, just as it came directly or indirectly to the prairies from Chicago, and to Vancouver from Los Angeles and San Francisco. It was heard remarkably early in Calgary, a city of less than 60,000, and relatively late in Toronto, where the population neared a half million. It flourished in Montreal, Canada's biggest city with almost 600,000 residents, and — as will be seen in Chapters 4 and 5 — it thrived in Winnipeg and Vancouver, the country's third and fourth largest cities with roughly 150,000 and 100,000 people, respectively. Significantly, the Canadian centres most hospitable to jazz also had a progressive history in various social, cultural and political matters; Toronto, still a bastion of Orange Protestantism at the turn of the 1920s, was quite reactionary in these same respects.

On New Year's Eve, 1916, the Auditorium Studios, a dance "academy" at the corner of Bleury and Ontario streets in downtown Montreal, provided for its revellers a "Special Orchestra with Saxophone," apparently from New York. Over the next several months, the Auditorium's ads in the Montreal *Star* documented the nominal introduction of jazz to the city, almost instrument by instrument. By May 1917, patrons were dancing to a "Saxophone-Banjo Orchestra." In September, finally, the academy inaugurated the Auditorium Jazz Band.[1]

The *Star* ads prompt several unanswerable questions. Was the same band in residence from December 1916 through the following September? Did its music actually change in the course of 10 months, perhaps reflecting the influence of the Original Dixieland Jazz Band and of novelty drummer Earl Fuller's Famous Jazz Band, whose recordings had carried some semblance of early jazz beyond New York during this same period? (Sheet music for the ODJB's *Livery Stable Blues* would be published under the title *Barnyard Blues* in October 1917 by Leo Feist of New York and could be obtained by mail for 25 cents.) Or, was this simply a case of opportunism, of jazz in name only — a description that had suddenly acquired considerable commercial value, no matter how accurately or inaccurately it was applied?

Significantly, two US bands active in Montreal during this same period made little or no reference to jazz in the way they billed themselves —

Wallace's Orchestra, a white New York band that worked intermittently at another Bleury Street nightspot, the Jardin de danse, as early as mid-1916, and Prevoa's Boston Colored Band, which was in residence at Stanley Hall on Stanley Street below Ste. Catherine for at least the last eight months of 1917.

Banjo (Joseph) Wallace used the "jazz band" designation briefly in September 1917 and again in January 1918, but on the whole preferred a variety of more general descriptions. By all surviving accounts, this was not in any event a jazz band; according to *Variety*, the Wallace ensemble that had worked at Rector's in New York in 1916 comprised three banjos, violin, piano, bass and Earl Fuller's 64 square feet of drums.[2] Wallace's recordings in New York for Emerson in 1916 and 1917 and for Okeh in 1921, bracketing his visits to Montreal and his other Canadian engagements in 1919 at Astor's Dansant, the Racquet Court and the Venetian Gardens in Ottawa, are apparently of little or no jazz interest.[3]

Meanwhile, Charles A. Prevoa, who maintained a Montreal address between 1917 and 1923 and was one of the city's first resident black dance-band leaders,[4] waited until 1919 to list Prevoa's Colored Jazz Band for the first time in the city's telephone directory.

Of course, the same questions asked of the Auditorium Jazz Band might well be raised with respect to the other early "jazz bands" that played in cabarets and dance halls across the country. The first dance-band recordings would not be made in Canada until 1920, and then only in Montreal and by musicians working in, or visiting, that city. In the absence of more than this random documentation, the stylistic particulars of any given resident or visiting band in Canada during the late 1910s — moreso even than the details of those acts that appeared, and were reviewed, on vaudeville stages during the same period — are simply lost to history.

The word "jazz," or "jaz," was employed by musicians appearing at cabarets in Alberta during the first weeks of 1917, concurrent with the Original Dixieland Jazz Band's early success at Reisenweber's Restaurant in New York and its initial recordings for Columbia and Victor.

Edmonton's Pendennis Cabaret announced the presence of an unnamed "jaz" band in the *Bulletin* as early as January 29.[5] Subsequent ads were suitably provocative, notable in two instances for their early metaphoric use of "heat" in the description of jazz. On February 1: "It's Warm! Where? Where you can hear that 'Jaz' Band play."[6] On February 17: "Our orchestra has just received some new songs 'hot' from New York and Chicago."[7] By the end of the month, however, the Jasper Avenue establishment was dark — and cold.

To the south, Calgary's Cabaret Garden introduced its own "jaz" band within days of the Pendennis Cabaret's first ads, an indication that the longstanding rivalry between the two Alberta cities extended even to their night life. Both Edmonton and Calgary had become much more than merely frontier communities by 1917, establishing themselves successfully as the province's northern and southern transportation and processing centres for agricultural produce from their respective hinterlands. Calgary alone had enjoyed a ninefold increase in its population during the first decade of the century.

The Cabaret Garden, which opened in 1916 in the basement of the six-storey Lougheed Building on 1st Street West, took its name from its decor:

the bandstand was framed in lattice work and hung with baskets of flowers. The cabaret's owners, Messrs. Kolb and McCaw, looked across the border for their musicians and by February 1917 had hired a black quartet — duly renamed the Cabaret Garden Jaz Band — under the direction of one L.B. (Lawrence) Morgan, pianist and vocalist.

"Here's a man," boasted the Garden Cabaret in its *Herald* ads, "who seldom ever looks at the keyboard of the piano when playing."[8] According to information obtained by the local constabulary on the occasion of Mor-

Lawrence B. Morgan, Edmonton 1917.
[Glenbow Archives, NA-625-20]

gan's arrest later in 1917 for living off the avails of prostitution, the pianist was 32, slightly older than many of the musicians who were just now introducing jazz throughout North America.[9] Morgan's fellow pianist and sometime pimp, Jelly Roll Morton, was then just 26.

The Garden Cabaret became the Plaza Cabaret in the spring of 1917 and Morgan thereafter shared the billing with his brother, Enzie (Enza), a

Morgan Brothers Syncopated Jaz Band,
Calgary Herald, 15 Dec 1917.
[Glenbow Archives, Calgary]

drummer also known as "Jazz" Morgan. The Morgan Bros' Syncopated Jaz Band remained in Calgary for almost two years before it was replaced in 1919 by a group under the leadership of the Morgans' banjo player, Arthur Daniels.

A Plaza ad in the *Herald* itemized the Daniels band's resources: "By engaging Chicago's greatest saxophone player and tenor vocalist, as well as two other musicians and singers, we are prepared to place our jazz music and quartette singing against any colored organization ever assembled for harmony, ragtime, jazz or classical selections, as well as perfect dance time."[10]

The vaudevillians Green & Pugh toured western Canada in the summer of 1919 and offered another list of the Plaza's attractions in a letter published by the Chicago *Defender.* "Then we blew into Calgary — one of the swiftest little towns in Canada — and found Mr. Daniels of Chicago leader of the big jazz band in one of the swellest cabarets in town, and Danny had everything and he turned it right on — chicken, beer, wine and things."[11]

With Daniels' departure for Los Angeles via Vancouver in early 1920, his place was taken in turn by Will Page, formerly of Chicago's State Theatre, and George Weaver of Milwaukee. Weaver's pianist, "Little" Jesse McLendon, stayed on with the Plaza Jazz Fiends until June 1922, extending the continuous presence of black American jazz musicians in Calgary well into a sixth year.

In a letter published by the *Defender* toward the end of the Fiends' engagement, McLendon referred to the Plaza as "Canada's only a la American cabaret" and identified his fellow musicians as Horten Wright, T. Tisdale, Bob Everleach [Everleigh, a saxophonist] and Enzie Morgan. "Jazz," McLendon noted, "is what these people out here crave for and you know that is where I shine."[12]

Arthur Daniels, pre-1920.
[Courtesy Grace L. Holden]

When Ben Greenhood, manager of the Royal Hotel in Hamilton, decided that his establishment's grand re-opening in September 1917 called for the presence of a jazz band, he looked to New York. After his initial efforts to engage musicians by mail and wire proved unsuccessful, he made the trip personally. "They are sending Jazz bands to Europe and all parts of the continent," Greenwood told the Hamilton *Spectator*, "and I consider myself lucky in being able to secure one."[13]

Greenwood had in fact contacted the Clef Club, a professional association established seven years earlier by New York's black musicians under the leadership of James Reese Europe. The Royal Hotel's new band, led by

DANCING

OPENING NIGHT

September 1st

And Every Evening at 8 o'Clock.

ROYAL HOTEL

Ladies Not Admitted Without Escort.

Dixieland JASS Band

Advertisement, *Hamilton Spectator*, 24 Aug 1917.

future Clef Club president, cellist Alexander Fenner, appeared nightly for five weeks. As would so often be the case with early jazz ensembles, the band's drummer was the centre of attention. "If [this] individual had been made of India rubber," marvelled a reporter from the Hamilton *Times* on opening night, "he could not have encompassed such a large field of operations more easily. He could be accurately described as being everywhere at once."[14]

On one occasion, Farmers' Night, Fenner's musicians shared the stage with an old-time group and square dance caller; according to the Hamilton *Spectator*, more than 1000 people attended.[15] The Clef Club band also seems to have inspired members of Hamilton's own black community to try their hand at the new music. Within weeks of the New Yorkers' departure, the Whang Doodle Jazz Band began rehearsing at the home of its drummer, Robert Harrison, a porter in the employ of the Royal Connaught Hotel.[16] The quintet of violin, banjoline, piano, cymbals and drums was clearly modelled on Clef Club bands of the day, with their preference for stringed instruments rather than horns. No evidence remains, however, to suggest that the Whang Doodle Jazz Band ever performed publicly.

There was little comparable activity in Toronto dance halls and cabarets until September 1920, when [Charles] Stone's Colored Jazz Orchestra[17] from Detroit began a month-long engagement at the Arena Gardens, establishing a connection between the Queen and Motor cities that would flourish later in the decade. Toronto's own dance-band leaders in the late 1910s, Ross Brown, Frank Wightman and Al Linton among them, did not include the playing of jazz among their advertised attractions.

In Ottawa, meanwhile, cabarets along Bank Street, a short walk down from Parliament Hill, provided the nation's capital with a succession of US bands in 1919. Astor's Dansant, for example, offered Banjo Wallace's Novelty Orchestra, the 5th Avenue Entertainers and the Broadway Five. The last included Saxi Holtsworth, a minor celebrity who would record with his own

Harmony Hounds in New York during the summer of 1920; for the moment, according to an evocative ad for Astor's Dansant in the Ottawa *Citizen*, Holtsworth could be found "mingling with the dancers on the floor with his saxophone as a dancing partner."[18]

Another American band, the Novelty Syncopators, appeared at the nearby Century Roof during the summer of 1920, promising fans of the new music "a demonstration rivalling the Original Dixieland Jazz Band."[19] With typical American bravado, the Syncopators offered Ottawa hopefuls instruction in "the true method of syncopation and ragtime taught by real musicians."[20] By then, however, Ottawa had already heard its first local group: drummer Tom Nagle's Home Brew Jazz and Novelty Band had taken residences the year before at a third Bank Street cabaret, the Winter Garden, and in Aylmer, Quebec, at Queen's Park.

Banjo Wallace and Charles Prevoa led just two of the many American bands that worked in the halls and cabarets around Bleury Street and along Ste. Catherine in downtown Montreal during the late 1910s and early 1920s. Most of these visiting bands travelled out of New York, but at least one arrived from Chicago.

Wallace's Orchestra, for example, was followed at the Jardin de danse by Munro's Jazz Band in 1918, and Munro by Tipaldi's Jazz Band in 1919. Meanwhile, a Clef Club Jazz Band, as well as the Famous Chicago Jazz Band and the Kentucky Serenaders, were all heard at the nearby Palais de danse. As will be seen, some of these groups became fixtures locally. The Famous Chicago Jazz Band was likely Millard Thomas' Famous Chicago Novelty Orchestra, the leading black jazz band in Montreal during the 1920s. Tipaldi's Jazz Band — with Billy Munro of Munro's Jazz Band at the piano — became the Melody Kings, the city's most popular white dance band of the decade.

American musicians, black and white, surely welcomed the opportunity to work in this most cosmopolitan of centres, the Paris of North America. By US standards — indeed, by Canadian standards — Montreal was "wide open," particularly with respect to the sale and consumption of liquor and to the related illicit activities of gambling and prostitution that were so much a part of a vibrant city's nightlife. Quebeckers led the way in Canada's rejection of the prohibitionist sentiment that swept the continent during and after the Great War, exercising their right under the "local option" clause of the federal temperance law, the Scott Act, by voting in April 1919 to allow the sale of beer and wine by the glass and bottle. Meanwhile, the Volstead Act, passed in the United States in 1919 and more restrictive than the Scott Act, remained in effect through 1933, making time spent in Montreal an attractive prospect for many Americans, entertainers and tourists alike.

Dave & Trossie, two black dancers who visited the city in the summer of 1921, voiced a typical sentiment in a letter to the Chicago *Defender.* "At last we are out of New York, the farthest since April was Philadelphia until this date, and, believe me, this part of Canada is great... Ten per cent beer [is] 30 cents a quart. Best brandy $1 a pint. Seems like living [i.e., a good life] up here, with the exception of meeting so many French people who do not speak English. But they are great people to be around. All nationalities look the same to them... The act is going great. You know they don't care much for talking acts, so as we have no talking and very little singing but a world of dancing, we are all to the mustard."[21]

Montreal's role in the early history of jazz in Canada was further bolstered by the city's active involvement in the burgeoning North American recording industry. Several foreign companies, including Columbia and Brunswick from the United States and Pathé from France, had established manufacturing and/or distribution centres in Toronto by the late 1910s and were releasing music from their international catalogues. Two Canadian companies in Montreal, on the other hand, were recording much of the music for their domestic labels locally: Emile Berliner's Berliner Gramophone Company of Canada, established before 1900 but not chartered until 1904, and the Compo Company, founded by Berliner's eldest son, Herbert, in 1918. Both companies drew their rosters in large part from musicians working in and around the city.

Initially, Emile Berliner pressed recordings in his St. Antoine Street factory from foreign masters, the majority licensed from the Victor Talking Machine Company, of Camden, New Jersey. The Berliner company used "His Master's Voice" (HMV) as its trademark; an illustration of a small dog,

Nipper, peering quizzically into the speaker horn of a gramophone, graced its HMV and Victor labels. By 1910, however, Berliner had opened a recording studio on Peel Street — the first in Canada. In 1916, under Herbert Berliner's managerial hand, the company introduced the HMV 216000 series, dedicated to Canadian and American artists who were recorded specifically for domestic release. Two years later, the company established a similar series, starting at catalogue number 263000, for the French Canadian market.

Compo, based in the Montreal suburb of Lachine, underwent a similar, though quicker evolution under Herbert Berliner's direction, pressing masters from US companies like Phonola and Starr-Gennett before introducing its own label, Apex, in 1921. Compo subsequently established an export label, Ajax, for "race" recordings — black jazz, blues and variety performances generally recorded in New York and intended for to the African-American market.

Both the HMV 216000 and the Apex series featured Canadian recordings of dance music, novelties, fiddle tunes, Hawaiian guitar selections, military pieces, patriotic songs, operatic excerpts and gospel material. Montreal musicians were well represented in both catalogues. So too, in time, were American dance bands, recorded either during extended engagements in the city — as was Simone Martucci's Orchestra while in residence at the Venetian Gardens — or on visits like the one described with such a flourish in this Berliner promotional release: "The Rega Orchestra of New York came to Montreal one morning completely saturated with Gotham's best dance music. They proceeded to skillfully place it in permanent form by way of the recording horn on the black discs bearing the symbol of the small dog [i.e., Nipper]. Two long days of strenuous work resulted...."[22]

It's not clear in the case of Yerkes' Blue Bird Orchestra, which went into the Berliner studio early in the summer of 1920, whether the musicians involved were working in Montreal at the time or had travelled to the city expressly at the recording company's behest. Harry A. Yerkes, a New York impresario, would send no less than four groups to Montreal cabarets between 1920 and 1922,[23] beginning with the his Novelty and Jazz Orchestra, which opened at the new Blue Bird Café, in the Wilder Building on Bleury Street, in May 1920.

Record label, 1920.
[Courtesy, Music Division,
National Library of Canada]

Yerkes, formerly a percussionist with the New York Philharmonic and Metropolitan Opera orchestras, was enjoying a productive career as the nominal leader of several white, interrelated recording bands, including the Jazarimba Orchestra, the Happy Six, the S.S. Flotilla Orchestra, Yerkes' Bell-Hops and Yerkes' Metropolitan Dance Players. Many featured the noted New Orleans trombonist Tom Brown and the early saxophone star Ross Gorman, as well as cornetist Earl Oliver, pianist Ted Fiorito and the virtuoso percussionist George Hamilton Green. Some of Yerkes' bands were jazzier than others, some scarcely jazzy at all.

At the Blue Bird Café, his eight unidentified musicians — each "a master of half a dozen instruments"[24] — played for late-afternoon tea *dansants* and as an *entr'acte* to the evening revue. At some point during the engagement, a band identified as Yerkes' Blue Bird Orchestra recorded seven tunes for the HMV 216000 series. While the proficiency of the performances in a variety of styles points to the participation of Brown *et al.*, the same musicians' nightly presence at the Blue Bird itself is open to question.[25] The Novelty and Jazz Orchestra left the Blue Bird Café in July 1920. A second Yerkes group, the Novelty Entertainers, arrived in October to inaugurate a Ste. Catherine Street cabaret, the Dansant Deluxe. By then, the Blue Bird Orchestra's first two 216000s were in release: *Dance-O-Mania*, issued in tandem with *Whispering*, and *Hold Me*, with *Frogs Legs*. Three more titles followed in November: *Kismet* (paired with a Diamond Trio recording) and *Just Like the House That Jack Built* with *Scandal Walk*.

Taken together, the seven sides offer far more novelty than jazz. *Dance-O-Mania*, however, is an interesting piece. The cloying violin that dominates five of the six other performances is absent. (The sixth, *Frogs Legs*, features a saxophone sextet.) Instead, cornet, trombone and two saxophones are heard in an ambitious, closely arranged scheme of breaks, modestly polyphonic ensemble passages (characterized by a degree of interpretive independence, if not collective improvisation) and two, 16-bar saxophone solos (one decidedly more daring than the other, though neither necessarily improvised). *Dance-O-Mania* is relatively sedate by the Original Dixieland Jazz Band's feverish standards, notwithstanding the occasional, dirtied cornet smear, but remains quite convincing as the first jazz record made in Canada.

CHAPTER FOUR

"Only a matter of time"

By profession, George Paris trained athletes.[1] He taught Vancouver's boxers, coached its runners and handled the Greenshirts, its lacrosse team. For many years, he ran the police department's gymnasium. It was said that Paris himself held an obscure world record for the 100-yard dash — in snowshoes.

Few if any members of Vancouver's small black community enjoyed greater prominence or respect throughout the city. When he died in 1947, he was paid tribute by Magistrate Mackenzie Matheson, who noted that Paris had served the court on occasion as a consultant "in matters pertaining to his race."[2] Vancouver's acting mayor attended his funeral.

By then, Paris' brief career as a jazz musician had been all but forgotten. Born in Truro, NS, in 1868, he was taken to Montreal as a child and left his family for the circus at 14. After competing as a runner in Canada, and serving as the trainer to boxer Jack Johnson in San Francisco, he settled in Vancouver. There, in 1909, he was reunited with Johnson, now the first black heavyweight champion of the world, and subsequently travelled during the early 1910s with the Galveston Giant's entourage.

Paris' early love of show business, born of the circus, appears to have been revived during his time with Johnson. The American often took vaudeville engagements between his title fights and in 1912 opened Chicago's first "black and tan," the Café de Champion, catering to a racially integrated clientele. Paris — back in Vancouver by 1914 — moved no less freely between the worlds of sports and entertainment, enjoying considerable local celebrity with his clean pate, lithe bearing, dazzling check suits and powerful Paige automobile.

Just as Johnson played string bass, danced and sang, Paris had some facility as a drummer, a logical application of the hand co-ordination required of a boxer. At the end of 1917 — according to the Chicago *Defender* — he was "organizing a jazz band for the Patricia Hotel,"[3] the East Hastings Street establishment that had opened its own cabaret in October.

A year later, a *Defender* correspondent reported that Paris — "the king pin of the drummers" — was now working at The Hole in the Wall with "a big orchestra."[4] The correspondent himself, one Elmer Pewee [sic] Malone, also played in the band on occasion; Malone otherwise took work with the Canadian Pacific Railway, establishing a pattern of split employment that many other black Canadian musicians would follow in the years to come.

George Paris, undated, *Vancouver Sun*, 2 Sep 1947.

Paris joined local 145 of the American Federation of Musicians in 1919 and remained a member until 1932, although he listed his occupation as "musician" in the city directory for only three years, 1920 through 1922, a particularly important period for jazz in Vancouver. Scattered references in the *Defender* to his activities during the 1920s suggest that Paris — then in his 50s and a generation older than the musicians who were emerging as leading figures in early jazz — saw himself in the role of man about town. He continued to associate with show people and entertained black American artists on their visits to the city. The producer and singer Joe Sheftell, a frequent recipient of his hospitality, described Paris to *Defender* readers in 1921 as "one of the pioneers of the Northwest"[5] and in 1924 as "the king of Vancouver."[6]

In retrospect, Paris was also the country's first identifiable jazz musician — the Canadian Buddy Bolden, as it were. By virtue of his direct exposure to contemporary black American popular culture through his travels with Jack Johnson, he was at a decided advantage back home when the jazz rage began in 1917. His countrymen could only await the music's arrival in Canada, as performed on record or by US bands in person, before taking it up for themselves. They caught on soon enough. Two white groups, the Westmount Jazz Band and Cyclone Jazz Band, were working around Montreal by the end of 1918. A third, Winnipeg's enterprising Jazz Babies, "The Original Canadian Jazz Band,"[7] followed in 1919.

The Westmount and Cyclone bands took their first engagements within days of the end of the Great War in November 1918, as if playing jazz would have been considered a frivolous, if not wholly disrespectful activity while the young musicians' contemporaries were dying on foreign soil. The WJB had, however, performed in support of war-related causes prior to the armistice.

The war over, the WJB immediately made Westmount's Victoria Hall its home, sponsoring dances there on a semi-regular basis until the building was destroyed by fire in 1920 and again, briefly, after it was rebuilt in 1921. The quintet of violin, saxophone, banjo, piano and drums also played for Canadian Grenadier Guards Association dances at the Armoury — at least until the Guards formed their own jazz band in 1920 — and for many charity events.

A brief item in the Montreal *Star* identifies only Howard Wyness by name among the WJB's musicians, noting that his drumming and xylophone work were "one of the [band's] big attractions."[8] Drummers were clearly the first Canadian musicians to capture the novelty, if not the nuance, of jazz, and with it the imagination of the public. Wyness, George Paris and other trapsmen like Tom Nagle in Ottawa and Roy Endersby in Saskatoon enjoyed a degree of local celebrity, modest though it was, that would elude other instrumentalists across the country during the late 1910s.

Like its Westmount counterpart, the Cyclone Jazz Band — with Gordon Bennett, Reg Dowling, Tom Maltby and presumably others[9] — appeared at Victoria Hall and elsewhere through 1920. With the precedent established, other Montreal musicians began to take jazz into neighbourhood halls; Eckstein's Jazz Band (led by violinist Jack Eckstein, brother of Willie) and the Regent Jazz Band were active by 1919, and (pianist Alfred) Vernham's Jazz Band by 1920. The city's downtown cabarets, meanwhile, remained the domain of New York musicians, as was seen in Chapter 3, thus establishing early the kind of stratification between Canadian and American musicians that would remain in effect in Canada for the rest of the century.

The Winnipeg Jazz Babies were "born" in the spring of 1919 during a particularly tempestuous period of the city's history. Winnipeg was in the midst of one of Canada's most infamous labour disputes, a six-week general strike that was widely regarded — in the wake of the October Revolution in Russia 19 months earlier — as the prelude to an incipient Bolshevik-inspired uprising. The confrontation peaked on Bloody Saturday, June 21, when a melee between strikers and police on downtown streets left one worker dead, several injured and many more under arrest.

The Babies made their initial appearances in May 1919 at the Strand and Orpheum theatres, then began in June to play for dances at the Alhambra and Manitoba halls. As if to add further portent to their emergence, the Babies' initial Alhambra engagement co-incided virtually to the moment with a tremendous summer storm whose winds — raging at upwards of 135 kilometres per hour and accompanied by thunder, lightning and rain — did extensive damage throughout the city.

Jazz had been a part of Winnipeg's musical life since the previous September, when Manitoba Hall on Portage Avenue presented "tea table dances" thrice weekly with a "Double orchestra (Jazz and the usual)"[10] in attendance, and the Alhambra on Fort Street introduced the first in a succession of generically named US bands. The Southern Jazz Orchestra, from Chicago, which appeared at the Alhambra in February 1919, was openly advertised as a "colored" band; by implication, the New York Society Syncopated Orchestra that preceded it, like the New York Jazz Orchestra that followed, were white.

"With the continued popularity of jazz music," observed the Manitoba *Free Press* in an announcement of a Jazz Babies performance for soldiers convalescing at a local military hospital in June 1919, "it was only a matter of time before some of the local artists devoted their time to this new form of entertainment. The Winnipeg Jazz Babies are a classy aggregation of jazz artists consisting of seven young boys, proficient on two or more instruments..."[11]

In the summer of 1919, jazz — as a commercial entity dating to the release of the first Original Dixieland Jass Band 78s — was in fact just two years old. But its development in Winnipeg, as in Montreal and other Canadian cities, was no doubt hastened by the draw of wartime service on

Winnipeg Jazz Babies, Spring 1919. From left: Cecil Taylor, Oliver Thomas, Leo Martin, Ab
Templin, Sam Friedman, W. Green, Sam Rosefield.
[Cecil Taylor Collection, photograph 11, Provincial Archives of Manitoba]

many of the country's established musicians. Younger men moved into their places — younger men with the newer ideas of a generation maturing under the formative influence of jazz, a music that offered their youthful energies full release.

A photograph accompanying the *Free Press* notice, with the musicians' names written in hand, identifies the Jazz Babies as saxophonists Cecil H. Taylor and Oliver Thomas, cornetist Leo Martin, trombonist W. Green, pianist Ab (Albert) Templin, banjo player Sam Friedman and drummer Sam Rosefield. And "babies" they were. Like Chicago's west-end Austin High [School] Gang of Jimmy McPartland, Bud Freeman *et al.* — which the Babies predated by three years — every musician was a teenager. Taylor, a future Winnipeg physician, had turned 18 only a month before.[12]

In mid-July, the Jazz Babies travelled west to Regina, where they performed in vaudeville, offering a 30-minute show at the open-air Pavilion, and then played for dances in the City Hall auditorium and the Arena; this, at a time when the city's only previous exposure to live jazz would have come through the Pantages acts that appeared at the Regina Theatre.

Word of the Babies' exploits preceded the band north to Saskatoon. A local musician, Ernest Knapp, whose orchestra appeared regularly at Butler–Byers Hall and played for barn dances in outlying communities, introduced Knapp's Jazz Babies in early August with Roy Endersby, from the Empire Theatre, featured on "the drums and things."[13] In view of either the local competition or the potential confusion, the Winnipeg musicians were advertised as the Original Winnipeg Jazz Babies for their own dances at

Original Winnipeg Jazz Babies, Fall 1919, *Regina Leader*, 22 Oct 1919. [Saskatchewan Archives Board]

Butler–Byers Hall in late August and early September. The name took: it can be found on a poster for their homecoming at Winnipeg's Royal Alexandra Hotel.

After reorganizing as a quintet — probably Martin, Thomas, Green, Templin and Rosefield — the OWJB returned to Regina and Saskatoon in late October, the first stops on an ambitious, indeed unprecedented, tour to the Pacific coast and back, a round trip of some 4500 kilometres. Beyond Edmonton, where the band appeared on Hallowe'en at the Allen Imperial Theatre and at Albion Hall, its westerly itinerary is unclear. Three weeks passed between the outbound Edmonton dates and a homeward stop in late November at Saskatoon's Butler–Byers Hall for a benefit dance that netted $20 after expenses for the Saskatoon *Star* Christmas fund. The OWJB's route east to the Manitoba border was probably typical of the entire tour: Vonda, Humboldt, Watson, Wadena, Invermay, Canora and Yorkton, seven stops in eight days at towns 50 to 80 kilometres apart on the Canadian Northern Railway line.[14]

So it was that a Canadian band introduced live jazz to many small communities whose access to the new music would otherwise have been limited to whatever was then available on record. At that, just three of the many 78s advertised in the 1919 Eaton's mail-order catalogue that serviced rural Canada were even remotely of jazz interest: one on Victor of foxtrots by the Brown Brothers Saxophone Sextet and two on Columbia by a group listed only as "Jazz Band" — in fact a group led by the black novelty and ragtime clarinetist Wilbur Sweatman, recorded in 1918 playing *Indianola, Oh You La! La!, Bluin' the Blues* and *Ringtail Blues.*

And the OWJB's music? It must have been fashioned in some measure from these same recordings, as well as the few others more readily available in Winnipeg stores, with details of stage deportment adapted from the immediate example of acts that appeared at the Pantages and Orpheum theatres — possibly even the Creole Band and Tennessee Ten — and of the Chicago and New York orchestras that played at the Alhambra. Whatever its sources, the new music was no mere passing fancy for these young men: several would be active during the city's first golden age of jazz, only a couple of years away. Indeed, a Winnipeg band in the early 1920s with Ab Templin at the piano generally also had an Original Dixieland Jazz Band tune or two in its repertoire.

Advertisement, *Edmonton Journal,*
I Nov 1919.

The OWJB's publicity photographs capture the teenaged musicians in demonstrative poses, instruments held rakishly at the ready — precisely the sort of image that brought jazz into disrepute with the Winnipeg local of the American Federation of Musicians in October 1920. By then, the Broadway and Chicago syncopated orchestras (the latter featuring Simone Martucci on saxophone) had taken residencies at the Alhambra over the winter of 1919-20, while the white Chicago novelty pianist Martin Mortensen was in place at the Hotel St. Charles with his Society Syncopators — the Los Angeles saxophonist Dick Newlin, the teenaged Winnipeg violinist Benny Loban, and two former Jazz Babies, Sam Friedman and Sam Rosefield.

Local 190 may well have had some of these musicians in mind when it passed a motion ruling jazz players ineligible for membership. The issue, so wonderfully overstated by the local's secretary F.A. Tallman (as quoted in the Vancouver *World*), was clearly one of conduct, not musicianship: "We want to get rid of this jazz stuff; the fellow who hangs over the piano when he plays, who stands on his head or leaps from one side to the other. The motion is aimed to eliminate the musician who plays a light instrument and dances around prodding ladies in the back and generally making a nuisance of himself."[15]

Increasingly, jazz was under attack. As it moved from vaudeville novelty to dance-hall staple, the theatre reviewer's bemusement gave way to the music critic's scorn and the moralist's outrage. To whatever extent the new dance music did, or did not, conform to the qualities that would come to be associated with jazz, *something* about it — the players' deportment, their musicianship, the questionable environment in which they worked, even the amount of money they commanded — was inflammatory.

"My own belief," averred S. Morgan Powell of the Montreal *Star* in June 1919, "is that 'jazz' is a distinct form of insanity... I can find neither music nor rhythm nor charm in the cacophonous riot of metallic yowlings, the blastings and blarings and strummings and [the] beating of drums and haphazard smashing of piano keys that constitute 'jazz' music."[16]

Rhynd Jamieson of the Vancouver *Sun* began a column in September 1919 on an ambiguously philosophical note: "King Solomon's challenging query: 'Is there anything new under the sun?' might well find an answer in the latest international sensation — 'Jazz.'"

Jamieson mused over its apparent ability "[to] stir real enthusiasm [in] a world wearied by a long and ghastly war — to draw sorrowful people from brooding over the loss of all they loved..." But he was unequivocal in his conclusions. "We are absolutely against this rotten dynamic nuisance known as 'jazz' and the only remedy appears to lie in the hands of civic authorities who should follow the example of the Portland [Oregon] city council who recently issued an order prohibiting all 'jazz' exhibitions in that place. What the public wants these days is the best of music. As for 'jazz' and the 'shimmy' Vancouver can do without these twin sisters of corruption."[17]

Jamieson returned to the subject in November. "Give us more community singing," he advised, with quaint optimism, "and 'jazz' exhibitions will disappear."[18]

In a vituperative, though inadvertently informative letter published the following April by the *Sun*, one M.F. Sheridan responded to a provincial government plan to tax local musicians. "I would suggest," Sheridan wrote, "that the government increase its revenues by taxing well the players of vulgar music such as jazz, rag, fox-trot and the nigger trash which the average Vancouver dancing audience only care to hear. The performers of this awful and harmful rubbish are too well paid for their services, the average from $7 to $9 per night. They are all engaged in commercial pursuits during the day, therefore they are reaping a large revenue daily, far more by many dollars than the poor musical artist who has to await an occasional call for his or her services. These calls unfortunately are too few, so on the artist's behalf I would ask the government not to drain his light purse, let him alone and tax the fakir [sic] who plays Traps, Gazoos and makes a pretense of being a musician."[19]

Sheridan surely applauded a dramatic headline in the Vancouver *World* six weeks later: "To Kill Jazz Music Aim of Clef Club."[20] In a follow-up article, William Pilling, president of this newly established professional association and the music director at the Orpheum Theatre, suggested more diplomatically that jazz was merely a passing phase. His observations were relayed in the newspaper's "Over the Footlights" column.

"But, [Pilling] said, one would scarcely believe the price jazz performers could command about a year ago. Jazz music really introduced the saxophone, and anyone who could learn to play that instrument could demand almost any sum he liked for his services. This also applied to a certain extent to the violin, and banjo, in fact, as Mr. Pilling humorously remarked, 'anything that could make a noise.' But such is not the case now. The Musicians' Union is not against Jazz Music, and if any cabaret wants music of that style, it is readily supplied, for as he said, it is an easy matter to make jazz music."[21]

Many a Vancouver cabaret, the Patricia included, did indeed want music of that style, and by 1920 was looking to black musicians from Los Angeles, San Francisco, Oakland and Seattle to supply it.

CHAPTER FIVE

Jelly Roll, Bricktop and Slap Rags White

*"Well, Will Bowman has opened a cabaret here and is doing fine. He has an
8-piece jazz band with Oscar Holden, Leo Bailey, Jelly Roll, Ada Brick-top
Smith and others..."*
Edw. Rogers, letter to the Chicago *Defender*, September 6, 1919[1]

Ferdinand "Jelly Roll" Morton (1890-1941) arrived in Vancouver toward
the end of an extended period of itinerancy as a pianist, vaudeville performer,
gambler, pool hustler and, as legend would have it, pimp. He had made his
first trip from New Orleans, the city of his birth, to Chicago around 1910[2]
and by 1917 was in Los Angeles, where he joined the small but growing
number of New Orleans musicians who were taking jazz up and down the
west coast from Canada to Mexico.[3] The coast remained Morton's stomping
grounds, as it were, until 1922. In the company of Anita Gonzalez — born
Bessie Johnson, sister of the Creole Band's Bill and Dink Johnson — he made
Vancouver a base for his activities, music not necessarily foremost among
them, from August 1919 to January 1921, a period of at least 17 months
corresponding with the halcyon days for black entertainment in the Terminal
City.

Morton was a few months shy of 29 on his arrival from the United States,
a mature artist who had already composed several of the compositions that,
once recorded in Chicago during the mid-1920s, would be hailed as
masterpieces of early jazz. What Vancouver thought of the pianist, diamond
in front tooth, went unreported; what Morton remembered of Vancouver
is documented in his Library of Congress interviews with Alan Lomax in
1938, the basis of Lomax's biography *Mister Jelly Roll*.[4]

With characteristic bravado, Morton set the stage for his arrival. He had
been gambling, he told Lomax, and started to lose money. "About the time

Patricia Hotel, late 1910s. The Patricia Café is the first door
to the right of the main entrance.
[Dominion Photo Co. Vancouver. Photograph 20402, Vancouver Public Library]

I got down to my last dime Will Bowman asked me to bring a band into his cabaret in Vancouver, Canada."

Bowman, also an American, had recently taken over the Patricia Café, now concluding its second year in business on the northeast corner of East Hastings Street and Dunlevy at the eastern limit of a bustling, four-block stretch that in 1919 included a dozen hotels, the Princess, Royal, Crystal and Empress theatres, several cafés and cabarets and — surely to Morton's delight — three pool halls. With Vancouver's docks just three blocks to the north, this was the heart of the city's commercial district at the time.

Morton to the contrary, however, various reports in the Chicago *Defender* clearly identify Oscar Holden as the bandleader at the Patricia (and in one instance as Will Bowman's business associate). Holden "was no hot man," Morton recalled to Lomax, "but played plenty [of] straight clarinet." Holden (1887-1969, originally from Nashville, via Chicago) was in fact primarily a pianist and, as such, would be an influential figure in Seattle after he left Vancouver in the mid-1920s.[5] Morton mentioned only one other musician in connection with the Patricia, a valve trombonist named "Padio" — Harold Patio[6] — who, "if he heard a tune, would just start making all kind of snakes around it nobody ever heard before."

Another Patricia musician, according to *Defender* reports, was the drummer Billy Hoy, previously a member of Harvey's Greater Minstrels. The café also had at least three entertainers: Seattle's Leo Bailey, Chicago's Ada "Bricktop" Smith and New York's Lillian Rose. Bailey had just left the vaudeville team Austin & Bailey of *Syncopated Hotel* fame; Bricktop (1894–1984), so-named for her red hair, would soon be enjoying international celebrity as a club owner in Paris. A fourth entertainer, the baritone Ralph Love, was also in Holden's employ for some of this period.

The Patricia's new attractions were not promoted in the local papers of the day — the *Sun*, *Province* and *World*. Nor were the activities of any of the other

Jelly Roll Morton and Ada Bricktop Smith, Cadillac Cafe, Los Angeles, 1917 or 1918.
From left: "Common Sense" Ross, Albertine Pickins, Jelly Roll Morton, Ada "Bricktop" Smith,
Eddie Rucker, Mabel Watts. [Floyd Levin Jazz Archives]

establishments mentioned by Edw. Rogers in his letter to the *Defender* in September 1919. "Tom Clark has a neat little cafe," Rogers wrote. "Reg Dotson still has the Lincoln club. Jean Burt and Perkins have opened a nice club and cafe, so Grandell [Granville] street looks like some parts of the Stroll [Chicago's State Street]."

However, the activities of three white Vancouver bands were advertised in the *Sun* during the fall of 1919. One was pianist Calvin Winter's Novelty Jazz Orchestra, then in residence at the Lodge Café on Seymour Street. The other two, Walmsley's Orchestra and the Famous Jazz Trio with clarinetist G.R. (Gilbert) Northey, appeared at the Winter Garden, which flourished briefly atop the Charleson Building at Robson and Granville. Ironically, when an opening-night report in the *Sun* of October 12 deemed pianist Hubert Walmsley's outfit "the jazziest jazz band that has been heard in Vancouver,"[7] Oscar Holden, Jelly Roll Morton and company had already been in the employ of the Patricia Café for at least a month.

The Patricia had a capacity of about 300 and apparently attracted a rough clientele. "Bowman's biggest customers — and I do mean big," wrote Ada Smith in her autobiography, *Bricktop*, "were the Swedish lumberjacks who came into Vancouver on their time off. Tall, strapping fellows, they could make a bottle of whiskey disappear in no time. Pretty soon they'd be drunk and ready to fight."

In one such brawl — "the fight to end all fights" on Christmas Eve 1919 — Bricktop sustained a broken leg.[8]

According to Morton, the engagement at the Patricia was short-lived. "I had good men," he noted, affirming his claim to the band, "but somehow that cabaret didn't do so good. Folks [in Vancouver] didn't understand American-style cabarets."

In fact, Oscar Holden remained in residence at the Patricia through 1920 with Bricktop and, very likely, Patio, Lillian Rose, Billy Hoy and — for a time early in the year — the banjo player Arthur Daniels, recently in the employ of the Plaza in Calgary. Meanwhile, the *Defender*'s Los Angeles correspondent, Ragtime Billy Tucker, reported in July that "Kid Jelly Roll and Ralph Love, the Whirlwind Entertainers, are doing their stuff in Portland,

East Hastings, looking east from Carrall Street, 1916.
[Photographer: R. Broadbridge. Photograph 8397, Vancouver Public Library]

en route to the Entertainers' Café in Seattle." Tucker also noted, perhaps to
Morton's chagrin, "Word comes from Vancouver, B.C., that Bill Bowman's
Patricia Café is the talk of the town."

Tucker added a wistful afterthought: "Then, too, that's a country where
you can 'crook your elbow' [drink liquor] and never be molested."[9]

British Columbia was in fact the second Canadian province — after
Quebec — to abandon prohibition, voting October 22, 1920 in favour of
government-controlled liquor outlets. Prohibition in any event had been
something of a sham on the west coast, as Bricktop made clear in her
autobiography. While she complained that "[British Columbia's] liquor laws
were so complicated that Vancouver was what we called a dry town," she
went on inadvertently to describe the relative ease with which alcohol could
be bought in the city. "Outside of private clubs and speakeasies, the only
place you could buy a drink was at someone's house. It was like those
after-hours places in Chicago, only in Vancouver you could buy a drink night
or day at someone's 'open house.'"[10] Bricktop and Lillian Rose established

just such an operation at their apartment, purchasing whiskey from a Chinese laundryman and selling it at fifteen cents a shot or two for a quarter.

Jelly Roll Morton returned to Vancouver later in 1920, taking a band into the Regent Hotel, two blocks west of the Patricia, near the corner of East Hastings and Main.[11] His musicians now included L.O. (Doc) Hutchinson, a drummer from Baltimore, and Horace Eubanks, "a beautiful hot clarinet from East St. Louis who had learned from New Orleans men."

Eubanks departed before the Regent engagement was over — "Horace had a lot of good offers and pretty soon he quit us" — leaving Morton in conflict with local 145 of the American Federation of Musicians over the need to bring a replacement from the United States. By Morton's account the dispute was resolved in his favour; Eubanks' replacement may have been Stewart Hall.[12]

Morton again worked with a singer at the Regent, as Anita Gonzalez revealed to Alan Lomax in an anecdote concerning Morton's jealous temperament. "One night... the girl singer got sick and, before Jelly could stop me, I went up and started singing and dancing. Right there Jelly quit playing and, because he was the leader, the rest of the band stopped playing too, but I kept straight on with my song. When I finished, there was stacks of money on the floor. Jelly was furious..."[13]

The Regent, Morton remembered, "did a hell of a business and other places started [b]ringing hot men in." Indeed, as Morton's Vancouver sojourn neared its end early in 1921, the Patricia continued to flourish — a *Defender* correspondent reported Holden now in charge of a 10-piece orchestra[14] — and the Lodge Café had brought in a black cabaret-jazz revue from Oakland with saxophonist Frank Waldron, trumpeter James Porter, trombonist Baron Morehead, pianist Olive Bell, drummer Adolf Edwards and several entertainers.[15]

CAN YOU KEEP A SECRET?

HERE'S ONE YOU DON'T HAVE TO KEEP!

Follow the Crowd to the Patricia Cabaret

One Block East of Empress Theatre
— AND —

Hear Miss Lillie Rose, Ada Smith
R. Love and the Eel

INTERPRET THE LATEST SONG HITS

Assisted by THE BRONZE JAZZ BAND

411 HASTINGS STREET, E.   MUSIC, 8 P.M. to 1

Ephemera, Patricia Cabaret, 1919.
[Courtesy Grace L. Holden]

Oscar Holden, undated.
[Courtesy Grace L. Holden]

At least two other important Oakland musicians arrived in Vancouver presently, pianist Henry Starr and saxophonist J.M. Henderson. The latter, a relatively old and somewhat mysterious west coast figure remembered by his colleagues as "a good jazzman for the times" and "a hot man at his age and tough to keep up with,"[16] spent at least seven months of 1921 in the city with his Maple Leaf Orchestra, perhaps following Morton at the Regent or working at the Monte Carlo Café nearby.

The Monte Carlo, located in the basement of a post office at the northeast corner of Main and East Hastings, had fallen into disrepute early in 1920, to the extent that the city's chief of police had deemed it "one of the dumps we want to get rid of."[17] It was nevertheless thriving as the year came to a close. "Jazz music reigns supreme," boasted the Monte Carlo's ad in the *Sun* on New Years' Eve, 1920, no doubt to Chief McRae's dismay. "We put the corn in the cornet and the slides and moans in the trombone."[18]

Two other itinerant black American jazz pianists arrived in Canada during Jelly Roll Morton's Vancouver sojourn — the young Stilgo (or Stillgo, later known as Bingie) Madison of Des Moines, Iowa, and the elusive James "Slap" (or "Slap Rags") White, said variously by his contemporaries to have been from either Louisville, Kentucky, or New Orleans.

Madison (1902-78) would make his name during the 1930s as a tenor saxophonist with Louis Armstrong and Luis Russell in New York. In his late teens, however, he travelled the west coast cabaret circuit as a solo pianist, working in Oakland, Sacramento and Seattle before crossing the border to play the "Club Sundown" in Vancouver — probably the Sun Club on East Hastings, across from the Regent Hotel. By 1921, Madison was in Montreal at the "St. Antoine Club,"[19] undoubtedly an establishment in the St. Antoine neighbourhood that was home to that city's black population.

Madison subsequently accepted an offer of work from alto saxophonist Bobby Brown and banjo player George B. McEntee, two Newark, New Jersey, musicians who were appearing in 1922 with drummer Brantley Eustey (or Eutsy) as the Royal Jazz Hounds in Hull, across the Ottawa river from Ottawa itself. The nation's capital was not without its own cabarets — the Century Rose Room was particularly popular, numbering Simone Martucci, Frost's Bostonian Jazz Band, the California Troubadours and Ottawa's own Orville Johnston among its attractions during the early 1920s — but its left-bank counterpart was the centre of the region's nightlife, taking full advantage of Quebec's relaxed liquor laws.

Several roadhouses, including the Broadway Inn and the Jardin de danse, flourished on the northly route out of Hull to the nearby town of Chelsea. As was the case in Vancouver, efforts would be made by municipal authorities to close these establishments in view of the illicit activities purportedly taking place on their premises; conditions on the so-called "Chelsea Road" in 1923 were described with revealing hyperbole by a local resident in the Ottawa *Citizen* as "worse than anywhere in the United States, not excepting the negro sections of the city of Chicago."[20]

George McEntee, a Mason, kept fellow Mason and *Billboard* columnist J.A. Jackson apprised of his activities, which included entertaining blues singer Mamie Smith and Harvey's Greater Minstrels during their visits to Ottawa theatres in 1922. According to Jackson's reports, McEntee took the Royal Jazz Hounds to Gatineau Point, west of Hull, for the summer of 1923 and was back briefly on the Chelsea Road with three white musicians at the Broadway Inn before returning in Stilgo Madison's company to Newark by year's end.

Just as Stilgo Madison probably crossed paths with Jelly Roll Morton on the coast, he may well have made contact with one of Morton's Chicago rivals,

James "Slap (Rags)" White, in Montreal. Details of White's career are unclear and in fact present enough inconsistencies to raise the possibility that two or more James Whites were active during the 1910s and 1920s.[21] If the songs, rags and blues published in Chicago between 1913 and 1917 (including *Pussyfoot March* and *Jazz Band Blues*, recorded by the Six Brown Brothers) were all the work of the same James White, then he was actually a more firmly established composer at the time than was Morton.

Like Morton, White was playing in a transitional ragtime/jazz style by the late 1910s. The *Defender* found "Slap Rags James White" with a quartet in March 1917 at the Hotel Badger in Milwaukee where, "from all reports, they are out-jassing all the other jass bands in the Beer Town."[22] Perry Bradford, another pianist and composer of the day, later remembered "Slap (Rag) White" among Chicago musicians of the 1910s for his "'hot' ragtime" piano style.[23] Morton himself, fully in character, suggested that White was one of several pianists in the Windy City who had come under his — Morton's — influence.[24]

In a rare contemporary reference to White's presence in Canada, the *Defender* noted in April 1927 that the pianist was then in the employ of one of Montreal's larger theatres and reported, "When prohibition went into force in the U.S.A. Slap packed up his duds and said, 'Goodby Forever.'"[25] He would thus have arrived in Canada in about 1920 and, in fact, the American Federation of Musicians' monthly, *The International Musician*, noted in September of that year that a "J. White" had recently deposited a transfer with Montreal local 406. The implicit reason for White's departure from the United States and choice of Montreal as his new home — prohibition — is consistent with a recollection from the Chicago percussionist Jimmy Bertrand that "Slap Rags... could write a song every day and sold them for almost nothing, being content to have a bottle and a cigarette."[26]

Despite the celebrity that White had enjoyed in and around Chicago, he spent his later — and apparently last — years in Canada in relative obscurity. He was not among the Montreal pianists who recorded locally during the early and mid-1920s for the Compo and Victor labels, which looked instead to his fellow American Millard Thomas, to the Strand Theatre's Willie Eckstein and to the Regent Theatre's Vera Guilaroff. Indeed little more than circumstantial evidence remains of White's time in Montreal: listings for a "White Jas music writer" in the city directories for 1925-26 and 1926-27 and a church certificate[27] noting the death of a James White in the city June 15, 1933. At 43, the deceased was Jelly Roll Morton's exact contemporary.

CHAPTER SIX
The Famous Chicago Novelty Orchestra

Millard Galwston Thomas of Collinsville, Illinois, was something of an anomaly among early black jazz musicians. Formally trained at the University of Nebraska, the pianist and composer was thoroughly familiar with the classics and would count among his credits in the post-Canadian years of his career an operetta, an oratorio and the lyrics for *Brown Buddies*, a Broadway musical.

By all indications, Thomas arrived in Montreal sometime between late 1918 and early 1920. He is known to have taken "a jazz organization of class"[1] from Shreveport to Chicago in June 1917, staying in the Windy City long enough to claim it as his band's point of origin from that time forth. Whether or not the Famous Chicago Jazz Band that appeared at the Palais de danse in Montreal between December 1918 and January 1919, as noted in Chapter 3, was in fact Thomas and his musicians, the pianist himself settled in the city within the next 12 months. For some part of 1920 he maintained an office as a music arranger on St. James Street West.[2] By September, however, he had moved on — to Quebec City, in fact, for the first of two winters with the Famous Chicago Jazz Band at the Princess Theatre.[3]

In this, Thomas is fairly typical of the black American musicians who worked in and around Montreal during the early 1920s. Most survive at best as fleeting shadows — here, there and gone. Like their counterparts living and working in other Canadian cities at this time — Oscar Holden and J.M. Henderson in Vancouver, for example, George B. McEntee in Hull and, as will be seen in Chapter 7, several musicians in Alberta — they were, simply by virtue of being *in* Canada, at some remove from the opportunities to make any sort of permanent mark on jazz history.

To the extent that a few of these early figures escaped complete obscurity — Holden, saxophonist Charles Harris, drummer Jasper Taylor, violinist Willie Tyler — they did so on the basis of their earlier or later achievements in the United States. Millard Thomas at least made several recordings in

Montreal; two other black American bandleaders active in the city during this same period, Charles Prevoa and George Wright, left no more than the occasional ad or "at liberty" notice in local newspapers to document Canadian sojourns of several years' duration.

As 1920 came to a close, Prevoa's Colored Jazz Band was looking for work. Prevoa had not appeared in the city proper for three years but likely found employment nearby, including an engagement during the summer of 1919 at the Hôtel Bureau in Bout de l'Ile, on the eastern tip of Montreal island, where he saw his orchestra Gallicized as Prevost's Celebrated Jazz Band.[4]

"Once again at the services of the public," he announced in the *Star* on his return to Montreal late in 1920. "Bigger and better, featuring the latest Jazz Novelties, The Laughing Trombone and Moaning Saxophones. Added material allows us to cater any affair requiring up to 15 pieces."[5] Four days into 1921, his new "Mammoth Colored Jazz Band of Boston," boasting an unprecedented 12 soloists, returned to the site of his extended engagement in 1917 — Stanley Hall — for a single night's work.

A second, no less provocative "for hire" notice published in the *Star* in November 1921 — "The original PREVOA, with entirely new band, including a few of the artists you have admired on your phonograph"[6] — appears to have brought the band further employment in the city over the winter of 1921-22, first at the Summer Gardens on Sherbrooke near St. Lawrence Boulevard, and then at nearby Prince Arthur Hall. Prevoa interrupted his Summer Gardens booking in December 1921 for yet another one-nighter at Stanley Hall, this time appearing on a bill with Gus Hill, a white singer popular locally. The Prevoa band was promoted for the occasion as "late of the Ritz-Carlton [Hotel],"[7] an engagement that would have put them in the midst of high — and white — Montreal society.

Prevoa, Millard Thomas and George Wright in fact played largely for white audiences, both in and outside the city, although they probably also appeared at social functions in Montreal's small black community; Thomas, for example, apparently performed for the local chapter of the United Negro Improvement Association in 1924.[8] Significantly the musicians themselves did not live among the city's resident blacks, who were concentrated in the

St. Antoine neighbourhood between the Canadian Pacific and Grand Trunk railway stations that were their community's primary source of employment. In the main, the expatriate Americans — those who stayed long enough to be listed in the city directory — took up quarters along Sanguinet, de Montigny (de Maisonneuve), Hôtel de Ville, St. Denis and other downtown streets just east of St. Lawrence Boulevard in a French neighbourhood that overlapped with the city's large red-light district.

Racial discrimination in Montreal, as elsewhere in Canada, would intensify during the 1930s in proportion to the impact of the Great Depression. For the moment, though, the city offered a relatively hospitable welcome to its black visitors. The clarinetist Randolph Whinfield, who emigrated from British Guyana in 1922 and moved on to Halifax in 1924, would remember the racial temper of Montreal on his arrival as muted. "It was like coming home to your mother's arms. The white musicians wouldn't let anyone call us those names. And the women loved us — they spoiled us!"[9]

Meanwhile, the enterprising Prevoa, whose local addresses between 1917 and 1923 included Dumarais and Lafontaine East in the same downtown east-end area, revealed himself to the Montreal public in a new guise in 1922, that of Eastern occultist, lecturing in August on "The Problem of Life" and "Divine Healing" for the Universal Spiritualist Mission.[10] As the year came to a close, however, he was again seeking employment for his Boston Jazz Band. "Clean, clever, classy," he boasted in a final *Star* appeal in November, just a few months before he left the city. "Ask anyone..."[11]

George D. Wright, probably a cornetist, arrived from Chicago to open the Roseland dance hall on St. Patrick's Day, 1921, playing opposite George Hume's Roseland Orchestra. Wright's musicians were initially advertised as the Original Darkey Jazz Band; discretion apparently prevailed and the band was renamed the Kings of Syncopation almost immediately.

The Roseland, one flight up in the DuBrule Building on Phillips Place, emphasized its respectability, proclaiming itself the "Home of clean dancing" and adding, "We invite Montreal's mothers to visit us anytime... Two matrons in attendance always."[12] Some 1000 people were present on opening night, according to the *Gazette*, which offered a vivid description of the hall's decor. "Roses entwined the great pillars of the lounge, the flowers showing effectively against a setting of dark foliage, and all the tints harmonizing with the dull ivory of the wood work and wall and ceiling decorations. Gay chintz hangings, introducing the rose design, and wicker furniture carried out the illusion of the pleasant surroundings..."[13]

The Kings of Syncopation, whose instrumentation was itemized in the *Gazette* as "saxophones, banjos and cornet, clarinet and piano, as well as tympani," stayed at the Roseland through the summer of 1921. They then played a series of dances at Stanley, Norman and Cluff halls with the violinist Willie Tyler, direct from New York, as a featured artist. Tyler, identified by Perry Bradford as "the first ragtime fiddler in the [United States],"[14] was an important if forgotten transitional figure in early jazz history, active both in vaudeville — he had just left a Loew's act with Joe Jordan — and as a bandleader. His Canadian sojourn would be brief: when the "Roseland 5 Jazz Kings" returned to Stanley Hall in May 1922, after an apparent absence of several months from the city, Tyler was in a New York recording studio with Edith Wilson's Jazz Hounds.

George Wright, meanwhile, remained in Montreal at least until 1926,[15] although the last reference to his band in the *Star* is an at-liberty notice published in October 1923 for "Montreal's only colored orchestra." The ad continues, "Organized March 16, [sic] 1921. A.F. of M. [American Federation of Musicians — i.e., union members] Sight readers, formerly of Dupere's."[16] In addition to the Chateau Dupere, an east-end rue Notre Dame hotel that apparently favoured black bands, Wright's musicians worked in 1923 in at least one Montreal theatre and were probably the "Colored Jazz Band" that appeared elsewhere in the city.

The Kings of Syncopation were not, of course, Montreal's only black orchestra in 1923. Millard Thomas' Chicago Novelty Orchestra was now mid-way through its busiest period in the city during the 1920s.

The Famous Chicago Jazz Band/Novelty Orchestra had been active in Quebec and the US northeast for at least three years. While Thomas was largely unknown in American jazz circles and thus not particularly newsworthy, his drummer during the FCNO's first three years in Canada, Jasper Taylor, enjoyed a degree of celebrity from earlier associations with W.C. Handy (the so-called "Father of the Blues") and Jelly Roll Morton.

The Chicago *Defender* reported during the summer of 1920 that he was at the Hôtel Bureau and "doing nicely"[17], while both the *Defender* and *The Billboard* carried items in early 1922 noting that Taylor and the FCNO were in their second season on "the Drapeau Canadian Circuit" — to wit, in winter residence at the Princess, one of several theatres operated in Quebec City by one Arthur Drapeau.

"I am syncopating on the xylophones and drums with the greatest of returns," Taylor wrote to the *Defender* from the Princess in January. Enclosing a newspaper review as proof, he added, "Excuse the clipping as it is a wee bit of French. It's all French through these parts."[18]

Taylor apparently sent a similar letter to J.A. Jackson of *The Billboard*, who complained pleasantly that reviews documenting the band's success in Quebec were "entirely to[o] Frenchy for my limited education." But, Jackson noted, "From reports volunteered by white showmen returning from the Far North it is gleaned that these people [Taylor and the Chicago Novelty Orchestra] have done much to make Canadians think well of our [i.e., black] artists."[19]

If not exactly the Far North, the FCNO's territory was nevertheless remote from the hotbeds of jazz. Indeed, at that historic juncture in the summer of 1922 when the young Louis Armstrong arrived in Chicago from New Orleans to join King Oliver's Creole Jazz Band at Lincoln Gardens, the FCNO was working in the small New Hampshire towns of Newport, Woodsville and Claremont. By September, however, the band had settled into a lengthy stay at the Starland Theatre in Montreal, where the *Defender* identified Thomas' musicians as Taylor, multi-instrumentalist Charles Harris, cornetist Daniel Smith and violinist Arthur E. Holiday.[20]

At the Starland, a burlesque house on St. Lawrence Boulevard below Ste. Catherine Street, the FCNO was part of a vaudeville show, *One Night in New York*, headlined by the legendary French-Canadian comedian Ti-zoune (Olivier Guimond *père*) and featuring the soubrette Effie Mack, along with 15 dancers. Initially, Charles Harris was heard on saxophone in *Dancing*

The Famous Chicago Novelty Orchestra. From left, putatively: Arthur Holiday, Millard Thomas, Charles Harris, Charles Gordon, Emmanuel Cassamore. Fourth from left may in fact be Jasper Taylor. [*La Presse*, 14 Jun 1924. Courtesy *La Presse*]

Fool, and Thomas at the piano in *My Baby's Loving Arms*, as part of a concert segment that also included an excerpt from *Il Trovatore*.[21]

The FCNO remained at the Starland through the winter but also began early in 1923 to perform in other Montreal theatres, the Dominion, Belmont and Papineau among them. With Jasper Taylor returning to Chicago in the spring and Charles Gordon in his place, the FCNO opened an eight-week stand at the Tétreaultville Island Park to the east of Montreal in June; at mid-month, the band was heard over CKAC, a station established a year earlier by *La Presse*.

The newspaper's radio column on the day of the broadcast noted the FCNO's "fréquentes auditions" [frequent performances] at the Ritz-Carlton, Mount Royal and Windsor hotels — three of Montreal's finest — and identified the musicians as Thomas, Harris, Gordon, Holiday and a trombone and cornet player, E. [Emmanuel] Cassamoir [Cassamore]. Listeners were promised a varied program that included the novelties *Fuzzy Wuzzy Bird* and *Yes! We Have No Bananas*, the jazz tunes *Running Wild* and *Wearied Blues* and an adaptation of Dvorak's *Humoresque*.[22]

However broad the FCNO's repertoire, though, and however flexible its style for engagements in Montreal's theatres, hotels, parks and dance halls, Thomas and his musicians played a rough, unvarnished form of jazz and blues when they recorded for the Compo company in the summer of 1924.

A total of eight FCNO titles were issued from six sessions held over an 11-week period in June, July and August.[23] Thomas subsequently recorded two piano solos, *Blue Ivories* and *Reckless Blues*, in October. The 10 sides were released in the United States under Compo's Ajax label; only the Thomas solos were also offered for sale in Canada as part of the company's domestic Apex line.

The recordings clearly were not intended to appeal to the FCNO's following in Quebec but to capitalize instead on the burgeoning demand stateside for recordings by black jazz and blues artists. (Three of the eight titles, *Black Star Lines, Hard Luck Blues* and *Papa Will Be Gone*, had previously been recorded in New York for the "race" market by minor blues singers, each accompanied by the pianist Fletcher Henderson.) As it was, no more than a dozen other black Chicago jazz bands had preceded the FCNO into a recording studio, although their number included vastly superior groups led by King Oliver, Jelly Roll Morton, Erskine Tate and Doc Cook[e].

Indeed, the FCNO's relatively unproductive output and its generally leaden performances on record[24] cast Thomas and his musicians at best as a second-rate band by contemporary standards, which may explain why the pianist found it expedient to remain in Montreal at a time when his contemporaries' careers were flourishing in Chicago.

Charles Harris, who is believed to have recorded in Chicago with Jelly Roll Morton in June 1923[25] and with the blues singers Ida Cox and Ma Rainey in early 1924, may have added some experience, as well as versatility, to the FCNO's ranks but he could not lift the band above its various limitations — specifically, the narrow range and lacklustre imagination of its cornetist and trombonist (one or both of whom may in fact have been Harris himself), the resulting middle-register congestion of its ensemble work, the dire efforts of its clarinetist and the sluggish nature of its tempos.

Curiously, the FCNO's very first effort, *Page Your Puppies*, is among its best, briskly paced by a banjo player; more curiously still, the banjo player does not appear on any of the subsequent recordings.[26] The two solo blues show Thomas to be a steady, two-handed pianist who used a modest degree of rhythmic dexterity to embellish an otherwise fundamental style.

With effectively no Canadian release, the recordings did little to enhance the FCNO's local standing; the band appears not to have worked extensively, if at all, in Montreal proper again. Thomas did, however, take an engagement with the FCNO, now a septet, at Royal Park in Hull, for some part of the summer of 1926, before following Willie Tyler, Charles Prevoa, Jasper Taylor, Charles Harris and George Wright in due course back to the United States for good. Not until the arrival in 1929 of yet another American orchestra, the Ginger Snaps, did Montreal again have a resident black band of any significance.

CHAPTER SEVEN
Shirley Oliver

The Lewis Bros. Annex opened February 20, 1920 in the Bell Building on 101st Street, just north of Jasper Avenue, in downtown Edmonton. Like the Plaza in Calgary and the Monte Carlo in Vancouver, the Annex was a basement cabaret; according to the Edmonton *Journal*, it boasted 78 tables and a particularly florid decor. "The entire floor is laid in maple and the decorations are carried out in a rich color scheme of green and rose. The walls have been fronted by green trellis work artistically overhung with purple wisteria. Dainty electric lights in the walls and ceiling, with rose colored shades, make a lovely lighting effect. A colored jazz band has been secured from Chicago and will supply all the best music."[1]

The Annex became the Alhambra in 1922, and the Alhambra in turn was renamed the Palais de danse in 1924. But the Palais was short-lived, and would soon be supplanted by Sullivan's in the Lafleche Building on 102nd Street as the city's most popular nightspot.

The Annex's Chicago jazz musicians came and went in anonymity. If Shirley K. Oliver was not actually one of their number, he would certainly have made their acquaintance during the engagement. Oliver, formerly the pianist with Charles (Doc) Cook[e]'s orchestra in Chicago,[2] had taken up residence in Edmonton by 1920, the circumstances of his arrival as mysterious as those of his eventual departure. He remained in the city through the decade and for several years played in Edmonton's leading white dance band, a not uncommon instance in Alberta during the 1920s — if scarcely anywhere else in North America at the time — of black and white musicians working together[3]. It would be another dozen years before Teddy Wilson broke the colour line with Benny Goodman in the United States.

Oliver and his family settled quickly into the black community that made up a small portion of Edmonton's 60,000 residents. A thousand or more American blacks, many of them Oklahomans facing disenfranchisement when the former territory attained statehood in 1907, had responded to a

Canadian government appeal for settlers to populate the western provinces. In the years around 1910 the new arrivals settled at Pine Creek (renamed Amber Valley) northeast of Edmonton, Junkins (now Wildwood) to the west and Keystone (now Breton) to the southwest, choosing such isolated locations precisely for their distance from white society. Nevertheless, when the region's short growing season and heavy bush thwarted their efforts to cultivate the land, many moved into Edmonton proper and found employment with the railway and in the meat packing plants that were a staple of the city's economy.[4]

Oliver himself took work as a porter to supplement his income from playing — and teaching — piano. Early in his Edmonton sojourn, he also travelled as an itinerant projectionist to remote communities in northern Alberta, showing movies where they had rarely been seen before. By April 1922 he was able to buy a home for his family in the Parkdale neighbourhood on the city's north side. The purchase was noted approvingly by Reverend George Slater, pastor of the new Emmanuel African Methodist Episcopal Church, in his weekly *Journal* column of social notes from the black community. "Mr. and Mrs. Oliver," Slater wrote, "are among our most progressive citizens."[5]

There were at least two other black American musicians living in Edmonton during the early 1920s. One, clarinetist Bob Everleigh, had travelled in the mid-1910s with the Rabbit Foot Minstrels and the Silas Green ("from New Orleans") tent show.[6] The other, Ernest Braxton, was a circus drummer and tightrope artist who may have been affiliated at some point with the Famous Georgia Minstrels.

Everleigh, like Oliver, was a member of the A.M.E. church. The two "professors" played for its social functions, all the while maintaining their place in the local world of jazz. Indeed, Reverend Slater's *Journal* column routinely tracked Everleigh's secular movements, first in Edmonton and environs with a jazz band at the end of 1921, and then on to Calgary, where the clarinetist joined pianist Little Jesse McLendon's Plaza Jazz Fiends early in 1922.

Everleigh was back in Edmonton for the fall season at the Alhambra cabaret with the Doo-Dad Jazz Fiends, a sextet led by erstwhile Plaza drummer Enzie Morgan. The band was filled out by white musicians: trombonist Victor Teasdale, saxophonist Tom Goodridge, pianist Art Fleming and the banjo player Dutch Lyons. (Fleming and probably Teasdale had worked with Morgan in an integrated band at the Plaza as early as December 1920.) On October 11, 1922, the Doo-Dads were heard from the studio of *Journal* radio station CJCA in a 45-minute broadcast that included *The Sneak, Sensation, Take It, Cause It's All Yours* and *Tiger Rag*, as well as a Doo-Dads original, *Barrell* [sic] *House Blues*.[7]

The Doo-Dads were followed on CJCA two weeks later by Shirley Oliver's new band, Gumps Jazz Hounds, with Ernest Braxton, cornetist Paul Poston and a banjo player, Frank Birch. The Hounds, described in a *Journal* preview as "the only colored dance band this side of Winnipeg,"[8] were certainly one of the earliest jazz groups in Canada made up of resident — rather than travelling — black musicians. (The pioneering activities of Vancouver drummer George Paris, noted in Chapter 4, must be acknowledged on both counts.) On October 25, the Hounds entertained radio listeners in northern Alberta with a selection of tunes that included the current jazz hits *Royal Garden Blues, Stumbling, Nobody Lied, Gypsy Blues* and *Everybody Step*.[9] The broadcast predated by nearly eight months the appearance of Millard Thomas and his Famous Chicago Novelty Orchestra on CKAC in Montreal.

Graydon W. Tipp was just one of the many white dance and jazz musicians in the city who had received his early training in the Edmonton [*Journal*] Newsboys' Band. In the fall of 1922 Tipp, a saxophonist, formed a six-piece orchestra for dances at Carlton Hall; by October 1923, when his Midnight Rounders filled in on short notice for an American act gone missing from a bill at the Pantages theatre, Shirley Oliver was at the piano. Many musicians passed through the Tipp band over the next several years.[10] Oliver alone was constant.

Tipp kept his musicians fully employed well into 1929. His band worked most summers at the Riverview Pavilion, which looked out over the North Saskatchewan River from 109th Street, and took extended engagements

Graydon Tipp and his Orchestra, Riverview Pavilion, circa 1925. From left: Raoul Esmonde, Milt Tipp, Len Dear, Graydon Tipp, Shirley Oliver, unknown saxophonist, Milt Weber, Russ Carter. [Photograph A.552, Provincial Archives of Alberta]

variously at Sullivan's, the King Edward Hotel and in local theatres at other times of the year.

Tipp's Orchestra, as it was generally known, mixed jazz hits of the day with lighter dance fare — everything from *Tiger Rag* to *The Swenska Polka*. The balance, however, leaned to jazz or at least to quasi-jazz "hot dance" tunes. Tipp's broadcasts from the Riverview on CJCA in 1924, for example, included the obscure *If You Sheik on Your Mama (Mama's Gonna Sheba on You)* as well as the future jazz classics *Somebody Stole My Gal* and *Limehouse Blues*. Tipp appears to have come under the influence of the Virginians, a New York studio band led by saxophonist Ross Gorman, then a member of the Paul Whiteman Orchestra and one of the foremost figures in "hot dance" music of the 1920s. Tipp employed the same eight-piece instrumentation as the Virginians and played *Mindin' My Business*, *Rose of the Rio Grande* and *I'm Goin' South*, tunes only recently recorded by Gorman with musicians that he had drawn from the Whiteman orchestra's ranks.[11]

Tipp maintained a similar stylistic balance in later years. His programs at the Riverview in 1927, as advertised in the *Journal*, included the jazz hits *Muddy Water*, *The Sphinx*, *St. Louis Shuffle*, *St. Louis Blues* and *Washboard Blues*, as well as a selection of waltzes like *Down the Lane* and *One Night of Love in Spain*.[12] This repertorial variety and corresponding stylistic range were noted by *Journal* critic "H.M.B.," who wrote that Tipp and his musicians, appearing at the Rialto Theatre, were "loudly applauded in all numbers, but especially encored in the livelier red-hot species of jazz."[13]

With Tipp's Orchestra providing a reliable income, Shirley Oliver was finally able to forego his job as a porter and in 1926 opened his own music studio downtown on Jasper Avenue. Such were his rising fortunes that he could take time off from the Riverview in the summer of 1927 for a return visit to Chicago. He made the trip home in his Studebaker "Big Six" sedan.

Neither Bob Everleigh nor Ernest Braxton matched Shirley Oliver's success at making a living solely as a musician in Edmonton. Everleigh had left the city by 1924; he spent the summer of that year in Calgary with a white band at the St. George's Island Pavilion before embarking on the travels that would take him by 1928 to Montreal, where he appeared in local nightclubs for many years. Of Braxton, meanwhile, little if anything had been heard since 1922. He, too, may well have moved away from the city for a time; when he resumed his musical career locally in 1927, he was in the employ of a 101st Street barber shop.

Braxton's first venture was probably a vaudeville act with a partner named Jones: as Jazz & Joker they appeared at the Rialto Theatre in April 1927. Two months later, the drummer returned with a full band, the Moonlight Syncopators — trumpeter Ollie Wagner, saxophonist Frank Sklove, violinist Seward Poston, pianist Josephine Barzey and the banjo player Carl Greene.

Braxton's Moonlight Syncopators, Rialto Theatre, 1927. From left: Carl Greene, Ernest
Braxton, Frank Sklove, Ollie Wagner, Josephine Barzey, Seward Poston.
[Courtesy Frank Sklove]

For Sklove, then 15, a member of the Edmonton Newsboys' Band and the
Syncopators' only white musician, the Rialto engagement marked the start
of a career that continued well into the 1990s.

Barzey may well have been one of Shirley Oliver's pupils, but Sklove
and Wagner were ultimately responsible for such jazz as the Syncopators
offered — a smattering of ideas drawn from recordings of the day. In Sklove's
words, "It was a bit whiny, but it was jazz."

Braxton himself was more than competent, according to Eddie Bailey,
whose family had given the drummer lodging when he first left the circus in
Edmonton. "He could *play* the drums, snare drum mostly, not all these
cymbals and things like they have nowadays. He could make those brushes
talk — and *walk*."

After a successful audition by telephone, Braxton's Moonlight Syncopators moved for the rest of the summer to the Lake View (or Alexandra)
Pavilion at Sylvan Lake, a popular resort spot southwest of Edmonton and
due west of Red Deer. Another group of Edmonton musicians, Frank Harvey
and his Red Tux Boys, "The Canadian band with the American rhythm,"[14]
played jazz in Red Nichols' spirited ensemble style across the street. Harvey,
a saxophonist, had the better band, according to Sklove, but Braxton met
with the greater success.

Sklove and Poston, best friends in Edmonton, naturally enjoyed their time away from the city. "We had a little cabin next door to the Alexandra," the saxophonist remembers, "and there was a restaurant in the dance hall. So we got our food and keep. Braxton got the money and he doled out a quarter every so often. You know, we were just kids. We were glad to be there. We had a lake to swim in..."

At summer's end, the band's two youngest members returned to school and Ollie Wagner, who was starting a career in music that would eventually take him to Calgary, Vancouver, Winnipeg and Toronto, went back to his job at the Swift's meat packing plant. Braxton reassembled the Moonlight Syncopators for at least one further engagement, a week at the Rialto in January 1928 with *Plantation Days*, whose familiar backdrop might have reminded Edmontonians of the Creole Band and Tennessee Ten.

The 20-minute act was described by "H.M.B." in the *Journal* as "a very pretty revue with an appropriate setting among the cotton fields of the south." Lest the racial inference be missed, the review turned explicit: "There were songs, dances and real darkey jazz with real picanninies taking part."[15]

Alberta's integrated bands, socially progressive though they were, must be seen in the broader context of race relations in Alberta in the 1920s. The Oklahoma settlers had met with considerable hostility on their arrival during the previous decade, both at the Canadian border and particularly in Edmonton, where nearly 15% of the city's population signed a Board of Trade petition protesting their presence. Efforts were made in 1924 by Edmonton's city commissioner to ban blacks from local swimming pools; the order was quickly countermanded by city council but similar exclusionary policies existed on a less formal basis in both the public and private sectors. The Ku Klux Klan, meanwhile, claimed 1000 members in Alberta by 1927,[16] and restaurants in the province freely advertised service exclusively by "all white help" throughout the decade.

What, then, to make of the Plaza and Alhambra groups with Enzie Morgan and others? Of Tipp's Orchestra with Shirley Oliver? Of the St. George's Island Pavilion Orchestra with Bob Everleigh? Of Ernest Braxton's Moonlight Syncopators with Frank Sklove? First of all, that racial attitudes among musicians were relatively relaxed. Secondly, that Morgan and Braxton were probably unable to find the musicians they required in the small black communities of Calgary and Edmonton. And finally, that Oliver and Everleigh possessed the sort of musicianship that transcended racial barriers.

Certainly Oliver's long association with a white band is evidence of a superior musician. There were other pianists available to Graydon Tipp in Edmonton, in particular Art Fleming and Tommy Mayo; the latter, a Native Canadian who had worked at the Savoy Hotel in London, England, in 1922, played instead for two of Tipp's rivals in the mid-1920s, the banjo players Dutch Lyons and Cecil Lord.[17] Yet Tipp chose to employ Oliver at a time when the presence of a black musician in his band undoubtedly would have cost it at least some employment opportunities.

Oliver's departure from Edmonton, possibly for Boston, in fact corresponds with the Tipp orchestra's dwindling fortunes. In the summer of 1929, Tipp, who was vice-president of J.L. Tipp & Sons Ltd., the city's leading tailor, turned the band over to his drummer, Murray (Red) Pawling. Work was scarce in the fall — Cecil Lord had moved into Sullivan's for the winter of 1929-30 — and Pawling was forced to advertise the Tipp orchestra's availability in the *Journal*. At year's end, as the Great Depression was beginning to settle over Canada, the orchestra was employed just one night a week at the King Edward Hotel.

Shirley Oliver had apparently left the city by then and would soon be forgotten outside the black community and beyond the small circle of white musicians who had played jazz in Edmonton during the 1920s. Eddie Bailey's older brother Harvey describes Oliver as "a hell of a piano player." Frank Sklove remembers clearly the lift that the pianist gave Tipp's Orchestra. "Let's put it this way, when he took a solo, I listened — *automatically*. And I was just a kid."

CHAPTER EIGHT
Jazz Week

If the Winnipeg musicians' union's ban on jazz of October 1920 had any effect at all, it was short-lived. However, the word "jazz" remained conspicuous by its absence from newspaper ads for local dance halls and cabarets until late 1921, when the Allen Theatre presented its first "All Jazz Week," setting off a remarkable 16-month flurry of activity in the city.

Jazz had been heard in Canadian theatres for seven years, dating back to the Creole Band's first Pantages tour in 1914. Musical presentations in general were taking on increased significance in theatres throughout North America as silent movies began to rival and then displace vaudeville as the primary popular entertainment of the day. Although many movie houses continued to offer a vaudeville bill with their main screen attraction, others relied on the "house" orchestra that accompanied the movie to supplement an evening's offerings with several selections of its own, hiring specialists or soloists as required by the material in hand. One way or the other, jazz took its place with the classics on these programs and Canadian "syncopators" were called — if only one night a week — from the bandstands of local dance halls to the stages of the city's largest theatres.

In Winnipeg, the Allen promised a 20-piece "syncopation orchestra" — in effect the theatre's regular orchestra augmented by local jazz musicians — with the featured motion picture, *Woman's Place*, during the last week of November 1921. A month later, the Allen Jazz Band, with saxophonists Dick Newlin and Harry Hill, the Winnipeg Jazz Babies' banjo player Sam Friedman, violinist William Einarson, pianist Harold Green and drummer Preston Purdy, appeared for the first of four consecutive weeks as a prelude to the screen presentation. A second All Jazz Week was mounted in February 1922, this time employing an orchestra of 35 as well as an outside group, the Pals' Club Syncopators. Management set aside 20,000 kazoos to give away with admission — 30¢ for the matinee, 50¢ for the evening show. A third

Ab Templin's Gate City Syncopators, 1923. From left: Harry French, Sam Friedman, Ab Templin, Ruby Rossiena, Harry Gault, Leo Martin, Ed Peterson. [Campbell Studios, Winnipeg. Courtesy Robert Templin]

All Jazz Week followed in April, again with the Pals' Club Syncopators ("fighting their way out of a storm of classics"[1]) and the kazoos.

Harold Green, otherwise the Allen's organist and scarcely a jazz musician himself, served as the syncopation orchestra's pianist and/or conductor. In September 1922 he introduced a Thursday-night series that continued through the following April — more than 30 half-hour performances altogether, each preceding the evening's motion picture and initially featuring an orchestra of 30, latterly scaled down to a dozen Allen All Stars. On occasion, smaller groups appeared as guest acts, among them two led by former members of the Winnipeg Jazz Babies, Oliver Thomas' Stellar Saxophone Quintette and Ab Templin's band from Baroni's cabaret.

The Allen, located across from the T. Eaton Company on Donald Street near Portage Avenue, was close enough to the city's dance halls and cabarets — Baroni's, the Alhambra, the Hotel St. Charles and, new as of October 1922, the Roseland Dance Gardens — to allow Templin and the others to play the 8:30 show and still start their evening engagements more or less on time. Indeed, the Allen's Thursday-night regulars included several musicians from local cabarets.

Sam Friedman, for one, was a member of the Pal's Club Syncopators, played in all of the Allen ventures and worked in turn with bands at the St. Charles, Baroni's and the Roseland. He also appeared on local vaudeville bills in *Banjology* and *Banjoland* accompanied by the pianist Burt Hook, a second Allen Theatre regular. Yet a third, the English-born violinist, Hugo Rignold, still in his teens, played with the St. Charles Syncopators over the winter of 1922-3 and then returned to London, where his Winnipeg experience served him well; by 1925 he was a member of Jack Hylton's Kit-Cat Band, whose recording of *Riverboat Shuffle* in October of that year was praised in the inaugural issue of *The Melody Maker* for "some real 'dirt' on the fiddle by that super-jazz artist, Hugo Rignold."[2]

The music performed by the Allen Theatre's syncopators apparently conformed to the musicians' union's two-year-old code of conduct. Following the first of the Thursday night concerts, the Manitoba *Free Press* reported, "Syncopation as rendered at the Allen is not of the blatant variety; it is of an entirely different color with the absence of weaving, standing on head and beating drums in the air."[3]

Nevertheless, Harold Green's programs, published in the *Tribune* and *Free Press* on the day of each concert, were right up to date. Many of the tunes performed were in circulation with the white "hot dance" bands recording stateside — the California Ramblers, Bailey's Lucky Seven, the Benson Orchestra and the Synco Jazz Band. Some of the local cabaret bands, moreover, had an even stronger jazz component to their repertoires. Ab Templin's musicians were heard at the Allen playing the Original Dixieland Jazz Band's *Ostrich Walk* and *Fidgety Feet*, as well as Johnny Dunn's 1922 hit, *Hawaiian Blues*. Ruby Rossiena, a popular local cabaret and vaudeville artist featured with Templin at Baroni's, sang *Got to Cool My Doggies Now*, a Mamie Smith hit of the same year.

The Allen closed soon after Harold Green's series concluded in the spring of 1923, only to reopen in the summer as the Metropolitan. Green remained in place and late in the year brought in Ab Templin's Gate City Syncopators from Baroni's on Monday nights. By then, however, the syncopation fad had passed in Winnipeg and the concerts ran a just a few weeks into 1924. Both Templin and Sam Friedman soon left the city, the pianist moving to Toronto en route to a career outside of music in the United States, and the banjo player to Chicago, where — switching to guitar — he took hotel, theatre and radio work. Harold Green, in turn, remained a fixture in Winnipeg music circles for another 40 years.

The Allen's early success with jazz in Winnipeg — initially the 2000-seat theatre was sold out on Thursdays — naturally had its imitators. Locally, the Capitol, managed by the xylophonist Oral D. Cloakley, featured violinist Earle C. Hill and His Syncopators for a week or two at a time in 1922; Cloakley himself was a featured performer, as was the pianist Martin Mortensen. Cloakley subsequently moved to the Capitol in Hamilton, mounting similar programs in 1923 with the bands of saxophonist Ernie Watson and the pianists Eke Chamberlain and Bill Stewart.

Other Allen houses across Canada also mounted jazz weeks with varying degrees of success. In Toronto, for example, violinist Luigi Romanelli — music director for the entire Canadian chain — fronted a jazz band with some frequency at the downtown Allen Theatre from late 1921 through early 1923. Romanelli was no more a jazz musician, and indeed probably less, than his Winnipeg counterpart, Harold Green. His presentations nevertheless caught rather more of the music's riotous spirit than did Green's decorous productions. "After Monday night's performance," boasted an Allen ad in the Toronto *Star*, "49 assorted buttons were found on the floor and 19 chairs had to be resprung."[4] A follow-up ad reported, "Five people almost fainted from laughter! To prevent this, attendants now mingle with the audience, squirting water on those unable to control themselves. No extra charge for this service."[5]

In Montreal, Simone Martucci from the Venetian Gardens and the Melody Kings from the Jardin de danse alternated Jazz Nights at the Allen Theatre in the fall of 1922. By year's end, both bands were appearing nightly on a circuit of United Amusement theatres, including the Plaza, Belmont, Regent, Mount Royal, Laurier and Papineau. Indeed, Montreal's theatre managers embraced jazz enthusiastically: no less than 10 of the city's movie houses were presenting jazz of some description as a supporting attraction during the first months of 1923.

Jazz weeks, or nights, as the case may be, also flourished briefly at Allen theatres elsewhere in the new year — in Vancouver with pianist Tom Andrews' Cotillion Hall orchestra, in London with Guy Lombardo's Winter Gardens orchestra, and in Edmonton, with a band led by Winnipeg pianist Dave Gussin at the Alhambra cabaret. By the end of 1923, however, most Allen theatres were dark. Jazz nevertheless continued to be heard sporadically in other movie houses across Canada until the arrival of "talkies" in 1928, followed by the onset of the Great Depression late in 1929, rendered musicians of any description a luxury that the majority of Canadian theatres could no longer afford.

The popularity of jazz on the theatrical stage, whether the music of American vaudevillians or of Canadian dance-hall syncopators, did not escape the shrewd eye of Captain Merton W. Plunkett, the leader and manager of The Dumbells. Under Plunkett's direction, the popular Toronto-based troupe was making the transition from a Canadian army concert party, with a distinguished service record in Europe during the Great War, to the country's leading vaudeville act of the 1920s. Its major attractions were songs, comedy and female impersonators, the last a holdover from the war years, when women were forbidden from travelling to the front.

Plunkett was not one to miss an obvious selling point. In 1922, with The Dumbells' third civilian revue, *Carry On*, he introduced a nine-piece jazz band sometimes known as the Overseas Orchestra. "Boy, Page Paul White-man, and when you find him tell him to look to his laurels,"[6] instructed Plunkett's promotional material, making bold comparison to the rotund New York orchestra leader whose orchestrated style of "symphonic jazz" had tempered the music's most boisterous aspects to great popularity.

The Dumbells took *Carry On* across Canada in 1922 and 1923, then followed with *Cherrio*. It was likely during their Montreal stops that they recorded eight selections for HMV's 216000 series, two from *Carry On* and six from *Cherrio*. Among the latter recordings were two instrumentals, *Winter*

Will Come and *L'il Old Granny Mine*, whose primary historical value may be
as examples of what passed in Canada as "jazz" at the time. Both are rather
stiffly rhythmic — perhaps befitting a band of quasi-military origin — and
each employs some familar elements of jazz texturing in its arrangement. But
only *Winter Will Come* offers any real improvisation, an unusual 32-bar,
two-piano break in which one of the pianists — perhaps HMV's star
recording artist, Willie Eckstein, in an uncredited turn — played a spirited,
novelty-rag embellishment over the other's stolid reiteration of the tune's
simple melody. Paul Whiteman needed not fear for his laurels.

The Plunkett orchestra's two titles were issued in February 1924,
competing for the Canadian record buyer's 75 cents with new American
releases by Whiteman himself, the Cotton Pickers (Phil Napoleon, Miff Mole
and others), Isham Jones, Benny Krueger, the Manhattan Merrymakers and
Fred Waring. These and other white ensembles and artists — the California
Ramblers, Ted Lewis, the Original Dixieland Jazz Band, Rudy Wiedoft and
Harry Yerkes' various units — dominated the lists of new dance-band releases
published each month in Canadian newspapers during the early 1920s.
Among the country's own recording artists, only the Melody Kings and the
trios of Willie Eckstein and his fellow pianist Harry Thomas enjoyed a
comparable profile on the Canadian market.[7]

Significantly, "race records" by black American jazz and blues artists
remained largely unavailable in Canada until the end of the decade. The
Compo Company of Montreal, for example, included just four items by the
Fletcher Henderson Orchestra (two as the Seven Brown Babies) and two by
Millard Thomas among the 600 titles in its domestic Apex and Starr-Gennett
series. Few, if any of the more than 120 "race" recordings that Compo
released in the United States under its export label, Ajax, were also issued on
the Canadian market.[8]

In fact, "race" material could be purchased in Canada only from private
agents in the black community[9] or by mail-order from outlets that advertised
in the Chicago *Defender* and similar US publications. Significantly, it was not
marketed through the lone black Canadian newspaper of the day, *The Dawn
of Tomorrow*, a London, Ontario, weekly that devoted its editorial coverage
in main to church-related activities in communities from Toronto west to

Windsor and typically paid jazz — and black popular culture more generally — scant attention.

In the absence of these same recordings, Canadian jazz musicians of the 1920s naturally looked for their lead to the white American bands that were far more readily represented in local stores and on US radio, as — in Edmonton, for example — Graydon Tipp evidently looked to Ross Gorman, and Frank Harvey to Red Nichols. Thus, to the extent that the finest black musicians and singers of the 1920s were heard at all in Canada, they were heard on the vaudeville stage, and even there only selectively and in performances tailored to theatrical presentation.

Mamie Smith, whose 1920 recording of *Crazy Blues* had touched off the blues craze and revealed the enormous potential of the "race" market in the United States, appeared with her Jazz Hounds in October 1922 at the Loew's theatres in Toronto, Montreal and Ottawa. The Hounds, who were featured on their own during Smith's many costume changes in each show, included tenor saxophonist Coleman Hawkins, then 17, as well as trumpeter Joe Smith and former Tennessee Ten drummer Curtis Mosby.[10] S. Morgan Powell, writing in the Montreal *Star*, dismissed the act briefly: "Colored jazz bands with colored minstrels seem to have gone out of date."[11] The singer personally proved Powell wrong when she appeared five years later at Montreal's Princess Theatre, now heading a cast of 40.

Of the other early recording artists to hold any significance in jazz history, only the black novelty clarinetist Wilbur Sweatman and the white drummer Earl Fuller preceded Smith on Canadian Time. Sweatman, whose pioneering ragtime and blues recordings for Pathé were available in Canada by 1920, appeared with his trio at Shea's Theatre in Toronto in April of that year; whatever the nature of his recorded repertoire, Sweatman made his vaudeville showpiece a rendition of *My Rosary*, played on three clarinets at once. Fuller, billed as "The Daddy of Jazz," travelled the Pantages circuit in Ontario and the west during the fall of 1922; his septet, which included Martin Mortensen, late of Winnipeg cabarets and theatres, was heard on the Regina *Leader* radio station CKCK in a program that included *Twelfth Street Rag*, *Wabash Blues* and *Dixieland One Step*.[12]

The American vaudeville circuits that brought Mamie Smith, Earl Fuller and the many other jazz acts of the 1920s to Canada's theatres generally integrated Canadian engagements on a regional rather than national basis. Smith, for example, was seen in central Canada but not in the west in 1922, as were Gonzelle White's Jazzers (with former Tennessee Ten cornetist Gus Aitkin) and drummer Sonny Thompson's Entertainers in 1923, and pianist and songwriter Luckyeth Roberts and his Browns in 1924.

Rare was the American jazz act that performed for audiences in both central and western Canada in the course of a single tour. Earl Fuller was one exception, enjoying a level of exposure that other artists could reach only by appearing on different circuits over several seasons. More typically, three black bands engaged for one Pantages season each — Robinson's Syncopators from St. Louis, George Morrison's Jazz Band from Denver and Carroll Dickerson's *Charleston Revue* from Chicago — were heard only in the west.[13]

Wilson Robinson's Syncopators, a 10-piece band, travelled on Canadian Time in late 1923. With changes in personnel (including Robinson's departure) and name (to the Missourians), it became the resident orchestra at New York's celebrated Cotton Club in 1925 and was taken over there by Cab Calloway in 1930. For Pantages audiences, though, the Syncopators dressed in plantation garb and performed before a backdrop painted with a watermelon, imagery that brought them notice in the Chicago *Defender* as the best act of their type since the Tennessee Ten.[14] Their closing number evoked the spirit of a revival meeting, with cornetist R.Q. (Roger Quincy) Dickerson in the role of the preacher and the band serving as his congregation.

George Morrison, billed as "the colored Paul Whiteman," toured the Canadian Pantages theatres late in 1924. His act mixed classics with jazz and featured Hattie McDaniel, who in turn was known as "the female Bert Williams" on the basis of some perceived physical resemblance to the great African-American comedian. Morrison's musicians, meanwhile, included the saxophonist and future Kansas City bandleader Andy Kirk.

The Charleston Revue, mounted under Carroll Dickerson's direction in 1925 to capitalize on the latest dance craze of the day, the Charleston, offered several entertainers backed by as illustrious a group of musicians as any to travel in Canada since the Creole Band: the influential pianist Earl Hines, along with reed players Dave Brown and Cecil Irwin, cornetists Willie Hightower and Natty Dominique, trombonist Honore Dutrey, a sousaphone player named Hall, banjo player Mancy Carr and drummer Alfred (Tubby) Hall.

Ironically, Hines would remember Dickerson's Canadian travels not for the cold, but for the heat. The musicians had been advised to wear long underwear during the trip; Hines complied, only to faint in the middle of a performance when the warming effect of liquor consumed in the wings was compounded by the heat of the footlights onstage.[15]

Charles Foster, known to his fellow musicians as Bass for his *profundo* singing voice, arrived at St. John's, capital of the then–British colony of Newfoundland, aboard the *S.S. Silvia* at 3 a.m. on January 31, 1924. Chester Hawkes and Pete Zabriskie were also among the ship's 25 passengers from New York and Halifax. Foster, Hawkes and Zabriskie were not new to travel by water — they had recently performed at the Palace Theatre in London, England.

Foster was a drummer, Hawkes a pianist. Zabriskie played banjo. All three sang. The trio specialized in "Playing all the latest New York 'Jazz Hits,' and Singing Rag Time Ballads and Southern Melodies," or so promised an ad in the St. John's *Evening Telegram* touting their first night at the Star Theatre.[16]

The *Evening Telegram* subsequently described their debut as "without a shadow of a doubt a success that remains unparallelled in the history of attractions in this city," adding as a rather coy qualification, "The fact of the performers being Colored quite naturally brought many [patrons] who do not usually attend a movie."[17] In short order, the theatre billed the entertainers as the Plantation Trio.

Hawkes confirmed their success in a letter published by the Chicago *Defender.* "The Star theater, seating 2000 people, has done the biggest business in its history since our opening and just when they will let us go is problematical." Indeed when Zabriskie left early in March, Hawkes and Foster carried on as the Plantation Team, drawing the engagement out to almost seven weeks. Hawkes wrote highly of the city's hospitality but noted, in wary self-congratulation, "Two other ofay [white] acts were here in opposition to us. They 'gypped' [stole] some of my brains (program stuff), but lasted just two weeks. The running was too hard for them."[18]

Charles Foster sailed again for St. John's the following January, this time aboard the *Rosalind*, opening three days late at the Star Theatre with clarinetist Ernest "Sticky" Elliott, saxophonist Bert Evans, violinist William Robinson and pianist Leroy Bradley for a month-long engagement. Foster again lowered his voice in song — *Asleep in the Deep* and *Bells in the Lighthouse Ring Ding Dong Ding* were two of his features — but the balance of the quintet's nightly program was instrumental. Foster had at least one noted jazz musician, Sticky Elliott, in his employ. The clarinetist was already a veteran of many recording sessions in New York, appearing on Mamie Smith's *Crazy Blues* and playing with trumpeter Johnny Dunn, singer Alberta Hunter and the studio bands of Fletcher Henderson and Clarence Williams. His showpieces during the quintet's three weeks at the Star included *Original Charleston Strut* and *Tiger Rag*.

The clarinetist wrote to the *Defender* from St. John's. "We arrived safe, but we had a rough voyage, five days' sailing, two from New York to Halifax... and the two days from Halifax to St. John's... We ran into a storm and I thought the old craft was going to tip over... [W]e are quite a novelty to these New Foundlanders [sic], they don't get to see much here. The population of the island is about 45,000 and there are only two Colored families here and they are [of] mixed [race]." Elliott again sounded the usual refrain: "We don't mind the cold here because the rum and Scotch flows gently all the time."[19]

Neither Charles Foster nor Pete Zabriskie were strangers to audiences on the Canadian mainland. Foster had sung on Pantages stages earlier in the 1920s with G. Wesley Johnson's Five Boys from Dixie, while Zabriskie travelled the Orpheum circuit in *Syncopation*, which starred the baritone and pioneering black songwriter J. Rosamond Johnson.

According to contemporary descriptions, these were less jazz bands than they were variety acts, broader in scope and as much vocal in nature as instrumental, their programs mixing the song, dance and comic traditions that predated jazz with jazz itself and, of course, with the latest recorded sensation — blues.

Similarly, two of the day's premier black recording artists, the singers Ethel Waters and Ada Brown, presented variety programs when they toured Canadian Time on the Orpheum circuit in 1924 and 1926, respectively. Unlike Mamie Smith with her Jazz Hounds, Waters and Brown sang to piano accompaniment alone; Waters, whose act was advertised as "Negro songs, sayings and dances," also worked with a partner, the entertainer Earl Dancer. She described part of their act in her autobiography *His Eye Is on the Sparrow*: "I opened up in my gingham apron for 'Georgia Blues,' did a smart eccentric dance, then a comedy routine with Earl [as a] build up for my comedy number, 'Mama Goes Where Papa Goes.'"[20]

The same black American vocal tradition had at least one Canadian proponent in the diminutive tenor Hiram Berry (1894?-1983), who was popular during the mid-1920s in his hometown of Hamilton (where he was otherwise employed as a bellman at the Royal Connaught Hotel) and elsewhere in southwestern Ontario.[21] Berry appeared in local theatres and sang songs like *Bringing Home the Bacon* and *Hard-Hearted Hannah* with several of the Steel City's white dance bands. On occasion, he performed with a fellow singer, the bass Byron Wade, who enjoyed a similar, though more modest career of his own; both men also sang spirituals and other traditional material, Berry serving as a church soloist and touring with the Canadian Jubilee Singers and Imperial Colored Concert Company.

Meanwhile, two stalwart US road shows, Harvey's Greater Minstrels and the Famous Georgia Minstrels, maintained their extensive itinerary of Canadian appearances throughout the 1920s. The latter company shared an unlikely Pantages bill in Toronto and Hamilton in 1923 with Robert Flaherty's celebrated film documentary of Inuit life, *Nanook of the North*.

New York's major black, post-minstrel productions also visited Canada, among them the groundbreaking Noble Sissle and Eubie Blake production of *Shuffle Along* (1921) and its less succcessful follow-up, *The Chocolate Dandies* (1924), as well as *Plantation Days* (1922) and the various *Blackbirds* revues mounted later in the decade by the white producer Lew Leslie. Each of these shows, and others that toured during the 1930s, promoted black popular culture to thousands of Canadians; during one week in the spring of 1925, Toronto audiences had their choice of *The Chocolate Dandies* — in its only Canadian performances — and *Plantation Days*, playing in direct competition at the Princess and Pantages theatres, respectively.

The Blackbirds of 1929 also brought an important Canadian jazz pioneer back home. Lou Hooper, who had been taken from North Buxton, Ontario, to Detroit as a child in 1897, was the pianist with this latest Lew Leslie production, playing under the direction of Allie Ross in a band that also included Johnny Dunn and Joe Smith. Hooper had spent most of the 1920s in Harlem, recording with Monette Moore, Ma Rainey, Mamie Smith, Ethel Waters and many other popular black artists of the day, either as a solo accompanist or with clarinetist Bob Fuller and the banjo player Elmer Snowden as the Choo Choo Jazzers.

As *The Blackbirds of 1929* drew its North American run to a close in May 1929, it stopped first in Toronto at the Princess Theatre and then in Montreal at His Majesty's. Hooper retraced the same Canadian route on his own in the early 1930s; as will be seen in Chapter 11, his decision to make Montreal his home in 1933 co-incided with the emergence of the first full generation of black, Canadian-born jazz musicians.

CHAPTER NINE

Melody Kings and Royal Canadians —
the "hot" dance bands

*"You know Guy Lombardo had it pretty rich too — he had a jazz band called
the Royal Canadians, the first time I heard them, they were a jazz band, with
a rich sound — and we were a jazz band too. Paul Whiteman had a jazz
band, didn't he? Lopez, Coon-Saunders, a whole lot of cats at that time had
jazz bands."*

Duke Ellington, 1965[1]

The music of the fabled Jazz Age — the years, roughly speaking, between
the Great War and the Great Depression — was not exclusively jazz as history
has come to identify it. A distinction has been drawn retroactively between
jazz, as played by Duke Ellington, for example, and jazz-influenced "hot
dance" music. Paul Whiteman, Vincent Lopez, the Coon-Saunders Original
Nighthawk Orchestra and many of the other white groups that recorded in
the 1920s — including the Canadian bands engaged by the Berliner and
Compo companies in Montreal — played to one degree or another in the
latter style, which typically presented pop material and novelties tightly
arranged to feature "hot" (embellished, if not wholly improvised) piano,
saxophone, cornet or trombone solos leading into a jazzy, modestly polyphonic finale from the full ensemble.

"Hot dance" music represented a marked departure from the more
expressive, loosely improvised and heavily polyphonic ragtime or blues-based
styles of the black Chicago and New York jazz bands of the same era, and of
the white bands that soon followed their example. In time, all but the hottest
of the "hot dance" bands — most notably, Phil Napoleon's Original
Memphis Five and Red Nichols' Five Pennies — would be pushed to the
margins of jazz history, and with them the few Canadian bands that were
fortunate enough to record.

Montreal's Melody Kings made their first recording in the fall of 1922. Fixtures at the Jardin de danse for three years now and a success in their recent "Jazz Night" appearances at local theatres, the Kings — led by the American Andy Tipaldi (1894–1969), a banjo player, and fronted onstage his cousin John, a violinist — had as high a profile as any dance band in the city. Indeed, their popularity gave rise by the end of 1922 to both Harmony Kings and Melody Boys, each group taking its place in Montreal dance halls and cabarets with US bands led by Simone Martucci, Millard Thomas and George Wright and the local ensembles of pianist Eddie Layton and the Le Grove brothers.

The Melody Kings' first record, a version of *Music (Makes the World Go Round)*, was issued by Compo under the Apex and Starr-Gennett labels together with *Where the Bamboo Babies Grow* by the New York studio band known as Bailey's Lucky Seven. *Music* was composed locally by the pianists Billy Munro and Willie Eckstein, with an additional credit given to the song's Montreal music publisher Sam Howard.

Munro (1893?–1969, of Grenada), a Melody King throughout the 1920s, had already enjoyed success with the song *When My Baby Smiles at Me*, written during a New York sojourn in 1919 and popularized by his employer at the time, clarinetist Ted Lewis, the High-Hat Tragedian of Song. It was Willie Eckstein, however, who was at the piano for the recording of *Music* and contributed its only "solo," 32 bars of counterpoint that set the melody of *Music* in the left hand against an elaborate rendition of the pop song *Nola* in the right.

The Kings made their next recordings early in 1923 for HMV's 216000 series, beginning with a second version of *Music* that features a different pianist, likely Munro, whose solo is unspectacular but nevertheless an improvement in strict jazz terms on Eckstein's extravagant effort.

The band recorded another 30 titles for HMV over the next year or so, most of generic dance music, but some also in the "hot dance" style. Two of the Kings' final recordings from this period, *Dimples* and a version of the popular jazz tune *Limehouse Blues*, offer quite competent cornet solos, possibly the work of Johnny Dixon, an American-born musician raised in Montreal and trained as a bugler while serving with the Canadian Army in France during the Great War. Subsequent to his association with the Melody Kings

Melody Kings, 1923. From left: Andy Tipaldi, Billy Munro, John Tipaldi, others unknown.
Detail from cover of sheet music for *Music*, Sam Howard Music Publishing Co.,
Montreal, © 1923. [Gene Miller Collection]

— he would remember them as a band "in the style of Phil Napolean's Memphis Five"[2] — Dixon moved on to New York and in 1926 returned to Europe where he recorded as a "hot" soloist on several occasions in Germany.

The Kings left the Jardin de danse behind in 1924, starting a three-year association with the Ritz-Carlton Hotel in mid-1925 and a two-year affiliation with the Palace Theatre in 1926. They continued to record for HMV until 1926, latterly under Andy Tipaldi's name, and broadcast regularly from the Ritz-Carlton on CHYC. As they moved up in Montreal social circles, they undoubtedly tempered the hotter aspects of their music; on occasion at the Palace they were heard in tandem with the pit orchestra in programs of light classics conducted by Guiseppe Agostini.

Such was the band's success during the 1920s, according to legend,[3] that each of the Tipaldis was able to amass a small fortune, only to have it wiped out in the stock market crash of October 1929. The Kings were on hiatus that year — John Tipaldi returned to New York — but took a final, extended engagement in 1930 at the Beaux Arts, a cabaret run by Andy Tipaldi at a Stanley Street address that would be famous in later years as the Chez Paree.

Between their cabaret engagements, hotel work and stage appearances, the Melody Kings dominated the Montreal scene of the 1920s. Recordings took their music to the rest of Canada. If such exposure made the Kings the leading dance band in the country, their status nevertheless came in some measure by default. While no other Canadian dance band made as many recordings during the 1920s, at least for the domestic market, very few Canadian dance bands (as distinct from the larger hotel orchestras led by Jack Denny, Sleepy Hall, Luigi Romanelli and others) were recorded at all in this early period — and none of them based in any city west of Toronto. Indeed, only two dance bands *from* Toronto, those of Harold Rich and Gilbert Watson, were recorded by Victor or Compo. Two other bands nominally of Toronto origin recorded while working abroad in the mid-1920s, the New Princes' Toronto Band in London and Dave Caplan's "Toronto-Band from Canada" in Berlin.

In the absence of recordings, Canadian dance bands — "hot" or otherwise — reached listeners outside their respective cities by radio. The airwaves were not yet crowded and early broadcast signals, though weak by

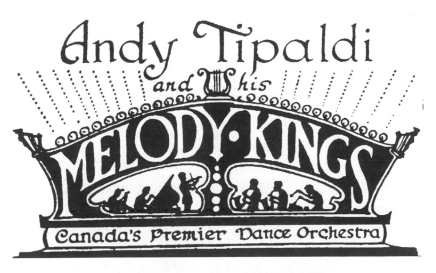

Detail, Advertisement, *Montreal Star*, 22 Jun 1925.

later standards, could carry great distances on a clear night. Newspapers routinely listed the programs offered by Canadian and US stations from one coast to the other; a newspaper that operated its own radio station, as many did in the 1920s, often published letters from listeners out of town, out of province and even out of country to support the claims it made for its station's range.

It may in fact have been through just such radio exposure that Gilbert Watson secured his initial opportunity to record. The Toronto *Star* station CFCA ("Canada's Finest Covers America") began carrying the Watson band in late-night remotes from Sunnyside Pavilion in July 1925. The broadcasts could well have brought Watson to the attention in Montreal of Compo's Herbert Berliner, for whom the pianist and his musicians cut their first six sides in early December 1925 and recorded six more the following November.

So it was in this still unregulated era of broadcasting that the syncopated sounds of Canadian bands swelled and faded freely with those of their American counterparts over radios on both sides of the 49th parallel. Canadian musicians would rarely, if ever, enjoy such unrestricted exposure in the US market again, short of moving stateside — as one band from London, Ontario, in fact did.

The Lombardo Orchestra was not quite four months out of Canada when it made its first recordings on March 10, 1924 for the Gennett company in Richmond, Indiana. Guy Lombardo (1902-77) and his brothers Carmen (1903-71) and Lebert (1904-93) had worked in the London area as early as 1919, when they took a summer engagement for $40 a week in an outdoor dance pavilion at Grand Bend on Lake Huron. Guy played violin, Carmen flute, and Lebert drums. Freddie Kreitzer, a pianist, made the first Lombardo "orchestra" a quartet.

In time, Carmen began to play the C-melody saxophone, copying his style from recordings by the American Benny Krueger. Lebert, though still the band's drummer, was fast becoming proficient as a trumpeter and soon would draw inspiration from Louis Panico's recorded solos with the Chicago orchestra of Isham Jones. The band as a whole took the Paul Whiteman Orchestra of the day as its model; Guy Lombardo does not reveal in his autobiography, *Auld Acquaintance*, whether the brothers were among the 900 in attendance October 27, 1921 when Whiteman — en route from Cleveland to Buffalo — made his Canadian debut at the Alexandra Academy in Hamilton. The Lombardos themselves had played the Alexandra just three weeks earlier.

In February 1922, the brothers began their first residency in London proper at the Winter Gardens on Queen's Avenue, staying until May and then returning in September for the winter of 1922-3. There were nine musicians in the band when it was heard November 14, 1922 on the London *Free Press* radio station CJGC; the program included two tunes from the Whiteman repertoire, *Hot Lips* and *Three O'Clock in the Morning*, as well as an early arrangement by Carmen Lombardo of *The World Is Waiting for the Sunrise*, a ballad written by the Toronto concert pianist Ernest Seitz in 1918 and popular with jazz musicians during the 1930s and 1940s.[4]

The Lombardo Orchestra also played in early 1923 for "Jazz Nights" at the Allen Theatre, where Carmen — lately returned from several months with the Wolverine Hotel Orchestra in Detroit — was usually the featured artist. After spending the summer at the Port Stanley Casino on Lake Erie, the Lombardos again returned to the Winter Gardens, but curtailed their season late in November 1923 to try their luck in the United States, first in Akron, Ohio, and then in Cleveland.

Soon enough, Guy Lombardo and his Royal Canadians — as they were now known — adopted the mellifluous "sweet" style that would be their trademark for the next 50 years. However, the first Lombardo recordings for Gennett reveal something quite different and presumably more typical of the range of music they had played so recently in London. Indeed Gennett, which in previous months had recorded Jelly Roll Morton, King Oliver's Creole Jazz Band and the Wolverines with Bix Beiderbecke, was known for the relative freedom it offered its artists to play in the manner they preferred.

The Lombardos' initial releases, *So, This Is Venice* and *Cry*, followed by *Cotton Pickers Ball* and *Mama's Gone, Goodbye*, were clearly the work of musicians thoroughly familiar and indeed quite comfortable with jazz. Three

Guy Lombardo and His Royal Canadians, Richmond, Indiana, 10 Mar 1924. From left: Eddie Mashurette, Carmen Lombardo, Guy Lombardo, Fred Higman, George Gowans, Francis Henry, Freddie Kreitzer, Lebert Lombardo, Jack Miles.

of the four tunes had been recorded within the previous three months by black US bands: *So, This Is Venice* by Cook's Dreamland Orchestra with former Creole Band cornetist Freddie Keppard, *Cotton Pickers Ball* by Fletcher Henderson and *Mama's Gone, Goodbye* by Piron's New Orleans Orchestra. The Canadians, while no match for their American counterparts, move quickly and confidently in their solos beyond the simple melodic paraphrase that so often passed for improvisation in this period; Lebert is particularly impressive in his use of mutes and growl effects. For that, for the band's rhythmic security, and for the music's textural variety, these are the finest of the Canadian "hot dance" recordings of the 1920s.

CFCA went on the air in late March 1922 and in its first weeks presented several bands that played what the newspaper described in front-page stories as jazz. A headline on April 19, referring to a performance by Frank

Wightman's orchestra, proclaimed "Radio telephone waves carry speech and jazz." A review on the 22nd of pianist Gordon Mitchell and his Syncopators noted, "the first [piece] was the familiar 'Song of India,' with its familiar aspect jazzed out of existence."

Harold Rich (1890?-1963, of Toronto) began broadcasting over CFCA in March 1923 and maintained his affiliation with the *Star* station throughout the decade, despite his band's many absences from the city. No other Canadian orchestra travelled as extensively in the country during the 1920s; Rich and his musicians finished out the season at London's Winter Gardens for the Lombardo Orchestra in May 1923, split the winter of 1923-24 between the Venetian Gardens in Montreal and the Rose Room in Ottawa and then toured nationally in 1924 and 1925 with Captain Merton W. Plunkett in the Dumbells revues, *Ace High* and *Oh Yes!*.[5]

The Rich band of this period survives on a single novelty recording, *Horsey! Keep Your Tail Up*, made late in 1924 under Plunkett's name for HMV's 216000 series. A cornetist — very likely Morris London — contributes the required whinnying to the tune's stop-time intro in the manner of Nick LaRocca's exaggerated lead with the Original Dixieland Jazz Band and later adds a vigorous, 16-bar jazz solo that reflects some awareness of other cornetists now recording in Chicago and New York. The program for a CFCA broadcast in April 1924, prior to the Dumbells tours, reveals even more clearly Rich's affinities in this period: *Turn on Your Radio, Limehouse Blues, All Over the Keys, Raggedy Ann, Unfortunate Blues* and *12th Street Rag*.[6]

London was given featured billing, and his cornet solos presumably received some prominence, when the Rich band — now known as the Versatile Canadians — went into the Palais Royale on the Toronto lakeshore in July 1926 and began broadcasting on CFRB. London, who had been with the pianist since 1922, rose to the status of co-leader by the time the band returned to the Palais, and resumed its CFCA affiliation, in May 1927.

The Canadians also had at least one other capable soloist at this time, Cliff McKay (1908-87, of Seaforth, Ontario), a teenaged saxophonist and clarinetist whose formative experiences with jazz were likely typical for the time. "I started playing and listening to jazz in Guelph [Ontario] when I was only 14," McKay explained in 1973. "First I listened to Phil Napoleon, then Joe

Venuti, and then Miff Mole. A bunch of us formed a band in high school. But a rather strict bandmaster wanted us to change things, so we went professional, playing at a local YMCA Saturday afternoons. I finally got a job with a bigger band in [nearby] Galt. My grandfather even bought me a little Ford roadster to get around in, and I thought I had made the big time. I made $5 a night — three nights a week."[7]

McKay, who apparently joined the Versatile Canadians at an even more impressive $100 a week, remained with the band through an engagement at the Hotel St. Charles in Winnipeg over the winter of 1928-29 but had moved on by the time it made its last significant appearance in Toronto at Old Spain — site of the future jazz club Bourbon Street — in the fall of 1929.

Hal Swain was one of two saxophonists in Harold Rich's CFCA orchestra in 1922 and 1923. Setting out on his own early in 1924, after the completion of the Rich band's Venetian Gardens engagement in Montreal, Swain organized a co-operative orchestra of Toronto's best young dance-band and jazz musicians to fulfill an engagement at Rector's in London, England. He was determined — according to a newspaper report published two years later — "to feature the fact that they were from the dominion and discover if the dancers in the empire's greatest city would evince the same interest in a jazz band from Toronto as they would in a New York importation."[8]

Seven other musicians were party to Swain's venture, at least three of whom — Swain himself, fellow saxophonist and vocalist Les Allen, and trombonist Bill Hall — would be returning to their country of birth. Trumpeter Alf Noakes, banjo player Dave Caplan, pianist Frank Walsh, tuba player Randall Garrison and drummer Ken Kenny also made the trip. Several were CFCA veterans, Allen and Noakes with Jack Kean's Harmony Sextette and Allen's own Radio Seven, Caplan with George Bouchard and his Royal Connaught Hotel [Hamilton] Orchestra, and Kenny with Eddie Worth's Novelty Orchestra. Allen, then 21, later described Swain's musicians as "a combination of mostly youngsters, all as keen as mustard."[9]

After a single appearance locally at the Alexander Academy in Hamilton, they left February 26, 1924 for England. While the band's departure was

New Princes' Toronto Band, Toronto 1924. From left: Les Allen, Hal Swain, Frank Walsh,
Ran Garrison, Ken Kenny, Dave Caplan, Bill Hall, Alfie Noakes
[Photographer: Charles Aylett.
Photograph NL 4562, Music Division, National Library of Canada]

front-page news in the Toronto *Star*,[10] its arrival in London proved less
auspicious: Rector's had closed while the musicians were at sea. Swain quickly
found work for his band playing opposite the popular British bandleader
Alfredo at the New Princes' Restaurant in London's Picadilly district. And
the city's dancers were indeed interested: the engagement lasted two years,
with sidetrips to Mansion House in Dublin. On Swain's return to Toronto
early in 1926, ostensibly to recruit another Canadian band, Dave Caplan took
charge at New Prince's, with Alfie Noakes (1903–82, of Toronto) serving as
his music director.

The British scene that greeted the Canadians in 1924 must have seemed
in some respects similar to the one that they had left behind at home. The
US influence was naturally less immediate, although the Original Dixieland
Jazz Band — which did not appear in Canada — spent 16 months in London
beginning in March 1919, and Red McKenzie's novel Mound City Blue

Blowers arrived toward the end of 1924. American "race" recordings were also in somewhat greater circulation, if the reviews that appeared in *The Melody Maker* are any indication. Nevertheless, early British jazz recordings, like the first Canadian efforts, were of the "hot dance" variety, among them releases by the bands of Jack Hylton and Bert Firman in 1925, each featuring British-born musicians with Canadian backgrounds, violinist Hugo Rignold from Winnipeg and trumpeter Max Goldberg from Toronto.

The New Princes' Toronto Band, as Swain and his musicians were known, did not in truth contribute significantly to the British jazz discography. Beginning in November 1924, the Canadians recorded more than 50 tunes for English Columbia, but few held any significance as jazz beyond the occasional, capable trumpet solo from Alfie Noakes.[11] The recordings did, however, launch Les Allen (1902-96) on what would be a major singing career in England during the 1930s.

Two other Canadian bands arrived in London during Hal Swain's New Princes' residency. One, known as the Buffalo Orchestra despite its Toronto origins, took a six-month engagement at the nearby Picadilly Hotel in 1924. The other, led by pianist Orville Johnston, moved from Ottawa's Rose Room into the Kit-Cat Club at the end of 1925. (A third Canadian band, led by the saxophonist Duart Maclean of St. Catharines, Ontario, worked at the Kit-Cat in 1929 as Art Maclean's Chicago Blew Blowers; Maclean had received his first saxophone lesson some years earlier from Carmen Lombardo.)

Orville Johnston and his musicians performed as Paul Specht's Canadian Band, taking the name of the popular American bandleader and agent who had set up the three-month booking. *The Melody Maker* detailed the orchestra's strengths: "A ten-piece combination, its members, who are all Canadians, between them account for thirty-five different instruments. There are three vocalists in the outfit, and the leader can extemporize on the spur of the moment about anyone or anything he notices. Among them [sic] is also a good ballad singer and a very clever 'rag' singer. Art Christmas, the first trumpet, is also a red-hot 'dirt' sax player, and the whole crowd is about as lively a bunch as one could wish for."[12]

Christmas (1905-61, of King- ston, Ontario) stayed with Johnston long enough to appear on the few recordings that the Ottawa band made in early 1926 for English Co- lumbia. He then moved at Alfie Noakes' behest to the New Princes' Toronto Band, joining the Toronto musicians in time for their final re- cording session in February and stay- ing on in Hal Swain's stead.

Art Christmas, pre-1930.
[Gene Miller Collection]

At the conclusion of its contract with New Princes', the Toronto band ef- fectively split in two. Alfie Noakes, Frank Walsh and Ran Garrison re- mained at the Picadilly nightspot as members of Alfredo's orchestra, while Dave Caplan took Les Allen, Art Christmas and five other musicians from London — Orville Johnston's drummer Lorne Cole among them — to Berlin for an engagement in August 1926 at the Scala Theatre. Appearances followed elsewhere on the Continent and in Glasgow, Scotland, before the band returned early in 1927 to London. There the Canadians reunited for a second engagement at New Princes' under Hal Swain's leadership.

Dave Caplan's "Toronto-Band from Canada" recorded more than 55 titles in Berlin for Deutsche Grammophon in October and November 1926. Again, there were novelties — *My Cutie's Due at Two-to-Two To-Day* was surely one — but the Caplan band had a stronger jazz component than its predecessor.[13] The German discographer Horst Lange compared it to the California Ramblers in his *Jazz in Deutshland: die deutsche Jazz-Chronik, 1990-1960*, noting that "The Toronto Jazzband was familiar with all styles and could play with this special 'American feeling' which pure European bands were lacking."[14] Indeed, one of the Caplan band's few surviving recordings, *I'm Sitting on Top of the World*, is a vigorous effort in the "hot dance" genre and is distinguished by Art Christmas' alto saxophone solo, a daringly virtuoso invention that displays a harmonic and rhythmic sophistication well in advance of its time.

Many of the Canadian musicians who travelled to England in the mid-1920s had returned home by the end of the decade. Dave Caplan, for one, was touring Eastern Ontario as "Europe's Big Musical Sensation"[15] in September 1929. Of those who remained in London, several became stalwarts of the British dance-band scene. Hal Swain continued to lead orchestras for several years, while Art Christmas, Max Goldberg, Alfie Noakes and Hugo Rignold were all part of a Canadian contingent that, by the early 1930s, also included trumpeter Frenchie Sartell and trombonist Tony Thorpe, both veterans of Toronto bands,[16] as well as the saxophonist Harry Karr from Winnipeg.[17]

Of these, Goldberg — born in London to Russian parents, raised in Toronto and a member in 1924 of the so-called Buffalo Orchestra — was especially celebrated in England for his ability as a jazz player, and even more so for his versatility. "'Hot' or sweet, straight and corny," the British discographer Brian Rust has written, "it was [as] one to him; he could play anything and did play everything."[18] In addition to his work with bands led by Bert Firman from 1925 to 1931, Goldberg was heard on recordings by the Gilt-Edged Four, the New Mayfair Dance Orchestra, Fred Astaire, Jay Wilbur, Ambrose, Benny Carter, Sid Phillips and many others. During the late 1920s he often played or alternated with the noted expatriate Americans Sylvester Ahola and Chelsea Quealey. Together, the three trumpeters dominated London's studios.

Gilbert Watson (1898-1959, of Glasgow, Scotland) brought a keen business sense to his musical endeavours. Raised in Midland, Ontario, and schooled in the classics at the Hambourg Conservatory of Music in Toronto, he began his career selling musical instruments. No doubt mindful of the popularity of Paul Whiteman's "symphonic jazz," he introduced his own Symphonic Dance Orchestra to Toronto audiences early in 1923. The orchestra, with

INSET: Gilbert Watson, undated. [Courtesy Douglas Watson]; Gilbert Watson and his Recording Orchestra, Toronto, circa 1925. From left: Doc Hollingshead, Gilbert Watson, Sam Ryle, Charlie Hayward, Curtis Little, Tony Thorpe, Tommy Gibson, Johnny Millard. [Photographer: Pringle & Booth. Courtesy Douglas Watson]

Les Allen, Alfie Noakes and others, made an unsuccessful foray to New York that summer.

By 1925, when public tastes had come to accommodate something a little closer to the true spirit of jazz, Watson obliged with the jazziest band in Toronto — jazzier than those of Harold Rich, Burton Till or J. Wilson (Jack) Jardine, who were his chief rivals for dancers and radio listeners when, in July, he started a year-long engagement in the Sunnyside Pavilion's Blue Room.

Watson was assisted in this new venture by Curtis Little, a trumpeter from Wilkes–Barre, Pennsylvania, who had arrived in Toronto some months earlier. In the opinion of saxophonist Ed Culley, who had joined Watson at Sunnyside by the end of 1925, Little was "the best Beiderbecker I've ever heard around here; he played a lazy type of trumpet in the [Bix] Beiderbecke style." Culley describes Little's role in the band as pivotal. "Curt was the boss with us. He'd say, 'We're doing it this way,' and we'd go along."

The band's development, presumably under Little's influence, can be traced through its CFCA broadcasts. Watson began in July by programming popular songs like *Waltz Me Lightly* and *Ukulele Lady*; in the following weeks he added *Hot Stuff* and *Hot Mittens*, tunes recently recorded by the American trumpeters Herb Wiedoft and Muggsy Spanier (with the Bucktown Five), respectively.

An unnamed radio columnist for the Toronto *Star* offered a clue as to the band's evolving style in early September, noting that "a friend walked in [during a Watson broadcast] and declared that he could always tell the [Vincent] Lopez orchestra when he heard it on air, and this was it."[19] Although Lopez's music, lately heard in Toronto from New York, was hardly the paragon of jazz, it was not without its "hot" elements.

By November, Watson's burgeoning repertoire included the jazz tunes *Sugar Foot Stomp, Copenhagen, Jimtown Blues* and *Milenburg Joys*. But when Watson took his musicians[20] to Montreal in early December to make his first recordings, he did not draw on his nightly repertoire but instead played new and unfamiliar tunes currently in circulation among New York's "hot dance" bands of the day. Three — *Bamboula, Who Loved You Best* and *Don't Wake Me Up (Let Me Dream)* — had been recorded by Bailey's Lucky Seven only weeks earlier.

These initial Watson sides, issued under Compo's Apex and Starr labels, have become collectors' items, though perhaps more for their rarity than their musical quality. Not all of the recordings have in fact survived. *Bamboula* and *That's All There Is (There Ain't No More)*, follow the standard "hot dance" format, although one of the band's two saxophonists, either Johnny Millard or Tommy Gibson, offers more than simple paraphrases in his solo, and its trombonist — either Robert Cawston or Tony Thorpe — shows some facility with tailgate effects in the ensembles. The band has a darker tonality than the Melody Kings, for example, and sounds more like a true jazz band than its other Canadian "hot dance" counterparts without actually making the transition complete.

As the Sunnyside engagement drew to a close, the *Star*'s radio columnist took note of the reasons for Watson's success: "This orchestra has remarkable adaptation. In a rapidly moving musical age, it keeps right up with the procession. Both its repertoire and its method of playing are constantly adjusted to the needs and feelings of the times."[21]

Watson's instinct for those "needs and feelings" would lead him back to a more commercial, or "sweeter," style by the end of the decade, corresponding with the passing of jazz as a popular trend.[22] For the moment, though, the pianist continued to include jazz tunes in his repertoire. He nevertheless hedged his bets when he returned to the Compo studios in November 1926.[23] Among the six new titles were the rather risqué novelty *How Could Red Riding Hood?* ("How could Red Riding Hood/have been so very good/and still keep the wolf from her door?") and a relatively straightforward reading of *Don't Be Angry with Me.* The band also recorded at least two jazz tunes — *I Want to Be Known as Susie's Feller* and *St. Louis Blues* — and probably a third, *Hot as a Summer's Day – Trumpet Fox Trot.*

The last, a feature for Curt Little, has not survived, if indeed it was ever issued at all, but *Susie's Feller* and *St. Louis Blues* reveal some favourable aspects of the band's development over the previous 11 months. *Susie's Feller* is looser rhythmically, the ensemble interplay comfortably informal without straying substantially from the core melodies. Significantly, there are several solos, including eight bars of Watson himself. In turn, *St. Louis Blues* is more moody than truly blue by virtue of its slow tempo, although Ed Culley and Curt Little are both heard in brief, smeared solos that reflect at least a passing aquaintance with the blues idiom.

"We didn't have any arrangers in the band, [so] we did our own arrangements," Culley remembered. "We had fun — that was the best band for having fun I ever played with; the rest were all work." While the recordings' informality support Culley's first assertion, the heaviness of the performances belies the second.

Back in Toronto, the Watson band spent some part of the winters of 1926-27 and 1927-28 at the Prince George Hotel. There, in April 1927, it played host to a still-unrecorded black orchestra from the Graystone Ballroom in Detroit, McKinney's Cotton Pickers. Their "battle of the bands" was broadcast on CKCL.

"That was quite a deal," Culley remembers, "to bring a coloured band into the Prince George Hotel." In the event, it was a modest coup: McKinney's musicians were welcome only as entertainers. "They played alongside us in the ballroom and then packed up and left right away. They didn't stay too long... People didn't like coloured people running around the hotels, you know?"

The Watson band summered in 1927 and 1928 at Ginn's Pavilion on Centre Island, latterly without Ed Culley. Curt Little also moved on presently, working with Luigi Romanelli at the King Edward Hotel and with Culley's older brother Fred at the new Royal York Hotel. The trumpeter's departure from Canada in 1930 apparently was sudden. According to Culley, Little had originally slipped into the country on the sly. "Somebody squealed on him — no two ways about that. They came and took him right off the stand at the Royal York — *right off the stand.*" Thus deported, Little spent the rest of his career in Buffalo.

Gilbert Watson, Harold Rich, the Melody Kings and the Lombardo Orchestra had many unrecorded counterparts across Canada during the 1920s. Among them: Ab Templin's groups in Winnipeg and Graydon Tipp's orchestra with Shirley Oliver in Edmonton, as well as Guy C. Watkins' Art Harmony Six in Saskatoon, the Merry Melody Men with drummer Roy Endersby in Regina and especially the Imperial Five — latterly Les Crane and his Canadiens — in Calgary and Vancouver. Even in the absence of recordings, some clues remain as to the nature of their music, if only programs for radio broadcasts or telling pieces of promotional hyperbole.

Les Crane and his Canadiens were, with but a single exception, Americans. They made their first Canadian appearances in the summer of 1922 as Harry J. Thompson's Imperial Five (or Imperial Jazz Orchestra), travelling as a vaudeville act with the noted black American baritone George Dewey Washington to theatres in Vancouver, Calgary, Edmonton and Regina. Presumably the tunes heard in an August 1922 broadcast from the Regina radio station CKCK were typical of the Imperial Five's repertoire: current jazz hits like *Virginia Blues, Some Sunny Day* and *Crazy Blues* as well as pop songs and a waltz.[24]

The Five discarded their clownish vaudeville garb in September and moved into Calgary's Plaza Cabaret, breaking the long run of black groups begun there in 1917 by the Morgan Brothers' Syncopated Jaz Band. Early in

1923, Harry J. Thompson mounted a new revue in Calgary, leaving the Imperial Five behind at the Plaza in Les Crane's hands. By April, the pianist had established the lineup that would stand until 1928: the banjo player Jean Pomeroy, saxophonist Lloyd Mansfield, drummer Laverne Walton and a young Calgary musician, violinist (and later trumpeter) Arthur (Bus) Totten.

Crane and his musicians effectively made Calgary their base of operations through 1925, continuing seasonally at the Plaza, broadcasting on CFCN, and appearing latterly at a First Street West dance hall known as The Isis. They also made frequent sorties to Edmonton, Regina and Saskatoon and in the summer of

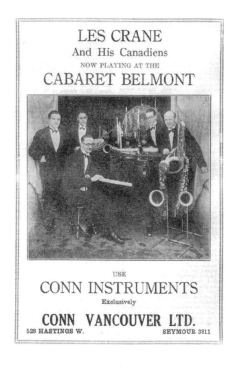

Advertisement, *B.C. Musician,* 2 Jan 1928. Arthur (Bus) Totten extreme left, Les Crane at the piano, others unknown.
[Courtesy Vancouver Musicians' Association]

1924 worked on a Pacific ocean liner sailing to the Orient. Inexplicably, Crane put Pomeroy's name on the marquee, billing the band as Jean Pomeroy's Imperial [Radio] Orchestra. Not until 1926, when the musicians followed Lafe Cassidy into Vancouver's Belmont Cabaret, with its CNRV wire, did they become Les Crane and his Canadiens, referring to themselves modestly as "Just five boys trying to get along."[25]

The "boys" would have found Vancouver a lively city during their two-year stay at the Belmont. The influx of black American musicians and entertainers at the beginning of the decade had long since passed, leaving the city's dance halls and cabarets largely the domain of local white musicians. Pianist Tom Andrews, saxophonist Fernie Quinn, the banjo player Art Thomas, trumpeter Jack (Tug) Wilson and saxophonist Ted Lander all led bands at Cotillion Hall on Granville Street at Davie, while Dick Gardner's Criterion Orchestra and Harry Karr's Rhythm Ramblers were heard at the Alexandra on Hornby Street at Robson.

To the north, across Burrard Inlet, two roadhouses operated at a safe distance from the watchful eye of civic authorities. The Grand Canyon Hotel, overlooking Capilano Canyon, and the Narrows, at Main Street and St. Denis, were known throughout throughout the Pacific northwest for their gambling tables and floor shows. Patrons crossed over from Vancouver via the railway bridge at Second Narrows, playing their first game of chance with the trains.

The Canyon Hotel imported US bands on occasion; saxophonist Joe Darensbourg and banjo player Freddy Vaughn, travelling out of Seattle, revived the presence of black Americans in Vancouver briefly in 1929.[26] Local musicians more routinely took the nightly, eight-hour shift — 10 p.m. through 6 a.m. — at the Narrows.

Al Ferris played drums with banjo player Roy Barry's quintet at both the Canyon and the Narrows in the late 1920s and early 1930s. "Hot spots," he calls them. "Over at the Narrows, we had 20 chorus girls, plus acts. But very few people danced, because all the upstairs was gambling. Anybody'd win a lot of money, they'd bring him downstairs, feed him, ply him with drink, have all the girls swirl around him — you know what I mean? — and the guy'd never have a chance to have a bit of a rest. Then back up to the tables again; he'd learn that he'd have to lose to get out."

By comparison, the downtown Belmont Cabaret — home to Les Crane and his Canadiens for two years — was a comparatively sedate Jazz Age operation. Mart Kenney, Canada's leading dance-band leader in the 1930s and 1940s, played saxophone there as a teenager in 1928 — just months after the Canadiens left for their final swing through western Canada.

"The Belmont Cabaret," Kenney wrote in his autobiography, "had a rather 'regular' clientele on weekends, but was inhabited on certain other evenings by what might be called 'the night people' — gamblers, bootleggers, madams and their entourages. They were all well-behaved and brought their own booze discreetly like everyone else."[27]

Guy C. Watkins, born in the United States but raised in Edmonton, began his career as a theatre and symphony percussionist in Calgary. Turning to jazz after the loss of his sight left him unable to play scored music, he moved in the early 1920s to Saskatoon, where he worked throughout the decade at the Art Academy with his Art Harmony Six. Watkins' leanings to jazz were revealed in remarks he made to a *Phoenix* reporter in 1924: "We use two distinct tempos, the straight jazz beat and that peculiar syncopated rhythm [i.e., ragtime] originated by Wilbur Sweatman, the famous darkie orchestra leader, switching from one to the other as the music demands."[28]

By the time Watkins had arrived in the city, Roy Endersby — identified as "the local drum nut" by the Saskatoon *Daily Star* in 1919[29] — had moved south to Regina. There, as a member of pianist Harry Pryce's Merry Melody Men, Endersby worked at the Regina Beach Pavilion over the summers of 1922 and 1923 and at the Great War Veterans' Association and Trading Company halls during the intervening winter.

A Merry Melody Men broadcast on CKCK early in 1923 included at least three tunes popular with jazz bands, *I Wish I Could Shimmy Like My Sister Kate*, *Choo Choo Blues* and *Struttin' at the Strutter's Ball*.[30] Endersby, moreover, was billed as "The Whirlwind Drummer of the West"[31] at a musicians' union dance later that year; the description suggests a musician with the energy and dexterity that typifies jazz. The Merry Melody Men were further advertised as "the Middle West's Fastest Dance Band"[32] on the occasion of their return, now nominally under Endersby's leadership, to Regina Beach in the summer of 1925.

Far fewer clues remain as to the nature of the many other bands active across Canada during the 1920s — from Eddie Gaudet's Melody Boys in Moncton to Hal Prince and His Hot Foot Four in Victoria. Rare was the group that openly declared itself "a jazz band in every sense of the word," as Vern's Revellers — led by pianist Vern Martin, with multi-instrumentalist Landon Muirhead ("a regular one-man band") and others — did in Regina in 1926.[33] Moreover, as the 1920s progressed and the Jazz Age wound down, the divarication of jazz from dance music grew more marked. No longer did a dance band necessarily include at least some "hot" elements in its music. The day of the "sweet" band was dawning.

"Dance music isn't noisy any more," the Vancouver trumpeter and bandleader Lafe Cassidy was quoted as saying in 1927. "Dance music, like dancing, is changing... A little while ago the demand was for noise and eccentricity; even the saxaphone [sic] became lost in the volume that dance orchestras were called upon to supply, but now the cooing of the saxaphone and the song of the violin can be heard among the dulcet strains of the best orchestras."[34]

The paths of jazz and dance music would soon cross again, however, with the advent in 1935 of the Swing Era.

CHAPTER TEN

Orange Blossoms and Red Hot Peppers —
Territory and travelling bands

Hollis Peavey's Jazz Bandits stole north for the first time in the summer of 1923 to play in the tiny, northern Ontario community of Emo, about 30 kilometres west of Fort Frances. The band's banjo player, Eddie Condon, just 18, was already a friend and admirer of the soon-to-be legendary cornetist Bix Beiderbecke and would later serve as rhythm guitarist, drinking buddy and employer to many other great dixieland musicians in Chicago and New York. He wrote about the Bandits in his autobiography *We Called It Music* and in *Eddie Condon's Scrapbook of Jazz*. "We played jazz," he noted in the latter book, "but we didn't come up the river from New Orleans."[1]

Peavey's Jazz Bandits in fact travelled out of Waterloo, Iowa. Hollis Peavey played saxophone and clarinet, and served as the band's chauffeur, driving a 1923 Packard around a circuit that included stops in Iowa, Wisconsin and Minnesota. The Bandits returned to Canada again late in 1923, this time by train, leaving a vaudeville engagement in St. Paul to work for Jack McGee at the Roseland Dance Gardens in the guise of the Roseland Dance Orchestra. They took over from Ab Templin's Gate City Syncopators; Templin immediately moved to Baroni's for the winter.

Condon described the Bandits' first night at the Roseland in his autobiography. The band opened with several current jazz hits — *That's A' Plenty, San, Farewell Blues, Panama, Eccentric Rag* and *Dippermouth Blues*. Jack McGee, apparently, was perplexed. Condon recorded his reaction: "'I've never heard anything like it,' he told Peavey. 'One minute it is beautiful and the next it is terrible. You don't seem to have any musicians. I can't pick out one who seems to know what he's doing.'"

Nevertheless, by Condon's account the band was enthusiastically received. "McGee shook his head. 'As long as [the dancers] keep coming it's all right with me,' he said. 'But I don't know what you're doing.'" Peavey diplomatically turned to lighter fare — *Last Night on the Back Porch, It Ain't*

Hollis Peavey's Jazz Bandits, Roseland Dance Gardens, Winnipeg 1923. From left: Harry French, Eddie Condon, Ruby Rossiena, Doris Peavey, Hollis Peavey, Harold Cranford, Gordon Leach, Cressey Whaylen, Tal Sexton.

Gonna Rain No More, Just a Girl That Men Forget, Wonderful One and *Charleston.* "But just as [McGee] thought things were back to normal," Condon wrote, "we broke out with our version of *Runnin' Wild* and he shook his head again."[2]

The Bandits were probably in place by late November, with only the palm trees and other tropicana painted on Harold Cranford's bass drum to remind them of warmer climes. The Roseland advertised Peavey's Christmas schedule in the *Tribune* and identified the musicians as Peavey, Cranford, Peavey's wife Doris (piano, accordion), Tal Sexton (trombone), Cressey Whaylen (trumpet), Gordon Leach (sousaphone), Harry French (saxophone and clarinet) and Ruby "Rossina" [sic] ("Entertainer de luxe").[3] French and Rossiena had previously worked at the Roseland with Ab Templin.

Peavey's Roseland orchestra was heard throughout the province on CKY, the Manitoba Telephone System's radio station that broadcast live from the Dance Gardens, and on CJGX, a Yorkton, Saskatchewan, station that carried the remote via a telephone hookup. Reverting to their original name,

Peavey and company also headlined an "All Jazz Week" at the Metropolitan — formerly the Allen Theatre — early in February 1924.

Condon, who would write fondly of the winter sports at River Park (likely referring to Winnipeg's carnival in mid-February), expressed the desire for greater musical challenges. He left the Bandits before the Roseland engagement was over.

"Our music wasn't bad but I couldn't forget Bix," Condon wrote in *We Call It Music*, explaining his early departure.

"'I think I'll go south for the rest of the winter,' I said to Peavey.

"'To Florida?' he asked.

"'No,' I said, 'to Chicago.'"[4]

Hollis Peavey's Jazz Bandits stayed on in southern Manitoba without Eddie Condon well into the summer of 1924, latterly working at the new dance pavilion at Winnipeg Beach, a resort spot located on the southwest shore of Lake Winnipeg and serviced by daily CNR runs. Peavey's primary competitor over the winter in Winnipeg, Ab Templin, led a band across the lake at Grand Beach.

The Jazz Bandits, who returned to the Roseland in Winnipeg as late as 1927, were among the earliest US territory bands to add Canadian cities to their itineraries. The territory band has at best played an unappreciated role in the history of jazz. By definition, it existed in relative obscurity, its activities regional rather than national in scope and usually conducted at some distance from the major jazz centres that offered opportunities to broadcast widely or to record. Indeed, some territory bands would be remembered only because a former member went on to greater renown, as Eddie Condon did. Others, including a few that travelled into Canada, lacked even this minor claim to posterity. Nevertheless, they sustained jazz — perhaps even introduced it — in the smaller, isolated markets in Canada as well as the United States that were not routinely serviced by the major attractions of the day. As such, territory bands arguably exerted a more direct influence on the development of jazz in Canada than their more famous counterparts.

A few obscure black groups — Carter's Jazz Band, for example, Bill

Moore's Plantation Orchestra and Bill Shorter's Ginger Snaps — made Canadian cities their bases of operation in the 1920s. Other bands, like the Chocolate Dandies, the Royal Ambassadors and Alphonso Trent's 12 Black Aces, operated out of American border cities, wintering in Detroit or Buffalo and summering — or, at least travelling frequently, as Bill McKinney's illustrious Cotton Pickers did — in southern Ontario. Still other US bands took single Canadian engagements of varying duration and significance: Smiling Billy Steward's Harmony Boys in Saskatoon in 1925, the Scott brothers in Hamilton and Jelly Roll Morton's Red Hot Peppers at Crystal Beach, Ontario, in 1927, and the white bands supplied by the Jean Goldkette organization in Detroit to Casa Loma in Toronto over a 10-month period in 1927 and 1928.

Of Carter's Jazz Band, little is known save that it appeared in Regina in January 1924 — an ad in the *Leader* for appearances at the Elite Café described the band as "well-known in Regina, having played at a number of popular dances here in the past"[5] — and was sighted at a Moose Jaw café in October 1925 by one of the Chicago *Defender*'s travelling correspondents, Smiling Billy Steward.

In the meantime, Moore's Colored London Orchestra opened a five-month engagement at Winnipeg's Alhambra Dance Gardens in September 1925. William J. (Bill) Moore, an enterprising pianist and promoter from Minneapolis, built his career on both theatre and dance hall work; his band had toured the Pantages circuit in Minnesota, the Dakotas and Wisconsin in 1923 and arrived at the Alhambra after a summer engagement at Minnesota's Detroit Lakes.

Bill Moore continued his pattern of split employment in 1926, establishing a "Plantation Revue" of 10 artists for work in Winnipeg and Regina theatres and halls. He spent the rest of the decade as the bandleader at Winnipeg's Columbia Theatre and by 1934 had become the music and stage director for vaudeville programs at the Beacon, holding the position until 1944, latterly — in what was now his customary white tuxedo, baton in hand — leading an all-women orchestra, the Melody Maids.

Advertisement, Regina *Leader*, 13 Oct 1925. Smilin' Billy Steward, with trumpet, sixth from left.

Smiling Billy Steward's Alabama Jazz Band of Peoria, Illinois, travelled in western Canada during the summers of 1924 and 1925 with Cullen's Minstrels. The band returned on its own in the fall of 1925, performing in Winnipeg, Brandon, Regina and Moose Jaw en route to a two-month engagement as the Harmony Boys at the Zenith Café in Saskatoon.

Steward, who played trumpet and saxophone, supplied the Chicago *Defender* with "Steward's Stewings" during this period and wrote from each of his Canadian stops. His column of news and gossip reveals the extent to which black American jazz bands were a presence in the Canadian west during the mid-1920s. In Winnipeg, Steward reported, he and his musicians crossed paths with Bill Moore's orchestra, now just starting its engagement at the Alhambra; in Moose Jaw, they were made welcome by the members of Carter's Jazz Band; in Saskatoon, the Harmony Boys in turn threw a party for the Carroll Dickerson orchestra, with Earl Hines, Honore Dutrey, Natty Dominique and others, travelling on Pantages Time.

By Steward's account, the Harmony Boys were a hit with everyone save the Saskatoon office of the American Federation of Musicians. "The boys," he wrote to the *Defender*, "were surprised to find Old Georgia [racism] in Canada but she is here. The local musical union has done everything it could against us here and up to date has failed to issue us a working permit. While we have taken the matter up with headquarters in New York, there seems to be no chance to get one, as they came out in plain English and told me our job was too good for us and that they did not want Colored orchestras on this job."[6]

The Harmony Boys nevertheless remained at the Zenith through November; according to an ad in the Saskatoon *Phoenix*, both band and hall could be rented for $45 a night.[7] But few were the takers, and by mid–December Steward had moved on to Minneapolis.[8]

The Scott brothers of Springfield, Ohio, formed their first band in 1919. Lloyd, a drummer, and Cecil, a saxophonist and clarinetist, had eight men in their employ by the time they travelled to New York to make their first records, *Harlem Shuffle*, *Symphonic Scronch* (or *Screach*) and *Happy Hour Blues*, for Victor in January 1927. Trombonist Dicky Wells, who had joined the Scotts by then, described their orchestra in his memoir *The Night People* as "a wonderful novelty band. We did all kinds of imitations — train effects, and so on. Oh, we had the gimmicks!"[9]

Two other brassmen also of later renown, trumpeters Bill Coleman and Frankie Newton, were in the band when it appeared in late June and early July — and again in November — at the Terrace, a summer dance hall that had opened three years earlier outside of Hamilton on the Niagara Highway.

Coleman recalled the initial engagement in his autobiography *Trumpet Story*. "We did not know anything about Canada except that it was supposed to be a cold country, so we took our overcoats and other winter clothes with us." Arriving in the first days of summer, however, the musicians found that "the weather was as nice and warm as it was when we left Springfield." Coleman lamented the limited availability of liquor in Hamilton but paid fond tribute to Canadian beer, noting "there was one label called White Horse Ale that I could get a good feeling from after two bottles."[10]

The Hamilton *Spectator* reported briefly but enthusiastically on the Scotts' opening night, concluding "The concensus of opinion... was that never has a better band been heard in this section of Canada."[11] Indeed, few black jazz bands had worked in Hamilton dance halls since Alexander Fenner's Clef Club musicians appeared at the Royal Hotel in 1917, although another Springfield band, now travelling out of Detroit as McKinney's Cotton Pickers, performed on three occasions at the Alexandra Academy late in 1926.

The Scotts' local reputation was otherwise secure: they were followed at the Terrace during the summer of 1927 by a succession of obscure US orchestras, including the Jazz Jesters, the Original Kentucky Masqueraders, Captain George Warmack's Algerian Syncopators and the Orange Peelers, as well as a third Ohio band, the Royal Ambassadors, then concluding the first of several sojourns in Canada.

By that same summer of 1927, Jelly Roll Morton, now based in Chicago, was living comfortably on the proceeds of his recording and publishing career. His west coast travels were four years behind him, his sporting ways no longer necessary to make ends meet. Morton had completed all of his recordings for the year early in June — just eight titles for Victor, the classic *Wild Man Blues*, *The Pearls* and *Wolverine Blues* among them. He then took over the Alabamians, a 10-piece Chicago band led by pianist Henry Crowder,[12] renamed them the Red Hot Peppers after his Victor recording ensemble, and joined the Egyptian Serenaders, Thelma Terry and her Playboys and Jolly Jack Crawford on a summer dance-hall circuit booked by the Music Corporation of America.

Morton returned to Canada in late July, following Thelma Terry at Crystal Beach, a popular Lake Erie resort spot that drew its clientele, largely by boat, from Buffalo. The steamers *Americana* and *Canadiana* sailed from Buffalo's Commercial Street dock several times daily. Morton's run at the $250,000 Crystal Beach casino lasted two weeks; an anecdote recounted by the Alabamians' banjo player, Ikey Robinson, who celebrated his 23rd birthday during the two-week engagement, suggests that the musicians stayed in Buffalo and travelled by boat with the city's dancers over to the Canadian side each night. Robinson and Morton were in conversation at the rail of the steamer when the pianist, who was toying ostentatiously with a diamond ring, blanched: he had just dropped it overboard.[13]

Only days after the Red Hot Peppers made their final trip from Buffalo to Crystal Beach, the Royal Ambassadors began an engagement at the Terrace near Hamilton. Morton, according to legend, toured during this period in a Lincoln, his musicians following in a well-appointed band bus. Lester Vactor and his Royal Ambassadors had the use of a single automobile fitted with an oversized wooden cabin that apparently held not only the musicians but their personal effects and instruments, the leader's tuba certainly not least among them.

As few as seven men, and as many as 10, the Royal Ambassadors travelled widely and no doubt uncomfortably in the late 1920s and early 1930s, taking engagements as far afield as Charleston, West Virginia, to the south and Montreal to the north.[14] After closing at the Terrace in mid-September 1927, they spent some part of the winter at the Mandarin Café in Buffalo and then, working through an agent in eastern Ontario, established a summer base in 1928 at Iroquois, south of Ottawa, on the St. Lawrence River.

The Shorter brothers, Bill and Andy — saxophonists both — were members of the Royal Ambassadors on their second Canadian trip, as was Myron Sutton, a young Canadian alto saxophonist who had been working in Buffalo since 1924. The Ambassadors played dance music and novelties, Sutton recalled in 1981, but they offered little in the way of improvisation. The band's selling point, at least with audiences in the smaller Ontario communities, was obvious. "They never saw coloured people before. The band was an oddity, and [the agent] played it for all it was worth."[15]

Sutton travelled with the Ambassadors until 1931; indeed, their core personnel remained relatively constant throughout their Canadian years — Vactor, Sutton, trumpeter Herbie Jenkins, trombonist A. Burroughs, pianist Vern Gudgell and drummer Roderick Ray.[16]

They had just started an engagement of several months' duration in or near Montreal when, on December 26, 1928, they recorded two titles for

Royal Ambassadors, circa 1929. From left: unknown, Herbie Jenkins, Roderick Ray,
A. Burroughs, Vern Gudgell, unknown, Myron Sutton, Lester Vactor.
[John Gilmore Fonds, P004/P186, Concordia University Archives]

the Compo company, *Get Off* (a blues) and *Ten Little Miles from Town*.[17]
Neither was issued commercially. The Ambassadors subsequently spent the
summers of 1929 and 1930 at Luna Park in Hull and also played at the
Gatineau Country Club in nearby Aylmer and at the Bayside Gardens, on
Collins Bay, among other eastern Ontario dance spots.

The band appears not to have returned to Canada for the summer of
1931. In any event, Myron Sutton, who introduced his own Canadian
Ambassadors at the Gatineau Country Club late in 1931, would — as will
be seen in Chapter 11 — take up where Lester Vactor had left off.

Construction on Casa Loma, the Toronto landmark that gave its name to
one of the earliest and most popular US bands of the Swing Era, began in
1911 on a crest of land overlooking the city from the north. Casa Loma's
owner, financier Sir Henry Mill Pellatt, lived in residence from 1914 to 1923
before abandoning the $1.7 million, 100-room castle in face of heavy
post-war tax increases levied by the city.

Various uses for the building were suggested after Pellatt's departure.
Gregory Clark, writing in the Toronto *Star Weekly*, reviewed the possibilities,

Henry Biagini Orchestra, Casa Loma, Toronto, 1927. From left, back row: Mike Kelly, Knox Pugh, Howard Hall. Middle row: Red Ginzler, Clem Johnson, unknown, Francis Grinnell. Front row: Spike Knoblaugh [Glen Grey], Ray Eberle, Larry Teale, Henry Biagini, probably Samuel Hersenhoren. [Courtesy Stan Kuwik]

which included a railroad station, a palace for visiting British royalty, an apartment house, a millionaires' club and a monastry. Clark deemed the last "the most intriguing of all the rumors, since the castle dominates, in its position, the most Orange [Protestant] City in North America."[18] By 1925, the decision had been made: Casa Loma would become a deluxe apartment hotel. It opened its doors April 19, 1927.

A Detroit orchestra led by saxophonist Owen Bartlett moved into the castle's wood-panelled conservatory in July. The band, one of several operated by impresario Jean Goldkette, took its name from a previous engagement at the Blue Room in Detroit's Book-Cadillac Hotel. Bartlett's Blue Room Orchestra was replaced in September by a second Goldkette band, this one led by violinist Henry Biagini and again carrying over its name from a previous engagement, the Orange Blossom ballroom in Delray, Michigan.

The Orange Blossoms remained in Toronto at least until early October and apparently continued in some variant form — billed as Goldkette's Orchestra or Goldkette's Casa Loma Orchestra in newspaper ads and for its broadcasts on CHIC, CKNC and CKCL — until May 1928. The engagement's length, and its proximity to Detroit, inevitably resulted in many changes in personnel. Trombonist Walter (Pee Wee) Hunt, for one, returned home soon after his arrival; a Pittsburgh teenager, Seymour (Red) Ginzler, was his replacement. Saxophonist Gene Prendergast left Casa Loma for Paris; his chair was filled briefly by Ed Culley from Gilbert Watson's Toronto band. Indeed, several local musicians played for Henry Biagini or for his designated second, saxophonist Glen Gray (Spike) Knoblaugh, during the eight-month engagement, including trumpeter Curt Little, saxophonist Joe Bernstein and guitarist Charlie Hayward — all also from the Watson band — and the violinist Samuel Hersenhoren.

The engagement complete, Goldkette's musicians returned to Detroit and worked at the Graystone Ballroom. After further personnel changes left Biagini, Knoblaugh, Hunt, saxophonist Ray Eberle and pianist Howard (Joe) Hall as the only veterans of the Canadian engagement, the Casa Loma Orchestra as jazz history would know it emerged in 1929. The musicians, now working along the eastern US seaboard, deposed Biagini as leader and in 1930 incorporated themselves on a co-operative basis. Initially their violinist, Mel Jenssen, served as frontman; he was supplanted in 1937 by Spike Knoblaugh, who by then had shortened his professional name to the far more distinguished Glen Gray.

The band's new members in 1929 included guitarist Gene Gifford, whose intricate, exciting arrangements of Casa Loma Stomp, Black Jazz, White Jazz and Maniac's Ball, recorded in 1930 and 1931, were not the "hot dance" pieces that had been so fashionable during the 1920s but true, full-blown jazz instrumentals.[19] Coupled with the Casa Lomans' penchant for rigorous rehearsal, Gifford's charts transformed this one-time hotel band into a formative swing orchestra. Although the band was often disparaged over its 20-year history for its brisk, parade-square precision, its popularity in the mid-1930s, as measured by readers' polls in the US trade magazines Down Beat and Metronome, rivalled that of Benny Goodman.

If the Casa Loma Orchestra bore little resemblance to the orchestra that had in fact played at Casa Loma, there were nevertheless Canadian connections to be found in its personnel. "Joe" Hall (1906?-58, of Stratford, Ontario)

The Chocolate Dandies, circa 1928. From left: Joe Brown (trumpet), Charles Victor Moore (trumpet), Nick Vaskey (tuba), Albert Holmes (piano), John Scott (banjo), Lanky Bowman (saxophone), Bill Canada (saxophone), Lorenzo (Rube) Waddell (saxophone), Elmer Jenkins (trumpet), Joe Johnson (drums). [Courtesy James A. Gallert]

remained with Glen Gray until 1942. Drummer Tony Briglia (1906?–83, of London, Ontario) joined the band in time for its first recordings in October 1929, having previously worked in London with Jack Pudney and in Detroit with Owen Bartlett. Briglia, whose deft, technically assured style was widely influential during the 1930s, stayed with the orchestra until 1944. A third Canadian, Toronto trombonist and alto saxophonist Murray McEachern, joined the orchestra in the fall of 1937 and left early in 1940 as one of the Swing Era's most distinguished soloists.

McKinney's Chocolate Dandies followed the Orange Blossoms to Toronto by a matter of only days. They too worked out of the Jean Goldkette office in Detroit, where they apparently served their manager, Bill McKinney, as a replacement band at the Graystone Ballroom for his better-known Cotton Pickers. The Chocolate Dandies saw the Cotton Pickers use their name for recording purposes in 1928, but the Dandies themselves remained at best a regional attraction in eastern Michigan and southern Ontario. A young Roy

Eldridge played trumpet with the Dandies briefly in 1928; he remembered them as "a little seven- or eight-piece band, and they could swing. They played a lot of good heads [unwritten arrangements], but they couldn't read too good..." Neither, at the time, could Eldridge, who must have felt right at home.[20]

Led at first by trumpeter Charles Victor Moore, the Dandies were working at Manitou Beach on Lake Michigan during the summer of 1927 before they arrived — "Hot as the sands of the Desert"[21] — at the new Silver Slipper in Toronto for a three-week stay. The Slipper, a $30,000 structure located a short distance beyond the Sunnyside amusement strip on the western Toronto shore of Lake Ontario, had opened as the Crystal Gardens a year earlier. By and large, it presented US orchestras during the late 1920s; the Dandies aside, white bands took the extended bookings while black bands — the Fletcher Henderson Orchestra and McKinney's Cotton Pickers, for example, in the spring of 1929 — were limited to one-night stands.

The Dandies returned to the Slipper in 1928 for the month of August, broadcasting thrice weekly on CFRB. The following year, apparently independent of McKinney's management and now travelling under the leadership of saxophonist Charles (Lanky) Bowman, they spent the entire summer in southern Ontario, making their first stop in mid-May at the Terrace near Hamilton and then returning in June to the Silver Slipper for four months. Again the Dandies were heard on local radio, now broadcasting from the Slipper via a CFCA remote. For some part of this final Toronto engagement, they played in competition with another black Detroit band, the Rhythm Rompers, led by alto saxophonist — and future Ink Spot — Billy Bowen, at a nearby Humber Bay dance hall, the Rendezvous.

By 1929, Bill McKinney's senior band, the Cotton Pickers, neared the peak of its success, rivalling the Duke Ellington and Fletcher Henderson orchestras as the leading jazz attractions of the day, both on record and in live performance. Under the direction of saxophonist and arranger Don Redman, the Cotton Pickers made many Canadian appearances during this period and on several occasions in 1929 and 1930 travelled through Ontario en route to recording sessions in New York. On one trip, in late January 1930, the band broadcast on CFCA from Columbus Hall in Toronto and on CKOC from the Alexandra Academy in Hamilton, likely giving listeners in each city a preview of the song that would soon be one of its most popular releases, *If I Could Be with You One Hour Tonight*, recorded on the final day of the month.

The Cotton Pickers crossed paths and locked horns on Canadian soil in 1929 with another of the great, if under-recognized and certainly under-recorded orchestras of the day, the Dallas band of Alphonso Trent. The pianist's 12 Black Aces, as they were billed, had split the winter between the Graystone Ballroom in Cincinnati and the Arcadia in Buffalo; they were nearing the end of a six-week, springtime engagement at the Port Stanley Casino, outside of London, when the Cotton Pickers' arrived on June 24 for a one-night stand.

According to Trent's frontman, violinist Leroy (Stuff) Smith, McKinney's musicians were clear winners of the inevitable "battle of the bands" that ensued — "the only [orchestra] that ever blew us down," Smith told author Stanley Dance. "I never heard such a band in my life! Don Redman was in charge and they had everything right."[22]

Alphonse Trent and his musicians were invariably described in no less exemplary terms by their contemporaries. The Aces included entertainers, a vocal trio and, in Smith, trombonist Leo (Snub) Mosely and (later) trumpeter Herbert (Peanuts) Holland, excellent jazz soloists.[23] For good measure, Smith noted, "We could play sweeter than any colored band you ever heard in your life."[24] Trent's few recordings (of which four, *Louder and Funnier*, *Gilded Kisses*, *Black and Blue Rhapsody* and *Nightmare*, predated his Canadian appearances) capture a band that could handle bold, challenging arrangements with precision and personality.

From the Port Stanley Casino, the Trent band moved to the Terrace. "If you like the Chocolate Dandies," suggested the dance hall's ad in the Hamilton *Spectator* on opening night, "hear this band."[25] The engagement, apparently arranged at the last minute, ran into mid-August, extending Trent's Canadian sojourn to three months. The Aces subsequently opened in early September at the Palais Royale in Buffalo but returned briefly to southern

Ontario in November for appearances at Hamilton's Royal Connaught Hotel and the nearby Brant Inn in Burlington.

The proximity of Buffalo to Hamilton allowed several other black American bands to border-hop for engagements as short as a single night. Honey Boy Carr appeared at the Royal Connaught Hotel during the winter of 1928-29, pianist Jimmy Harrison's Ginger Snaps performed at the Alexandra Academy in April 1928 and February 1929, and Captain George Warmack and his Algerians were heard at the Terrace on Hallowe'en of 1929. The Ginger Snaps, who may have included the trombonist J.C. Higginbotham at the time, also worked at the Rendezvous in Toronto for some part of the spring, and possibly the summer, of 1928.

By and large, the traffic went one way, although a St. Catharines band led by saxophonist Duart Maclean and the Buffalo-born banjo player Billy Bissett worked in upstate New York in 1927 before taking engagements in US vaudeville. Another Canadian band shared a Christmas engagement in Buffalo with Louis Schwab and his Illini Orioles from Illinois in the late 1920s. One of the Orioles, saxophonist Bill Reinhardt, later remembered the occasion. "There was a band from Canada playing opposite, five or six pieces, and each man had a sock [hi-hat] cymbal, [and] played with this heavy sock thing. The audience loved them; ignored us."[26] The Canadians were probably the Arcadians (formerly the Harmony Shieks), a Hamilton band that used hi-hats in just this manner.

Meanwhile, the Chicago-Montreal connection established around 1920 by Millard Thomas' Chicago Novelty Orchestra and carried on by "Slap Rags" White and George Wright was revived with the arrival of former Royal Ambassador Bill Shorter and *his* Ginger Snaps in the summer of 1929. "The Ginger Snaps," reported the Chicago *Defender*, "are in Montreal, Canada, where they expect to remain one year. The Boys are from Chicago. William H. Shorter, leader. They are playing the most exclusive hotel in that section..."[27] Shorter, who subsequently took the Ginger Snaps into the Palais d'Or (formerly Stanley Hall) for the winter of 1929-30, in fact remained in Montreal for the rest of his life.

CHAPTER ELEVEN
Canadian Ambassadors

Fewer than 20,000 Canadian residents, from a population exceeding 10.3 million, identified their racial origin as "Negro" for the census taken in 1931.[1] Of these, slightly more than a third were living in Ontario,[2] based for the most part in cities and towns from Toronto west to Windsor.

The first blacks arrived in what was then Upper Canada during and after the American Revolution (1775-83), either as slaves to British Loyalists or, in a few cases, as Loyalists themselves, freed for their service to the Crown. Upper Canada signalled its disdain for slavery in 1793 with a law requiring that the colony's black population be gradually emancipated and prohibiting any further importation of slaves. By the time slavery was abolished throughout the British Empire in 1834, Upper Canada was firmly established as a haven for American blacks escaping slavery in the southern states or fleeing oppression in the north.

The so-called Underground Railroad, a system of safe houses and secured routes for blacks on the run, was in place by 1820 and saw its heaviest traffic between 1840 and 1860. Many refugees crossed into what was now Canada West at Detroit or Buffalo, initially settling in towns along the St. Clair River and Niagara Peninsula and later moving inland to other southwestern Ontario centres, including Hamilton, London and Toronto. They also attempted to establish their own communities, most notably at Buxton, near Chatham.

With the end of slavery in the United States, marked by the American Civil War (1861-5), the pattern of migration began to reverse. Over the following decades, American-born blacks and their Canadian-born descendants were drawn in number to the large and increasingly self-sufficient black sections of northern US cities, where the new arrivals enjoyed a greater range of employment prospects and a stronger sense of self-identity than they would have found as members of Canada's overwhelmingly white society.

So it was that the first Canadian-born blacks to have significant careers in jazz were taken as children to the United States by these same Ontario emigrants: the pianists Lou Hooper (1894-1977, of North Buxton) and Kenny Kersey (1916-83, of Harrow) to Detroit, the pianist and arranger Lavere (Buster) Harding (1912-65, of North Buxton) and the bassist Albert Lucas (1916-83, of Windsor) to Cleveland, and the bassist Bob Rudd (1920-71, of Toronto) to distant Omaha. The songwriters Shelton Brooks and Fred Stone were also taken to the United States at an early age from Amherstburg and Chatham, re-

Al Lucas, Toronto, 1943.
[Photographer: Clyde Clark.
Courtesy Clyde Clark]

spectively. Of these seven, only Hooper, Harding and Rudd returned to live in Canada in later years, Hooper and Harding in 1932 and Rudd around 1948.[3]

Significantly, there is no comparable group of noted jazz musicians originating in any other part of Canada, including Nova Scotia, the one province whose black population exceeded that of Ontario. The lone anomaly appears to be the Chicago pianist, composer and arranger Hartzell Strathdene (Tiny) Parham (1900-43), reportedly born in Winnipeg and raised in Kansas City.[4]

Young black musicians maturing in the United States would have had a decided advantage over their counterparts in Ontario — indeed, anywhere in Canada, save possibly Montreal. The cities of Detroit and Cleveland, for two, offered far greater opportunity for instruction and employment, as well as for contact with older musicians living in, or passing through, the black neighbourhoods. Blacks in Ontario communities, meanwhile, remained few in number, marginalized by white society, lacking in their own economic infrastructure and very much in the reactionary thrall, socially and culturally, of the Christian churches — in all, not a context in which jazz would readily flourish.

Typically, two of the earliest black jazz bands in Ontario appear to have had, at best, a fleeting existence: Waldon's Five Sharps and Flats in Stratford in 1926, and Harry Coursey's Coloured Merrymakers (or Night Hawks), active in the London area briefly in 1930.

A third, Douglas Wark's Canadian Ambassadors, made a stronger, if still passing impression, in 1931, undertaking more than 30 engagements during the final three months of the year, including a weekly dance at the Dominion Rubber Company in Wark's hometown of Kitchener, as well as several trips to Hamilton and occasional visits to Elmira, Galt, Guelph and Stratford. Ads in the Hamilton *Spectator* for the Ambassadors' appearances locally at the Markeen Gardens promise "Step Dancing" and "Those Sizzling Blues,"[5] leaving no doubt as to the nature of the band's performances.

Douglas Wark's Canadian Ambassadors played their final engagement on Christmas night, 1931, at the Markeen Gardens. Two days later, Myron (Mynie) Sutton's Canadian Ambassadors opened at the Gatineau Country Club in Aylmer, Quebec. The two bands seem to be connected, if only circumstantially: Sutton, who was living in Guelph, little more than 20 kilometres east of Kitchener, in late 1931, appears to be the alto saxophonist in a photograph of the Wark band — a photograph used on a poster found in a scrapbook that Sutton kept of his own career as a musician.[6]

By the advent of the Canadian Ambassadors, Sutton (1903-82, of Niagara Falls) had been working professionally for about seven years, starting his career in 1924 with a band led in Buffalo by pianist Joe Stewart.[7] Sutton left Canada as a trained musician but typically required a few years stateside to become seasoned in the more informal ways of jazz. By 1927, he was capable enough to play in drummer Eugene Primus' Birds of Paradise beside three musicians of some renown, the one-armed trumpeter Theodore (Wingie) Carpenter, the trombonist J.C. Higginbotham and the pioneering jazz violinist Robert (Juice) Wilson.

Higginbotham and Wilson, each a little younger than Sutton and already well-travelled, were not long for Buffalo. Both men moved to New York in 1928, the trombonist joining Luis Russell's orchestra and the violinist working with Lloyd Scott and Luckyeth Roberts before leaving for Europe in 1929 with Noble Sissle.

Higginbotham apparently encouraged his Canadian bandmate to show similar initiative. "Higginbotham wanted me to go to New York, and guys like that figured I was qualified *to* go to New York," Sutton recalled in 1981. "But New York sounded big to me, and I just didn't want to be bothered."[8] Instead, Sutton travelled from 1927 or 1928 until early 1931 with Cleveland's Royal Ambassadors, work-

Kenny Kersey, 1949.
[Courtesy Sheila Vaughan]

ing on a circuit that introduced him to the possibilities that existed for a black band in Ontario and Quebec — possibilities that he would all but exhaust on his own with the Canadian Ambassadors during the 1930s.

The Canadian Ambassadors spent about a year at the Gatineau Country Club, broadcasting locally on CKCO. Mynie Sutton aside, at least two of the other original Ambassadors could boast US experience. Saxophonist Lloyd Duncan of Guelph had played with Joe Stewart, Captain George Warmack and Jimmie Lunceford, probably in the Buffalo area, while drummer Terry Hooper of North Buxton was working in Cleveland immediately prior to the Gatineau engagement. The remaining Ambassadors were all members of the Guelph local of the American Federation of Musicians: Lloyd Duncan's brother Clyde, who played banjo (and later bass), Benjamin Rogers (possibly a saxophonist), Oscar Summers (probably a trumpeter), and John Waldon, a pianist.[9]

Lloyd and Clyde Duncan were relatively constant to the Ambassadors through the 1930s. Otherwise, the turnover in personnel was high, reflecting Sutton's struggle to maintain a consistent level of musicianship while dealing

The Canadian Ambassadors, Gatineau Country Club, circa 1932.
From left: Terry Hooper, Buster Harding, Clyde Duncan, Lloyd Duncan, Mynie Sutton,
possibly George Bennett, possibly Oscar Summers. [Photographer: Dery, Hull.
Mynie Sutton Fonds, P019/P11, Concordia University Archives]

with the vagaries of such employment and remuneration as were available to
the Ambassadors. John Waldon, for one, was found wanting as a pianist and
ordered replaced by management at the Gatineau. The Duncans, Terry
Hooper and Summers were still with Sutton when he left Aylmer for
Montreal at the turn of 1933, but George Bennett was now playing
saxophone, while Brad Moxley and then Buster Harding — summoned from
Windsor and Cleveland, respectively — had followed Waldon at the piano.[10]

Of the 25 or more musicians who played for Mynie Sutton in a variety
of configurations during the 1930s,[11] only Harding and *his* replacement, Lou
Hooper, have been accorded a place in jazz history. Harding was 20 when
he joined the Canadian Ambassadors in 1932, already a veteran of travels in
Ohio and Pennsylvania with the Cleveland territory band of saxophonist
Marion Sears. Harding had just turned 21 when he left the Ambassadors in
the spring of 1933; Lou Hooper remembered him at this time as "already a
promising pianoman in the Earl 'Fahtha' [sic] Hines tradition." In his
unpublished autobiography *That Happy Road*, Hooper noted that Harding

was playing at a St. Urbain Street spot, the Paramount Grill, and "soon became a sensation in Montreal."[12]

Harding, who may have rejoined the Ambassadors for a time in Montreal, appears to have returned to Cleveland in 1934 or 1935. He later made his way to the east coast — first to Boston and then, by 1939, to New York. There, through the 1940s, he wrote arrangements for the orchestras of Teddy Wilson, Coleman Hawkins, Count Basie, Cab Calloway, Benny Goodman, Earl Hines, Artie Shaw and Roy Eldridge; his rhythmically assertive and harmonically rich charts were relatively advanced for the time and proved to be highly influential on the swing idiom.

Lou Hooper, 18 years Harding's senior, had already made a modest contribution to jazz history in New York with his recordings as an accompanist to blues singers during the 1920s. His Harlem piano style was rather older than, and certainly different from, Harding's more modern, Hines-based approach, the contrast exemplifying the problem that Mynie Sutton faced as he tried to develop a cohesive band from the limited number of black Canadian musicians at his disposal.

Hooper returned to Canada from Detroit in 1932 as a member of the Hooper Brothers Orchestra, also known as the Dixie Dandies. The seven-piece band, based briefly in Toronto, was led by Arno[ld] Hooper, a violinist, and included two other southwestern Ontario musicians, trombonist Warren Lewis from the Buxton area and tenor saxophonist Bill Kersey from nearby Dresden. A Toronto band, the Harlem Aces, served as the Hooper Brothers' main competition locally; work for both bands was scarce, however, and

Lou Hooper, 1937.
[Lou Hooper Fonds, photograph NL 17288, Music Division, National Library of Canada]

most of the Detroit musicians soon returned home. Staying on alone, Lou Hooper was playing at a Toronto chicken shack when the Canadian Ambassadors, without Buster Harding, came to the city in April 1933 for an engagement at the Oriole Gardens. Hooper was an Ambassador himself when they left the following month to open a new, east-end Montreal nightspot that would take its name from a popular Harlem cabaret, Connie's Inn.

On their arrival in Montreal in 1933, the Canadian Ambassadors found a small though centralized black community that in many social and economic particulars parallelled its larger counterparts in the northern United States. Some 1650 residents of Quebec identified their racial origin as "Negro" in the census of 1931;[13] the vast majority lived in or near the St. Antoine neighbourhood of the working-class St. Henry district of Montreal.

The CPR, whose lines into Windsor Station separated "Little Harlem" or "Black Bottom" from the city's main commercial district to the north, was the community's primary employer. The heads of most St. Antoine households were sleeping-car porters; many of the district's families were of US or recent West Indian origin.

Several black establishments flourished along St. Antoine Street in the lee of Windsor Station, among them in 1933 the after-hours Terminal Club, the Nemderoloc ("Coloredmen" spelled in reverse) Club and Rufus Rockhead's Mountain Hotel. Rockhead, a former CPR porter who had made a small fortune smuggling Canadian liquor into the United States while working the Montreal-Chicago run, converted his hotel's second and third floors into Rockhead's Paradise. The Monte Carlo Grill — later known as the Ideal Gardens and most famously as the Café St. Michel — opened across from Rockhead's on Mountain Street in the spring of 1934.

Indeed, Mountain and St. Antoine became the hub of black nightlife in Montreal. Known to one and all simply as The Corner, it served as a magnet for venturesome Montreal whites and visiting black show business personalities and sports figures alike. Here, to scale, was Canada's version of New York's famed 52nd Street — the so-called "street that never slept."

As had been the case 10 years earlier, the black bands working in and around Montreal during the early 1930s were led by American musicians.

Charles Prevoa, Millard Thomas and George Wright had given way in the interim to the saxophonist and drummer Eddie Perkins, the pianist Art Davis, the trumpeter Jimmy Jones and Mynie Sutton's fellow former Royal Ambassadors, saxophonists Bill and Andy Shorter.

Perkins, who may have been from Boston, led a band at the short-lived Plantation Inn in 1930 and would frequently be in the employ of the Terminal Club through the rest of the decade. The stout, cigar-smoking Davis — Mister Five by Five — first made himself known to Montrealers in 1930 with his Chicago orchestra at the Paramount Ballroom. The Shorter brothers' Ginger Snaps (sometimes also known as the Chicagoans) had played in various local dance halls since 1929. Jones, who is thought to have arrived with the Shorters, led his own Swinging Aces at the Silver Slipper in the summer of 1933.

The Americans would have found Montreal variously attractive at this time — in Lou Hooper's words, "a wide-open city with [a] flourishing red-light district, booze unlimited; no labour strikes and no bank robberies."[14]

According to Allan Wellman, who began his career as a trumpeter with Andy Shorter at the Ideal Gardens in the late 1930s, there was another explanation for the city's lasting hold on visiting black American musicians. "You have to give the French Canadian white woman all the credit in the world because she was the nicest woman to all the black musicians... If it wasn't for the French Canadian women, all the black musicians who came from anywheres, and stayed, would have starved to death. And don't forget the French Canadian families — the father had to love his daughter enough to say, 'Well, okay, if you love this man, he's welcome.' Otherwise [the musicians would] all have starved, they'd have had to go back [to the US] and take that Jim Crowism [racism]. But most of them were sheltered by the French Canadian white woman."

The earliest of the St. Antoine community's own jazz musicians — the Halifax-born Wellman as well as drummer Freddie Blackburn, the saxophonists George and Hugh Sealey, and the pianist and saxophonist Harold (Steep) Wade — were still in their teens. The Sealeys and Wade apparently took lessons from an American teacher, Milton Smythe, who lived in Montreal from about 1927 to 1937. "All the good musicians — all the *Canadian* musicians — that ever learned anything, went to him," remembers Wellman, who was too poor to follow suit. "I just learned music by hanging around with musicians."

Mynie Sutton, now nearing 30, was effectively the first black Canadian bandleader of any significance in the city and, according to Wellman, brought a higher standard of musicianship to Montreal than had hitherto been the norm. "Mynie Sutton and all those fellows from Ontario, they were good musicians. They didn't look up to the American musicians. They were better than the American musicians because, to tell you the truth, most of the American musicians who came over to Canada weren't good readers. That's *why* they had to come to Canada."

In Sutton's own estimation, the Canadian Ambassadors — an organized band with a growing repertoire of original arrangements, including a number of Buster Harding's early efforts — represented something new for Montreal. "I don't think there was that much jazz in Montreal at all, actually, until we got in there and started to experiment and started playing the music that we were capable of playing, eh? You went to the Terminal Club and they had maybe Smitty [pianist Elmer Smith] and a drummer and a saxophone player named Boston Herbie [one of two US musicians in Montreal named Herb Johnson]. But it wasn't the type of jazz we worked it up to be."

If the Ambassadors recorded during the 1930s, as Sutton suggested they did, the results were not issued.[15] Beyond Sutton's personal preference for the sensual lyricism of Johnny Hodges over the plainer style of Benny Carter — Hodges and Carter were an alto saxophonist's primary models at the time — particulars of the band's "type of jazz" survive only in the most general of descriptions.

"Our band was a swing band," Sutton said, "and we just swung, that's all. That's all we knew how to do... We never made ourselves *known* as a jazz band, but they just took it for granted that we was a jazz band." His words echo those of his Kansas City counterpart Andy Kirk, who noted in his autobiography, *Twenty Years on Wheels*, "anytime people saw a colored band, they immediately expected it to play jazz and jazz only."[16]

When the Canadian Ambassadors left the Gatineau Country Club in 1932, they also left the American Federation of Musicians. According to the union's monthly publication, *The International Musician*, for February 1933, Mynie Sutton, George Bennett, Clyde and Lloyd Duncan, Terry Hooper and Oscar Summers had all been "erased" as members of Ottawa's local 180.[17] Having set their sights on the bright lights of Montreal, the Ambassadors likely had no choice but to adopt non-union status; with the Great Depression deepening, work growing scarce and the number of Montrealers on relief nearing one in three by the end of 1933, the city's AFM local, 406, had ceased to welcome black members.

Many US cities in this period had two AFM locals, one for whites and one for blacks, each with its own executive. Musicians in Chicago, Buffalo, Cleveland and New Orleans, for example, were segregated in just this manner. New York, on the other hand, had a single local, 802, which accepted both white and black members.

Canadian cities also maintained single AFM locals, of which some — those in Montreal and Toronto, in particular[18] — were effectively open during the 1930s only to white musicians. While black musicians affiliated with US locals were accommodated as "travelling" (as opposed to "transferring") members when they passed through such a jurisdiction, resident blacks appear to have been excluded from membership.

In practical, if not official terms, this represented a change in policy from the 1920s, when several black musicians had been affiliated — however briefly — with local 406, among them the banjo player W. (Wiley) Teasley and the trombonist E. (Emmanuel) Cassamore, men whose names are distinctive enough to be recognized in reports sent by the Montreal office to *The International Musician* in New York. Black musicians are conspicuous by their absence from the same reports submitted more sporadically by local 406 during the 1930s; not until April 1940, when the former Shorter Brothers trombonist Frank Johnson is identified as a new member, do they begin to appear again.[19]

In Toronto, according to drummer Willie Wright of the Harlem Aces, "They didn't want any blacks at all in the union." By Wright's account, local 149 blocked the Aces from appearing on radio during the Depression by insisting that membership dues of $500 per man be paid in advance. "Who could afford $500 up front at that time?"[20]

The exclusion of blacks from some, if not all, of the AFM's Canadian locals was consistent with membership policies practised by the country's unions in many other sectors and reflected a general move during the Depression to marginalize further those people who were already on the fringes of society. The federal government, for example, would deport some 30,000 impoverished immigrants to their country of origin by 1935.

The unions' policies also parallelled the colour bar that existed in many other areas of Canadian society, including the operation of some dance halls. The Palais Royale in Toronto, for example, routinely turned away black patrons wishing to hear the name American bands of the day. One young Earl Hines fan, Roy Johnston, suffered just such an indignity in October 1942.

"What really hurt," Johnston recalled years later, "is that while I was arguing with the man that we had every right to go in and my money was as good as everyone else's, a drunk stinking of vomit was let through the door after making a mess of himself in the parking lot."

A protest was organized; its leaders appeared before the police commission in search of guarantees that they would have access to a forthcoming Palais appearance by Duke Ellington. "A compromise was reached," according to Johnston, "and Ellington was booked into the Royal York [Hotel] instead of the Palais Royale — and we were able to hear him without any problems."[21]

The Chez Maurice Danceland in Montreal had a similar, if subtler policy. "They'd always have a good excuse," Allan Wellman remembers, recreating a typical scenario at the front entrance: "'Well, we'd like to give you a seat but we're filled up... That seat there? Well, it's reserved.'"

The small number of musicians directly affected by the actions of locals 406 and 149 made the union's position all that much easier to promote. In Montreal, which had substantially the largest number of black professional musicians of any Canadian city, clarinetist Sydney Flood could muster only 23 men — Mynie Sutton, Lou Hooper and the Duncans, Sealeys and Shorters among them — in his efforts in late 1934 or early 1935 to revive the Canadian Clef Club.[22]

The Clef Club — called the Canadian Coloured Clef Club at its inception in 1928 — was a self-help collective in the tradition of the quasi-union established by James Reese Europe for black musicians in New York 18 years earlier. Sydney Flood's new initiative co-incided more broadly with the challenge offered in 1934 to the AFM's authority in Canada by the newly formed Canadian Federation of Musicians. The Canadian union adopted the AFM's American model of segregated locals in Montreal, reserving local 10 for white musicians and establishing local 11 in July 1935 for the Clef Club. Some 21 musicians were listed as charter members of local 11, including several men and women not associated with the Clef Club's recent revival.[23]

The Clef Club established its quarters in September 1935 at the address of the former Nemderoloc Club, mid-way between the Terminal Club and Rockhead's Paradise on St. Antoine Street. Jam sessions there were frequent, and members magnanimously welcomed those white Montreal musicians who wished to participate. Violinist Willy Girard, pianist Bob Langlois and tenor saxophonist Eddy (Adrien) Paradis — all French Canadians — were three who frequented the Clef Club, among other St. Antoine rooms.

The Clef Club survived the demise of the Canadian Federation of Musicians in 1939 but drifted to an uncertain conclusion around 1944. By then, local 406 was admitting black musicians in number. Developments during the years of the Second World War, including the acceptance of blacks in the Canadian armed services, had rendered the union's discriminatory policy of the 1930s anachronistic.[24] Several Clef Club musicians, including Lou Hooper, Allan Wellman, Jimmy Jones, the Duncan brothers and trumpeter Wilbur (Mack) Mackenzie, were enlistees themselves.

The Canadian Ambassadors' stay at Connie's Inn, from May 1933 to early 1934, was one of three extended engagements in the band's eight-year history. The Ambassadors moved from Connie's Inn to the Hollywood Club in March 1934 for 16 months, and later spent a year — beginning in September 1937 — at the new Café Montmartre. All three clubs mounted black floor shows for a white clientele and were located within a block or two of the intersection of St. Lawrence Boulevard and Ste. Catherine Street in the heart of city's red-light district.

In each case, Sutton and his musicians accompanied singers, dancers and other variety acts, the majority imported from New York. According to Lou Hooper's *That Happy Road*, a young Billie Holiday sang with the Ambassadors at Connie's Inn. Holiday, in her autobiography *Lady Sings the Blues*, recalled being "booked into a French joint in Montreal. This was my first date outside New York and I enjoyed it. I tasted champagne there for the first time — hated it and still do." Holiday, however, did not receive quite the same warm welcome that her male counterparts enjoyed. "I met a wonderful Canadian boy up there... He was a fine fellow, but his family caught onto what was going on and they broke it up but quick."[25]

The Ambassadors' superior reading skills were put to the test by the turnover of headliners every second or fourth week; only during the dance sets between the floor show did the musicians have the leeway to improvise at any length. Whatever its limitations in the latter respect, though, this was the same role that had launched the Duke Ellington and Cab Calloway orchestras from Harlem's famous Cotton Club just a few years earlier. It also offered the Ambassadors a degree of stability rare during the Depression years.

Lou Hooper, who was with the band at the Hollywood, described the musicians' life in his autobiography. "In our free time, we went to the beaches to swim and we even had our own baseball-team; also by now we had weekly broadcasts (remote-control) direct from the club [on CHLP], not to mention the numerous jam-sessions that had a way of materializing, mostly at the black clubs or bootlegging joints (in Black-Bottom) but attended by white musicians too."[26]

Between these extended engagements, Sutton took smaller bands into the Terminal Club — *Down Beat* sited the Ambassadors there in late 1937 with a photograph[27] — and organized several summer tours of Ontario dance pavilions and halls, travelling as far north as Kirkland Lake. At least two stalwart Ambassadors became bandleaders in their own right during these sometimes fallow periods, Clyde Duncan in 1935 at the Stoney Point Cabaret in Lachine, Quebec, and Lou Hooper in 1936 at the Monte Carlo Grill.

Sutton made his one and apparently only attempt to take the Ambassadors to the United States in 1934. Coming at the height of the Depression, his efforts brought a letter from the US House of Representatives advising

The Canadian Ambassadors, Silver Slipper, Toronto, 1938. From left, back row: Benny Montgomery, Willie Wade. Front row: Frank Johnson, Mynie Sutton, Steep Wade, Lloyd Duncan, Brad Moxley (without instrument), Clyde Duncan. [Photographer: W.H. James. Mynie Sutton Fonds, P019/P12, Concordia University Archives]

somewhat awkwardly that "a showing has not been made that labor of like kind unemployed is not obtainable in the United States"[28] — in effect, that American bands deemed comparable were readily available to fill whatever stateside engagements the Canadian Ambassadors had lined up.

Sutton was philosophical. "We knew we were missing out on more fame and money, but we were having fun... I never wanted to go back to the States, really. I knew I couldn't stand that pace. I would have been dead by now if I had gone [in 1927] to New York." Other Canadian musicians on the Montreal scene shared Sutton's sentiment toward the United States, mindful of stories told by their American colleagues about encounters with racism far more severe than anything blacks routinely experienced in Montreal. "Why would I want to go to the States," asks Allan Wellman bluntly, "make $2 and get killed?"

The Canadian Ambassadors left the Montmartre in August 1938, but not before Mynie Sutton had sketched out *Moanin' at the Montmartre*, using a simple riff that bore more than passing resemblance to the opening notes of *Christopher Columbus*, a popular jazz theme written by the American saxophonist Chu Berry. Sutton's choice of title was catchy but misleading: the Ambassadors had little reason to be unhappy at the Montmartre. Indeed, they would never hold such secure employment again.

Montreal's east-end cabarets were moving in the late 1930s to white floor shows and, with them, to white bands. Over in St. Antoine on The Corner, the position of bandleader at the new Ideal Gardens had gone to Bill Shorter, who in due course passed it on to his brother Andy. Thus the Ambassadors were again forced to look outside the city for work and in September 1938 returned to Toronto, spending a month and a half at the Silver Slipper, followed by a shorter engagement at the Hollywood Hotel in Windsor.

The Slipper, summer home to Detroit's Chocolate Dandies during the late 1920s, was now a non-union hall that paid Sutton and his seven musicians a total of $200 for each week's work. By comparison, the 11 musicians of the Trevor Page band from Vancouver would appear the following year at Sutton's old haunt, the Gatineau Country Club, for a reported $440 weekly. "The boys won't starve," noted Don McKim in *Down Beat*, "but they won't take champagne baths either."[29]

By the fall of 1938, the Ambassadors had long since ceased to be exclusively Canadian. Sutton still had the Duncan brothers and Brad Moxley from his original Ontario contingent. Steep Wade was the band's third saxophonist; just 20, he had already drawn praise in *Metronome* for "a hot alto technique seldom heard in these parts."[30] But the remaining musicians on the tour were Americans: trumpeter Benny Montgomery from Washington, DC, trombonist Frank Johnson and the exuberant drummer Willie (or Bill) Wade.

At the Silver Slipper, Sutton also featured a local teenager, Phyllis Marshall (1921-96), who was making her nightclub debut after a year of radio work with the CBC orchestras of Percy Faith and Jack Arthur. Fats Waller had apparently offered her a spot with his stage show around this time, as did Cab Calloway several years later; though too young to go on the road with Waller, she spent eight months in 1946 and 1947 touring in the United States with the Calloway revue. Her later CBC work on the radio shows *Blues for*

Phyllis Marshall, Toronto, 1938.
[Courtesy Sheila Marshall]

Friday and *Starlight Moods* and, in the 1950s, on the TV series *The Big Revue* and *Cross-Canada Hit Parade* gave her the highest profile of any black performer in Canada, rivalled only distantly by Eleanor Collins in Vancouver. With the Canadian Ambassadors in 1938, Marshall sang songs like *Embraceable You* and *In My Solitude*, taking the first steps toward developing the direct, sultry style that made her so popular in later years.

Bill Wade — his drums and his band, Montreal, circa 1946.
From left: Al King, George Sealey, Allan Wellman, Bill (Willie) Wade,
Steep Wade, Hugh Sealey. [Photographer: R. Gariépy.
John Gilmore Fonds, P004/P90, Concordia University Archives]

With the Ambassadors' return from Windsor to Montreal late in 1938, their horizons narrowed further. There would be no new engagements of any duration, just a final summer tour of Ontario in 1939 with Lou Hooper back at the piano. The band was playing at the Ridley Dance Pavilion in Port Sydney, near Huntsville, when the Second World War broke out in September.

Sutton, now in his late 30s, began the final stage of his professional career as a musician, making the rounds of the old Montreal neighbourhoods for the last time. He returned in 1940 to the Terminal Club — George Sealey, now 22, was his tenor saxophonist there — and played in 1941 at the Rendez-Vous on St. Lawrence Boulevard near Ste. Catherine Street. Summoned home later that year to Niagara Falls on a family matter, Sutton began to work outside of music and eventually took a factory job as a welder. He continued to lead bands in the area, however, and in 1946 again drew the attention of *Down Beat*, this time as the black leader of an otherwise all-white orchestra.[31]

Even in his absence, though, Sutton's influence continued to be felt in

Montreal as former Ambassadors became fixtures on the St. Antoine scene of the 1940s. Willie Wade and Lloyd Duncan, in turn, were bandleaders at the Café St. Michel, Wade taking over in 1946 when Duncan moved across Mountain Street to Rockhead's Paradise. Duncan gave way at Rockhead's the following year to the Sealeys, George, Hugh and their younger brother Milton.

Steep Wade, who eventually put aside his alto saxophone in favour of the piano, would be a dominant figure on The Corner throughout the 1940s, often alternating at the St. Michel and Rockhead's with Art Davis. Indeed Wade and Davis remained unchallenged until the emergence of a younger St. Antoine pianist, Oscar Peterson. And there, too, Mynie Sutton apparently played a small role: when word of Peterson's extraordinary abilities began to spread throughout the neighbourhood, the boy was invited to join the Canadian Ambassadors for a few rehearsals.[32]

CHAPTER TWELVE
Ollie Wagner and the Knights of Harlem

"...that colored genius at the Rowning [sic] *Club, Kenora, is Ollie Wagner."*
George Beattie, *Down Beat*, July 1939[1]

Twelve years had passed since Ollie Wagner played trumpet with Ernest Braxton's Moonlight Syncopators at Sylvan Lake, Alberta. In the interim, Wagner moved between western Canada's four largest cities and travelled as far north as Stewart, on the British Columbia-Alaska border, and at least as far east as Kenora, Ontario.[2] He established his own swing band, the all-black Knights of Harlem, in 1935, and by virtue of his versatility, if not his genius, he found employment with many other groups, both black and white.

At the Kenora Rowing Club, a large hall built out from the shore of the Lake of the Woods, Wagner was a member of Eddie Franks' Modernaires, an otherwise white Winnipeg band that offered "a new style of schmalz [sic] and a bit of wide open swing," according to *Down Beat* correspondent George Beattie. "Only 8 pieces, it has extra power in super trumpet and saxman Ollie Wagner."[3]

The trumpet was Ollie Wagner's first instrument but the saxophone would be his main horn. Tenor and alto — tenor primarily. He was not recorded during a career that spanned six decades, leaving only the descriptions offered by his fellow musicians to document his style and, by all accounts, his considerable skill. Wagner, they agree, played classic, Swing-Era tenor. "Like Coleman Hawkins," remembers his nephew, the Winnipeg drummer Del Wagner, who adds a loyal, if improbable qualification. "Maybe a little better, though."

Hawkins, first of the great tenormen in jazz, was widely influential from the mid-1920s through the 1940s, initially for his work with the Fletcher

Henderson Orchestra and then for his recordings with his own bands, culminating in an unsurpassed ballad performance of *Body and Soul* in 1939. His brimming sound and boldly harmonic approach to improvisation were the primary models for tenor saxophonists in this period — at least until Lester Young, first heard with the Count Basie Orchestra in the late 1930s, proposed a lighter, more relaxed and essentially melodic alternative. Indeed, it would be more noteworthy had Ollie Wagner *not* sounded like Hawkins.

"He was on the lines of Coleman Hawkins, Don Byas, the old-time guys," recalls the Toronto saxophonist Don Carrington, who played at Wagner's side in the Cy McLean Orchestra of 1946 and 1947. "I'd put him in that class."

Another Winnipeg drummer, Bill Graham, who knew of Wagner's playing in the mid-1940s, puts a finer point on the Hawkins influence, noting a sweeter and more lyrical quality. "It wasn't [just] the Coleman Hawkins thing, but the Coleman Hawkins thing through Herschel Evans... It was lighter, but it wasn't like 'Lester Young' light. He had that Hawkins thing. He was pretty fast, but he could play a *melody*."

As for Wagner's alto style, the Winnipeg trumpeter Paul Grosney, a Wagner sideman in 1942 at Lido Plage, remembers the influence of Benny Carter, an impression perhaps compounded by the fact that Wagner — like the American Carter — was also a trumpeter, arranger, pianist and singer. The Regina drummer Jim Moffatt, who backed Wagner during an Edmonton concert in the early 1950s, describes the saxophonist's playing as "hard-driving... more in the Louis Jordan school. He really swung."

Wagner's trumpet playing was less advanced but still highly effective in a straightforward, melodic manner. "He didn't have the range on trumpet," notes Paul Grosney. "He didn't play 'high' and even his sound was thin. But he played with such heart that it came through the horn... Sometimes he'd play the simplest things. You know how simple Louis Armstrong played? That's the essence of great music, to make it simple."

"Ollie could have crossed the border and worked for anybody — *any* band," asserts Everett Williams, who drummed with the Knights of Harlem during a Regina engagement in 1942. Ironically, Wagner showed little interest in working stateside, even though as an American by birth — in Witchita, Kansas, circa 1907 — he would have been free to return to the United States without confronting the exclusionary policies of US immigration that invariably limited the career aspirations of his Canadian-born contemporaries.

Wagner, however, was wary. According to family legend, his father, born into slavery, had spent several years in a US prison for manslaughter before taking the family to the Athabaska district north of Edmonton around 1910. The senior Wagner was a bitter man; young Ollie took his father's experiences to heart and declined to return to the United States, no matter how restricted the opportunities for a black musician in Canada. Instead, he travelled widely from west to east during the mid-1930s and the 1940s, becoming a link figure between the small, black jazz scenes from Vancouver to Toronto.

On occasion, though, he must have cast an envious eye south. Indeed, at some point during the 1940s he sent a few of his arrangements to one of the Dorsey brothers — either Tommy or Jimmy, both then enjoying great success with their respective orchestras. His submissions were neither acknowledged nor returned.

The Wagners, like many of the Athabaska settlers, eventually moved to Edmonton, where Ollie — one of four children — received his first trumpet from the Salvation Army. A career as a musician would surely have seemed like an attractive alternative to the jobs that were otherwise available to Canadian blacks as sleeping-car porters, shoeshines and, particular to Edmonton, labourers in the city's east-end meat-packing plants.

For Wagner, who in fact worked at Swift's during his late teens, the example of two older black Americans in Edmonton, Shirley Oliver and Ernest Braxton, must have been by turns encouraging and cautionary. Oliver was finally able to make his living as a musician after several years as a porter, but Braxton continued to work as a barber. In any event, both men eventually moved on — back, in fact, to the United States.

Sports offered a similar means of advancement. Wagner's older brother Walter was a baseball player of sufficient skill to catch on for a time with the Texas Giants, a team that travelled as part of a carnival in western Canada, although he too would eventually take work at Swift's. Other Edmonton blacks were involved in both music and sports. Les Bailey played clarinet and hockey, his skills on the ice bringing him the nickname "Tiger Ace" after the great Toronto Maple Leaf forward of the day, Ace Bailey. Jessie Jones, meanwhile, was a pianist, trumpeter and, in the words of Les Bailey's brother Harvey, "one of the runningest dudes that ever hit Edmonton; he beat the British Empire champion and beat him without even a pair of spikes — beat him in his stocking feet."

Harvey Bailey himself was a professional boxer who had tried his hand at trumpet in Edmonton and would later be pressed into service as a drummer around Winnipeg. A third Bailey, Eddie, played trombone. "You wanted to find something to do during the day," he notes, of life during the years of the Great Depression. "That's why we fell back on music. And you could make the odd dollar-and-a-half, which was a lot of money."

There were several social occasions in the black communities in and around Edmonton that called for a musician's services — picnics and other church functions, dances and holiday celebrations. At the same time, Ollie Wagner's early work with Ernie Braxton in 1927 at the Rialto theatre and at Sylvan Lake would have opened his eyes to the opportunities that existed outside the community — opportunities that would need to be explored further if he were to make music his career.

Wagner had some success initially as a singer on radio station CFRN, where he was introduced as The Lark of the Air. *Pennies from Heaven* was apparently a favourite song. He also worked occasionally for Louis Biamonte, an Italian bandleader who employed another black musician, Wagner's brother-in-law Joe Boyd, on a regular basis at the Palace Gardens. After Wagner's example, Boyd played trumpet and saxophone and was also an arranger. Indeed, Boyd may have been the first of the many musicians that Wagner taught, formally or informally, over the next 20 years — in some cases simply to fill an empty chair in one of his bands.

In 1934 Wagner left Edmonton for Calgary and in May 1935 introduced a new band, the Knights of Harlem, at an Eighth Avenue cabaret called the Green Lantern. It was a bold initiative, coming at a time when the effects of

Edmonton musicians, 1930s.
From left, back row: Mel Crump, Ollie Wagner.
Front row: Harvey Bailey, Timmy Mayes.
[Courtesy Mel Crump]

the Depression were hitting western Canada with particular severity; Wagner watched in early June with other Calgarians as more than 1000 men from unemployment relief camps in British Columbia passed through the city en route to protest their plight on Parliament Hill, picking up supporters along the way for what came to be known as the On to Ottawa Trek. The Knights of Harlem nevertheless succeeded by late June in acquiring the sponsorship of the city's York and St. Regis hotels for what was billed as a "coast-to-coast tour."[4]

Wagner was not the only black bandleader to try his luck on the road in Canada that difficult summer: two Montreal groups, Jimmy Jones' Harlem Dukes of Rhythm and Mynie Sutton's Canadian Ambassadors, were barnstorming in Ontario and Quebec. As the On to Ottawa Trek continued eastward, only to be stopped by the combined force of the Royal Canadian Mounted Police and local police in Regina, the Knights of Harlem worked around southern Alberta and then headed west — via the Elks' and Athletic Association halls in Kamloops — to Vancouver, where they opened in early November at the Roxy Ballroom.

Wagner had six musicians in his employ when he arrived on the coast, including the Calgary pianist Verne King and the Winnipeg trumpeter Frankie Nelson. By the end of the month, when the Knights left the Roxy, he had added a seventh, Lionel Mitchell, just 18, on tenor saxophone.

There were four brothers in the Mitchell family, Stan — the eldest — Elliott, Lionel and Les. Their father, Greenwood Mitchell, a logging engineer, had arrived in Vancouver as a travelling musician from Montgomery, Alabama, via Chicago; mindful of his sons' limited prospects in British Columbia outside of logging and, of course, the railroad, he encouraged their interest in music, providing instruments and some semblance of instruction.

Initially the Mitchell boys performed together as a trio: Stan played alto saxophone, Elliott, piano, and Lionel, drums. In the early 1930s they were heard on CJOR from La Fonda, a 4th Avenue roadhouse near Jericho Park. When Les, barely into his teens, joined the band as a drummer around 1933, Lionel switched to tenor saxophone.

Adding a fifth musician, and sometimes a sixth, the Mitchells worked in the city's overlapping black and sporting districts around Main Street and East Hastings. Their longest engagement, circa 1934, found them backing shows at the Royal Theatre, a burlesque house next door to Jelly Roll Morton's old Hastings Street haunt, the Regent Hotel. By night they played for dancing at the Three Monkeys, a nightclub on the Kingsway.

There were few other black musicians in Vancouver during the 1930s. Most were pianists, among them Tommy Thompson, Joe Wilson and a fellow known only as Shebo. Thompson, according to Elliott Mitchell, was the most advanced of the three; he worked for the white trumpeter Sandy De Santis at the Venice Café on Main Street. Wilson, a former boxer, had a rough but exuberant style in one key and one key only, F-sharp, which used the piano's raised — and thus easily struck — black keys. Shebo, meanwhile, played ragtime. Both Wilson and Shebo entertained at Rosa Pryor's famous Chicken Inn on Keefer Street, as did Mitchell around 1932 and again just before he moved to Seattle late in the decade.

Mitchell, Wilson and Shebo also found employment at Buddy's, the Scat Inn and other bootlegging "joints" that flourished in Hogan's Alley, a laneway running between and parallel to Prior and Union streets, very near the city's

Main Street railway terminal. Austin Phillips, a guitarist who moved from northern Alberta to Vancouver in 1935, remembered, "There was nothing but parties in Hogan's Alley — night time, anytime, and Sundays all day. You could go by at 6 or 7 o'clock in the morning, and you could hear juke boxes going, you hear somebody hammering the piano, playing the guitar, or hear some fighting, or *see* some fighting, screams, and everybody carrying on."[5]

Elliott Mitchell picked up pointers at the keyboard from both Shebo and Tommy Thompson, as well as from Don Flynn, a white pianist who worked downtown at the Commodore Cabaret. Stan, Lionel and Les Mitchell had no such immediate examples and looked instead to the visiting American musicians who frequented the black neighbourhood after playing shows at the nearby Beacon Theatre.

All of the brothers also listened closely to recordings. Lionel, naturally, took Coleman Hawkins as his model. "Somebody," remembers Les Mitchell, "had taken Coleman Hawkins' *Body and Soul*, written it out and printed it in *Down Beat*. Lionel put that up and tried to play it — for hours, he tried..." Indeed it was precisely Lionel's work ethic, according to Les, that set him apart from his brothers. "Either you're a musician or not, and he *was*. It seemed like it was no effort for him to sit down and practise for hours. He couldn't get enough of it. You'd wonder when he was going to quit. Whereas, the rest of us... when a job was finished, it was finished."

For his diligence, Lionel Mitchell would come to be highly regarded by his black Canadian contemporaries, indeed the only musician praised years later in terms otherwise reserved for Ollie Wagner. And like Wagner, Mitchell was forced into a career of itineracy, working in Seattle, Portland and Edmonton before taking charge in 1940 of a band in Vancouver at the former Venice Café, now a black cabaret known as the Log Cabin Inn. He subsequently joined the US army around 1942, serving as a band musician at Fort Leonard Wood, Missouri. Mitchell later travelled in the east — Chicago, Detroit, Toronto — before returning in the 1950s first to Seattle and then to Vancouver, where he died in the 1960s.

The Knights of Harlem broke up soon after their engagement at the Roxy Ballroom. Verne King, for one, was back in Calgary by March 1936, entertaining at Duke's Barbeque. Ollie Wagner and Frankie Nelson remained in Vancouver, each working casually with the Mitchells. Came summer, Wagner and three of the brothers, Elliott, Lionel and Les, sailed up the British Columbia coast to Stewart, a small town on the Alaska border, nearly 200 kilometres north Prince Rupert. "Some dude conned us," Elliott Mitchell remembers, of the ill-fated hotel engagement. "We went broke up there... practically had to walk our way back to Vancouver." The four musicians in fact took a boat back to Prince Rupert, played locally, then jumped a freight train across to Prince George, spending three nights there in jail for their transgression. Wagner continued east from Prince George to Edmonton, while the Mitchells, "instruments and all," hitchhiked south to Lillooet. They again performed locally — "so we had a little change" — and then rode the rails back into Vancouver. "It was no hardship, really," Elliott says mildly, in retrospect. "The weather was good."

The first Knights of Harlem had lasted less than 10 months, possibly as few as seven. It was nevertheless an eventful period, one that found Ollie Wagner in the company of at least a few musicians whose resolve was similar to his own. Lionel Mitchell was one, Frankie Nelson another; the trumpeter subsequently worked in Winnipeg in 1938 with drummer Joey Jampol and in Montreal during the early 1940s with saxophonist Herb Johnson.

Back in Edmonton by the fall of 1936, Wagner watched as the city's first Canadian-born black musicians came of age. Some had already started their careers, including a teenaged Elnora Proctor, who was singing on CFRN; as Eleanor Collins, she would be a CBC radio and TV star in Vancouver during the 1950s and 1960s. Others were simply biding their time until they were old enough to find work "on the road" — as porters.

Although highly temperamental, and disinclined to suffer those who took music lightly, Wagner gave instruction to several younger musicians, among them his nephew Del — son of Walter Wagner and the singer Zena Bradshaw — and Del's friend Bill Hayes. Del studied saxophone; Hayes, trumpet. Both were mere boys at the time. Wagner was a very good teacher, Hayes recalls, but tough. "You'd better learn your lesson or you'd get hit upside the head."

Tiger Ace Bailey and his Knights of Swing, Edmonton, late 1930s. From left: Joe Boyd, Lionel Mitchell, Tiger Ace (Les) Bailey, Mel Crump, Gene Lane, Verne King.
[Courtesy Mel Crump]

By the late 1930s, Edmonton's black musicians had organized themselves into two bands. Jessie Jones formed the Harlem Aces with his wife Ruth at the piano, Bert Proctor (Elnora's uncle) on guitar, Ida Proctor (Bert's wife) at the drums and Eddie Bailey on trombone. Bert Proctor was the Aces' arranger and, like Ollie Wagner, a figure of some influence locally; he later led the Swingsters, a family band, in Calgary.

Tiger Ace Bailey, meanwhile, established the Knights of Swing with Joe Boyd, Verne King, guitarist Gene Lane, drummer Mel Crump and, summoned from the coast, Lionel Mitchell. The Knights of Swing were the better band of the two, and enjoyed greater success, eventually working downtown at the Cameo Cabaret on Jasper Avenue.

The Aces' engagements were rather more modest. "We used to go out in the country, 40, 50 miles out, and play little dance gigs," recalls Eddie Bailey. "We didn't get as good jobs as the Knights of Swing. They were making $7 a week each [at the Cameo]; we played the Exhibition one week in Edmonton, down near the CPR station, for a dollar-and-a-half for the whole week."

Ollie Wagner apparently performed only occasionally with the Knights of Swing and not at all with the Harlem Aces. Indeed, by the time the Knights of Swing went into the Cameo Cabaret in December 1939, Wagner had finished the season with Eddie Franks at the Kenora Rowing Club and was starting to work in the Winnipeg area with a new version of the Knights of Harlem.

More than 60 men were present in May 1934 when a Colored Musicians and Entertainers Association opened its rooms on Main Street in Winnipeg's north end.[6] The number may, however, be misleading: the city's two most prominent black musicians during the 1930s, Bennie Starks and Bill Moore — both Americans — found it necessary to lead white bands.

Starks belonged to the important lineage of St. Louis jazz trumpeters that included the older Charlie Creath and Dewey Jackson and the younger Clark Terry and Miles Davis. He was in fact a member of Jackson's orchestra before heading north to Winnipeg, where he opened at the Roseland Dance Gardens in September 1932 with eight white musicians. He then spent the following summer in Alberta at Sylvan Lake's Oriental Gardens, making appearances en route in Calgary. Starks' presence at the lake would likely have been known to Ollie Wagner and the other young black musicians in Edmonton, 150 kilometres to the north; Wagner, of course, had worked there with Ernie Braxton five years earlier. Back in Winnipeg by September 1933, Starks played for dances at Legion Hall, the Hollywood Dance Gardens, Steiman's Hall and the Trianon. He also appeared in 1934 on CJRC and CKY.

Starks was the first jazz trumpeter heard by Paul Grosney, not yet a trumpet player himself. "Like all black trumpeters," Grosney remembers, "[Starks] was very Louis [Armstrong]. And at that time it was almost a tradition if you played trumpet you had to sing. And he sang, but he sang *really* well, and he played the usual thing, ending up on a high note."

Curtailing his CKY broadcasts and Trianon appearances in November 1934, Starks moved on to Montreal, where he joined the Canadian Clef Club and found work with Mynie Sutton's Canadian Ambassadors.[7] By March 1935, however, he had apparently left the country; Winnipeg *Tribune* radio columnist Denny Brown reported, "According to unconfirmed rumors, Benny Stark [sic], former local musician[,] is making good with Cab

Bennie Starks, Winnipeg, early 1930s.
[Courtesy Stewart Barnett, Vancouver
Musicians' Association]

Calloway's orchestra."[8] Starks was back in Winnipeg later in the decade but eventually returned to St. Louis. There, during the 1940s, a young Clark Terry would occasionally sit at his side in the Jeter-Pillars Orchestra. For Starks' Canadian exploits, Terry remembers, he was known to St. Louis musicians as "Mountie."

While Bennie Starks' white band went unremarked, a similar organization led by Bill Moore at the Tarantella Dance Gardens in the summer of 1937 made headlines internationally. Moore, a 12-year veteran of Winnipeg vaudeville stages and now the music director at the Beacon Theatre, may well have seen the novelty and/or publicity value of a racial arrangement that he — like Starks before him — apparently had no choice but to adopt if he were to lead a dance band in Winnipeg. This was the same musician, after all, who would introduce the all-women Melody Maids as the Beacon's house orchestra in 1941, at a time when the Second World War had drawn away many of the city's male musicians.

"Scoop... Race Fleshite Directs All-White Band in Winnipeg, Canada," proclaimed a headline in the Chicago *Defender*, over a photograph of the maestro, in a white tux, with his 10 musicians.[9]

"Canadian Upper Crust Turn-Up Nose As Negro Leads White Band," reported *Down Beat* more provocatively. "Despite the efforts of a certain snooty clique that turns up its nose at dancing to a white band conducted by a sepia gentleman," wrote Philip A. Novikoff, "Bill Moore's swingsters are going great guns at the new and classy Tarantella Dance gardens at River Park." Novikoff, who had been present on opening night, marvelled, "...when I stepped into the spot, I thought I had entered the torrid den of Duke Ellington at the Cotton Club." Novikoff added a cryptic postscript. "In Bill we have an Ellington and Calloway rolled into one, though he prefers the high-brow stuff."[10]

Ollie Wagner liked to call the Knights of Harlem "the only colored band in the West."[11] At the very least, they were the only black band based in Winnipeg during the early 1940s. In any event, the billing was intended to appeal primarily to a white audience which — if it cared about the veracity of Wagner's claim at all — had no way of knowing about the activities of Tiger Ace Bailey in Edmonton or Lionel Mitchell in Vancouver. At the same time, word of Bailey's Knights of Swing or of Mitchell's band at the Log Cabin Inn surely travelled quickly in the black community given the number of part-time musicians who criss-crossed the west in the employ of the railroad.

Wagner found most of his new Knights of Harlem locally, drawing on trumpeters Clarence Lewsey and Tucker Williams, tenor saxophonist Cecil Lewsey, pianist Percy Haynes, bassist Alva Bradshaw and drummers Dave Saunders, Everett Williams and Al Thumbler. His former sister-in-law, Zena Bradshaw, now married to Percy Haynes, sang with the Knights on many occasions in 1939 and 1940.

Wagner also looked to Calgary and at one point even put out a call for Lionel Mitchell. "We started to get [the Knights of Harlem] together," Cecil Lewsey remembers, "with Lionel Mitchell, Ollie Wagner, myself and a couple of other fellows. And before we could even play the first job, Lionel and Ollie fell out. We never even had a chance to play together!"

Wagner, according to Lewsey, was "a pretty hot-headed guy; you couldn't tell from one night to the next what he might be doing." Everett Williams identifies one source of Wagner's volatility: "Ollie was a perfectionist, man. He'd be ready to take you out in the alley if you made too many mistakes. Oh yeah, he was tough."

Wagner's wife Alice concurs. "It had to be perfect. He could be a block away and he'd hear the band [playing]. He'd go in: 'You made a mistake here, you made a mistake there. Do it again.' And he'd make them do it for maybe an hour at a time — the *one* piece. He wanted perfection, because he was a perfectionist himself."

Under the circumstances, though, Wagner's expectations surely were unrealistic. He had only a small pool of musicians in Winnipeg on which to draw, and their level of skill varied, as did their availability — the latter subject to the demands of their other jobs, most often on the railroad. In turn, Wagner could offer only limited employment: one night a week at the Oddfellows, St. James or Columbus halls and summer appearances at Selkirk Park and River Park. The Knights would also make the occasional barnstorming run over the dirt roads of southern Manitoba and Saskatchewan. "They'd all pile in a car," remembers Everett Williams, "and away they'd go."

Luck, moreover, did not often work in Wagner's favour. The Knights of Harlem, down to just a quartet, lost a steady job at Regina's Oriental Gardens in early 1942 when one of their number, a minor, was fined $300 or six months in jail on a charge of bootlegging. The offense, which involved a single glass of whiskey, resulted in the suspension of the Gardens' license by local politicians who wanted to make the Scarth Street establishment an example for other Regina nightspots.[12]

Back in Winnipeg that summer, Wagner led a band that included Paul Grosney and a second white musician, tenorman Al Sprintz, at Lido Plage, on the Assiniboine River near Headingly, outside of the city. Grosney casts Wagner's perfectionism in a different light. "He knew exactly what he wanted. That was the great thing [about Wagner], because most of the guys I played with in Winnipeg weren't good musicians. They didn't know what they wanted; they wouldn't know whether you were playing the right note or not."

Grosney also recalls the telling visual image of Wagner's arrangements. "He couldn't even afford manuscript paper. They'd be written on ordinary paper; he'd draw in the five lines."

When the Knights of Harlem were at liberty, Wagner worked for white Winnipeg bandleaders like Teddy Burton and Frank Staff. The Staff band, known as the Happy Boys, played "oldtime" music on a weekly circuit that included the Oddfellows' Hall and the Normandy and Aragon ballrooms. For several months in the summer of 1943 Staff gave Wagner featured billing in the small, classified ads that the Happy Boys placed in the *Free Press*.

By his versatility, if perhaps not his temperament, Wagner was ideally suited to an old-time group; he could make a band seem much larger in its radio broadcasts than it in fact was, moving unseen from saxophone to trumpet and on to piano in the course of the dance medleys that were common in old-time music. He would also sing and had the opportunity to solo.

"There was always jazz," remembers the drummer Billy Graham, of Winnipeg's old-time bands. "You'd play songs and you'd play waltzes and you'd play polkas, but there was always blowing."

At some point in 1943, Wagner also found work outside of music, taking a job with the CPR — not as a porter, though, like the Lewsey brothers, Tucker Williams or Percy Haynes before him, but as a labourer, shovelling coal in the powerhouse. It would be only a matter of time before Wagner again moved on and, indeed, by March 1946 he was living in Toronto. The local tabloid *Hush* announced his presence: "Cy McLean, piano virtuoso at the Lobster Restaurant, tells us that we should hasten down to the Yonge Street spot and get a load of the tenor sax work of Ollie Wagner, who according to Cy, is 'out of this world'..."[13]

Cy (Cyril) McLean (1917-86, of Sydney, Nova Scotia) was the latest in a succession of black bandleaders in Toronto dating back at least to Noel Allen, an alto saxophonist whose Harlem Aces were active as early as 1931. "Although juniors," reported *The Dawn of Tomorrow*, "[the Aces] are making the best showing of any colored orchestra attempted in Toronto. They have rhythm, time and the music."[14]

Harry Lucas, a pianist, had succeeded Allen as leader of the Aces by the fall of 1932. Lucas in turn was replaced by Charlie Winn, a trumpeter; Winn, together with several other Aces, then worked for "Singing Sam" Morgan's Harlem Knights at mid-decade.[15] Like the Aces, the Knights played at dances held in meeting rooms along College Street near Spadina Avenue — the Oddfellows and Belvin halls, for example, and especially the Universal Negro Improvement Association's quarters. Both bands also performed for sports

Harlem Aces, Toronto, circa 1933. From left: unknown, Charlie Winn (seated), Roy Worrell, Willie Wright (drums), unknown, Reggie McLean (seated), Nevis (Duke) Rigby. [Courtesy Lloyd Williams]

events and social functions sponsored by the city's black community, including its annual August picnic at Port Dalhousie, near St. Catharines.

Employment prospects outside the community were otherwise limited by the bands' exclusion from local 149 of the American Federation of Musicians. Ironically, black bands affiliated with US locals of the union were able to take jobs in Toronto nightspots that remained closed both to the city's resident black musicians and, in some instances, to its prospective black patrons.

Willie Wright, known as Kingfish after a character on the popular American radio program *Amos 'n' Andy*, played drums for both the Aces and the Knights. *Tiger Rag* was one of his features; he would blow across the loosened wires of his snare drum to create the required roar. The Aces, Wright remembered in 1989, played for Italian weddings and occasionally travelled to small communities like Kincardine, Southhampton and Owen Sound, where they would be presented "direct from New York" to unknowing dancers. Sam Morgan, meanwhile, an entertainer more than a musician, and a hustler above all, had greater success in finding engagements in and around Toronto. The Knights worked in 1935 at the Holland Inn, east of the city on Kingston Road, and also performed at the Cameo Club on Danforth Avenue in the city proper; according to Wright, Morgan's stagy renditions of *The Prisoner's Song*, *River Stay 'Way From My Door* and especially *Mammy* were popular with the clubs' white clientele.[16]

Cy McLean, a small, hunchbacked man, moved from Sydney to Toronto in 1934, following in the footsteps of his older brother Reggie, who played piano with the Harlem Aces. The McLeans each worked in turn for Sam Morgan, and by 1937 Cy was leading some of Morgan's old musicians under his own name. Indeed, the story of the black Toronto jazz scene during the 1930s is effectively that of a single, slowly evolving band that passed from one leader to the next, its impermanence a function of the small number of players in the city — both Morgan and McLean had to employ white musicians on occasion[17] — and of the lack of work necessary to keep a group together for any length of time. Here, as elsewhere in Canada, many of the city's black musicians curtailed their careers to work on the railroad, among them Willie Wright and a younger drummer who first worked with Cy McLean at the age of 16, Phil Williams.

By his own account, Cy McLean simply assumed leadership of the Rhythm Rompers, a band established by a former Harlem Ace and Harlem Knight, trumpeter Roy Worrell.[18] Apparently it was a friendly takeover: Worrell remained with the McLean band through its peak years, 1944–7, contributing solos in the powerful style of Roy Eldridge and serving as a featured vocalist.

McLean maintained his predecessors' ties to the black community, but looked even further afield for the engagements that would sustain his band long enough for it to develop a distinctive style and recognizable name. He spent the summer of 1939, for example, at Chemong Lake near Peterborough and worked for much of 1941 at the former Holland Inn, now the Casa Manana, where tenor saxophonist Ray Coker was a featured soloist. By 1944 the band, still non-union, had also played at the Ambassador Hotel, the Strathcona Club, the Bloor Casino and out of town at Crystal Beach.

McLean had eight musicians in his employ when he went into the east-end lakeside Fallingbrook Pavilion in the summer of 1944: Worrell, trombonist Albert Marsen, saxophonists Lloyd Salmon and Wilf Williams, guitarist Henry Wright, bassist Vivian (known later as Austin or Ozzie) Roberts and drummer Sammy Richardson, the last well known locally as a track star who had competed in the broad jump against the American Jessie Owens in the 1936 Berlin Olympics. "Tiny" Marsen was the band's ballad tenor — Worrell handled the "scat" material — and Roberts, recently returned from New York, served as its principal arranger.

By now McLean had attracted the attention of the Club Top Hat, which had been presenting US stars like Fats Waller, Red Norvo, Lee and Lester Young, Sabby Lewis, Coleman Hawkins and Louis Jordan to Toronto jazz fans for a week or more at a time since 1942. With pressure from the Top Hat, McLean and his musicians were finally granted admission to local 149 during the summer of 1944 and took the first of several engagements at the Sunnyside nightclub in the fall.

McLean remained associated with the club, which had a CKEY wire, until 1947, expanding his orchestra there to as many as a dozen men — the only fullscale black swing band in Canada. He also worked with some frequency in 1945 at the Hotel Genosha in Oshawa, east of Toronto, and led a small group with Ollie Wagner and others for three months in early 1946 at the Lobster Restaurant downtown.

McLean was billed in this period as "Canada's Count Basie," a promotional tag that was in equal parts truth and hyperbole. There were indeed Basie arrangements in the book — *Every Tub*, for example, and *Jumpin' at the Woodside* — but McLean used the Les Brown hit *Twilight Time* as his theme at the Top Hat. His piano playing, meanwhile, approximated Earl Hines' enthusiasm as much as it echoed Basie's economy. "Old Earl, he's my buddy," McLean said in 1969, by which time he had made Hines' acquaintance. "I've been listening to him a long time."[19]

Dillon O'Leary, who had started a jazz column, Hot Platter Patter, in the *Globe and Mail* in April 1945, departed early in 1946 from his usual subject — records — to comment on McLean's "superb hot piano" at the Lobster. "Heard him Thursday night," O'Leary wrote, in telegraphed style, "and

Cy McLean and his Orchestra, Toronto, circa 1945. From left, back row: McLean (at piano), Roy Worrell, Henry Wright, Phil Williams, Nick Sotnick, Wilf Williams, Ollie Wagner. Front row: Syd Blackwood, Alfred (Tiny) Marsen, Lloyd Salmon, Vivian Roberts.
[Courtesy Phil Williams]

(later) recalled he didn't play one boogie number, which is a relief these days... But he has a rugged beat, ideas and technique."[20]

However, Helen McNamara, who began to write a similar column, *McNamara's Bandwagon*, for the Toronto *Telegram* in January 1949, would describe the pianist's music in rather different terms, referring to "the unmistakeable McLean trademark" as "light, polite jump..."[21]

In the summer of 1946, a McLean band with Ollie Wagner, Roy Worrell and others was in the employ of Lever Brothers, touring southern Ontario dance halls and pavilions to promote the company's Lifebuoy brand of soap. Billed as the Lifebuoy Debonaires, the seven musicians received about $80 a week each, a not inconsiderable sum for the time, and travelled in a new 1946 panel truck and two cars driven by employees of their sponsor.

A black dance band on the road in rural Ontario was more often the object of curiosity than of hostility, although at one stop, guitarist Henry Wright recalled, the musicians were refused service. "In other places people would line up to peer through the restaurant window to watch us eat. They had actually never seen blacks before."[22]

For one of the Debonaires' young saxophonists, Syd Blackwood, the experiences of the tour were "nothing any worse than the life I had to lead anyway. It was a lot of fun. We never encountered any discrimination that was harmful... We would blow into some town like Mount Forest, where they didn't see very many black people — probably *never* saw any unless they were part of a [base]ball team. We always found the dining room of the best hotel, and that's where we would have dinner... One or two guys would walk into the dining room, then another... First thing you know, management comes running out of the kitchen to see what's going on. And the inevitable statement would be made — 'How many of them *are* there?' — as though there was some kind of invasion going on. We sat down, we had our meal, and we moved on. That night we entertained at whatever the function was and everybody in town would turn up. 'Oh, [they would say] *that's* what it's all about.'"

For the most part, Ollie Wagner played tenor saxophone with the McLean band, sharing the solo load with Roy Worrell, Tiny Marsen and the pianist himself. On occasion he also sang; more rarely he played trumpet. McLean may have had some of his arrangements in the band's repertoire alongside those of Vivian Roberts and, latterly, a white writer, Art Snider.

The other saxophonists who sat at Wagner's side at the Lobster and on the Lifebuoy tour in 1946, and at the Top Hat through 1947, were either section players or relatively inexperienced youngsters. One of the latter, Don Carrington, benefitted both from Wagner's example — and his informal tutelage. "He taught me how to play a solo. He used to take me aside — 'Hey, do this, do that.' He was a tough teacher but he was a good teacher. He used to teach me in between the jobs we were working, on the breaks. Used to say, 'Hey, Kid' — he called me 'Kid' — 'bring your horn.'"

Wagner, the senior man in the band save possibly for the Texas trumpeter Stan Hardee at the Top Hat, was otherwise an aloof and often forbidding figure to his colleagues. He did get along well, however, with Cy McLean, nine or 10 years his junior, no doubt appreciating from personal experience the pianist's efforts — and, for the moment, his success — in maintaining a black band in Canada. At that, McLean's orchestra ran its course at the Top Hat in 1947. The pianist took his next extended engagement, an interrupted stand at the Colonial Tavern from March 1948 into early 1950, with a quartet.

Indeed, only a few other black bands were active in Canada during this same period. The Sealey brothers, George, Hugh and Milton, were in residence at Rockhead's Paradise in Montreal, Charlie Adams and Les Bryan led bands in Halifax, former members of the Knights of Harlem continued to work together casually around southern Manitoba, and Ernie King's Harlem Kings flourished briefly in 1948 in the west.

A young Ernie King heard Ollie Wagner and the Knights of Harlem during their Vancouver sojourn in 1935 at dances in the black community. "Everybody went," King remembers. "Young, old — it didn't matter. Even if you were a babe in arms, you went to the dance."

King, born in Edmonton to an Oklahoman mother and Texan father, was now about 15, and had started to play trombone. The Knights of Harlem clearly made an impression: nearly 60 years later, he could still recall the refrain from the band's theme song.

Hello, Knights of Harlem, Hello
We're here tonight to put on a great big show
Scoot, scat, like this and like that
Hello, Knights of Harlem, Hello

Through an older sister who was friendly with musicians, the teenaged King met Jack Washington, a Hamilton singer and guitarist working as a CPR porter, and Lawrence Brown, the influential trombonist with Duke Ellington's orchestra. Washington advised King to find a teacher, while Brown offered moral support, leaving the young man "more determined than ever to play trombone."

King's first band was something of a family affair. His brother Leroy played piano. A cousin originally from Calgary, Virgil Lane, was the drummer. Bill Hayes, one of Ollie Wagner's Edmonton pupils, played trumpet.

Lane, in King's words, was "a flash drummer." Like King, Lane had received encouragement from a touring American musician, in this case the showman Kid Lipps Hackett, who was drumming in 1944 with an otherwise all-woman orchestra led by arranger and trombonist Eddie Durham. "He sure gave Virgil some bad advice," King remembers of Hackett. "Told him: 'To be heard and to be seen, play loud!' So Virgil always had about 10 pairs of sticks down the neck of his jacket. He'd be twirling them and throwing them in the air; by the time he'd finish a solo there'd be sticks all over the place! But he had a hell of a beat."

By 1945, Lane had caught the eye of Don Williamson, a white bandleader working at a West Pender Street dance hall known as Melody Lane. Leaving Williamson, Lane introduced his own 13-piece swing orchestra in 1946. He and Ernie King were its only black members; in one Vancouver *Sun* ad for an engagement at Happyland, Lane was billed a little too obviously as "Vancouver['s] Lionel Hampton."[23] After sporadic appearances around town, the band went on tour during the summer, playing one-nighters as far east as Lethbridge, Alberta, before running out of work and finding itself stranded on the road.

Lane repeated the misadventure in the summer of 1947. This time, however, he travelled without Ernie King, who had formed a smaller group of his own, drawing on the the "jump" style of small-band swing and formative rhythm-and-blues popularized during the 1940s by the American saxophonist Louis Jordan. King had a mixed sextet with Leroy King, Bill Hayes and tenor saxophonist Frank Risby, as well as a white guitarist and drummer. Learning from Lane's mistakes, King toured the same smalltown circuit but picked his spots and routing with greater care and made more than $4000 during the summer.

Suitably encouraged, King signed in 1948 with an agency that promised a coast-to-coast Canadian itinerary and a profit of $6000. In return, King would supply an all-black band. To that end, he hired Lane, Hayes and four musicians from Seattle, alto saxophonist Roscoe Weathers, tenor saxophonist Noble Perkins, pianist Oscar Richardson and bassist Milton Garred. Weath-

Harlem Kings, Edmonton, 1948. From left: Verne King, Noble Perkins, Jerry Bates, Virgil Lane, Bill Hays, Ernie King. [Courtesy Ernie King]

ers, originally from Memphis, had worked with Jay McShann and Horace Henderson and was one of the first and finest beboppers in the US northwest. King hospitably incorporated some bop material into his repertoire of "jump" hits and original tunes; the band's theme song was a ballad, *Lullabye of the Leaves*.

The Harlem Kings, as the septet was called, got no further than Kamloops, BC. Heavy rains in the spring of 1948 had created extensive flooding in western Canada, leaving the band's route east all but impassable. Weathers, Richardson and Garred returned to the United States, but Perkins stayed on and travelled with the trombonist to Edmonton, where the Harlem Kings reorganized on a more modest scale.

Now a sextet, the band included pianist Verne King from Ollie Wagner's original Knights of Harlem 13 years earlier, as well as Perkins, Bill Hayes, Virgil Lane and an alto saxophonist summoned from Winnipeg, Jerry Bates. Heading south, rather than east or west, the Kings worked their way into Montana and broke up after an engagement in October 1948 at the Trianon Ballroom in Lethbridge.

Ollie Wagner returned to Winnipeg by 1950. Within a couple of years he moved back to Edmonton, where he made his home — with one interruption — well into the 1970s. In failing health after an automobile accident, he died at a nursing home in Camrose, near Calgary, in 1985.

Like most of Canada's black jazz musicians of the day, Wagner led a double life in the 1950s and 1960s. Cy McLean worked as a courier for Imperial Oil and played with his trio in Toronto hotel lounges, while Ernie King ran a trucking company by day and operated an East Hastings Street bar, the Harlem Nocturne, by night. Wagner, though no longer a young man, worked in Edmonton as a roofer. He nevertheless continued to play and to give music lessons. It was on the offer of a teaching post that he took his family briefly to Vernon, BC, in the late 1950s. When the position fell through upon his arrival, he was left with no recourse but to open a shoeshine stand.

CHAPTER THIRTEEN

The Kings of Swing

By all accounts, Benny Goodman launched the Swing Era in August 1935 at the Palomar Ballroom in Hollywood. The clarinetist and his 15-piece orchestra were at the end of their first extended road trip out of New York, ostensibly capitalizing on the national exposure they had received during the previous winter over NBC radio's weekly broadcast, *Let's Dance*.

The tour had not gone well. Audiences were unreceptive to Goodman's hot, swinging style, preferring generic, "sweet" renditions of current pop tunes over the dynamic Fletcher Henderson arrangements that had so recently given the Goodman band its new identity. Goodman's NBC work seemed to have had little or no beneficial impact; in fact his post-midnight spot on *Let's Dance*, following Kel Murray's sweet band and Xavier Cugat's Latin orchestra, was too late in the evening for the young listeners who would have been his natural audience.

Not until a chastened Goodman reached California, where *Let's Dance* had concluded at the reasonable hour of 10:30 p.m. Pacific Standard Time, did he get a sympathetic hearing. Here, to his initial bewilderment, the sweet repertoire that had sustained the band for the past several, frustrating weeks now fell on deaf ears. With little to lose in this, the final engagement of the tour, Goodman made a serendipitous decision on opening night, the 21st, to return to his Henderson arrangements, the public's fickleness be damned.

The response, as legend records it, was tumultuous. Within months, swing, as played first by big bands and then adapted to small groups, became the most popular music of its day, the only style of jazz to achieve such a distinction at any time during the 20th century. And with greater heed to rhyme than reason — jazz would seem to hold more to a republican rather than monarchist ideal — Goodman was hailed as the King of Swing.

The Swing Era lasted through the Second World War and, though waning, on into the late 1940s. It made greater or lesser stars of Count Basie, Bunny

Berigan, Tommy and Jimmy Dorsey, Duke Ellington, Coleman Hawkins, Woody Herman, Harry James, Gene Krupa, Jimmie Lunceford, Glenn Miller, Artie Shaw and many others, including two Toronto-born musicians, Murray McEachern (1915-82) and Georgie Auld (1919-90).

Initially, swing gave expression to the hope and renewed energy of a society that was beginning to move out of the Great Depression. Swing's largest audience had come of age during this most desperate of times; its young fans naturally turned away from the sentimental, post-Jazz Age music favoured by their elders — what Dillon O'Leary later described as "a sad mess of syrupy notes."[1]

Swing satisfied the growing need for release and new excitement and in short order gave rise to a generational sub-culture of fans and followers — "gates" or alligators, wildly energetic jitterbug dancers and, by the early 1940s, the sartorially extravagant zoot-suiters whose stylized jackets (padded in the shoulders and hung almost to the knee) and high-waisted pants (voluminous to the knee and tapered to the ankle) were considered an affront to a society that had survived the privations of the Great Depression and now faced renewed austerity in support of the war effort.

In musical terms, swing was a style of arranged, large ensemble — "big band" — jazz that alternated and blended improvisation with formal orchestration. It had its origin in the evolving music of black bands from the 1920s and early 1930s, Fletcher Henderson's defunct New York orchestra prominent among those in the east, and the Bennie Moten Orchestra with Count Basie at the piano foremost among those in the Southwest. Among white bands, the Casa Loma Orchestra — now several years out of Toronto — was also a formative model.

Swing — the very word suggests effortless movement — gave the vertical clip of early jazz rhythms a smoother, more relaxed and subtly inflected lean; swing's solos showed a similar fluidity in their melodic construction and benefitted from the technical assurance that was increasingly common among the style's finest improvisers. Moreover, the loose collectivity of older New Orleans and Chicago jazz was replaced on one hand by powerful brass, reed and rhythm "sections" that functioned as disciplined, interdependent units, and on the other hand by the new prominence accorded individual performers, instrumentalists and vocalists alike. A swing band found its identity in this apparent dichotomy — in the signature strokes of its arrangers and the personalities of its featured soloists. According to the material in hand, up-tempo "flagwaver" or slow ballad, the result could be tremendously exciting or remarkably formal, in each case capturing the public's imagination to an extent previously unknown in jazz.

Radio, which had played such an important role in the emergence of Benny Goodman, introduced Canadian listeners without delay to this new craze. New, but not entirely unforeseen: there were some indications the year before that musicians in Toronto, for example, had anticipated just such a change in popular tastes.

Jack Evans, an alto saxophonist who led bands at Columbus Hall for many years, predicted in the Toronto *Star* late in 1934 that "...'red hot' rhythm is coming back again and will soon take the place of slow, sweet music as dispensed by Guy Lombardo."[2] Multi-instrumentalist Bert Niosi was apparently showing the way; his band was described as "the Casa Loma Orchestra of Canada" in a British music publication, possibly *The Melody Maker,* earlier in the year.[3]

Meanwhile, in a studio atop the Royal York Hotel, Rex Battle was rehearsing a 14-piece big band that included some of the city's finest jazz musicians.[4] Battle, a British-born concert pianist who served as the hotel's music director, had hired Johnny Burris, an American pianist with connections to the Casa Lomans, to write arrangements for the band.

Even at this early date, Battle understood the crucial role of an arranger in distinguishing one band from the next. Many a Canadian orchestra in the Swing Era simply relied on generic "stocks" purchased through US publishers or, latterly, from the Toronto arranger Eddie Graf. The country's leading swing bands, however, would invariably have arrangers of their own.

According to one of Battle's musicians, cornetist Jimmy (later "Trump," as in trumpet) Davidson, the first Burris "charts" were in the riff-based Casa Loma style. "Then he got the idea of trying to make a big band sound like an improvised group. The first arrangement he brought in was *Milenberg Joys.* It was semi-arranged, with a couple of guys playing jazz through it: the clarinet, trumpet and trombone — the dixieland combination. The rest was written. We thought, '*This* is really *it*, we've got something here!' Everyone was quite excited about it."

After nearly a year in rehearsal, Battle's Maple Leaf Orchestra took its one and only engagement during the summer of 1935 at Bob-Lo Island, an amusement park near Windsor on the Detroit River. There, however, the Toronto musicians heard a new US band led by Bing Crosby's brother, Bob, playing in a similar dixieland-based style on a radio broadcast from the Blackhawk in Chicago. "It just wiped us out," Davidson remembered, "because this was *exactly* what we were trying to do."

The revelation diminished the Maple Leaf Orchestra's achievement only slightly. "It was a real good band," Davidson claimed many years later, "and compared favourably with anything in the States." Nevertheless, an effort to take the Canadians to the United States after Labour Day for a cross-country tour foundered on their inability to obtain the necessary work visas.

As swing music moved quickly into the mainstream of American popular culture, it enjoyed the full support of the US entertainment industry, showcased not only on radio, but by the recording (and related juke box) industry and in such Hollywood films as *The Big Broadcast of 1937*, *Cabin in the Sky*, *Jam Session* and *Wintertime*. In short, its influence throughout North America was pervasive, although at no time did it displace sweet music entirely.

Just as one generation of Canadian musicians had taken up jazz enthusi-astically in the late 1910s, another, younger generation embraced swing in the mid-1930s. The Toronto guitarist Rudy Spratt was leading what he described as a swing band — albeit a quartet — at the Ambassador Hotel within two months of Benny Goodman's success at the Palomar Ballroom in 1935. But Canada's fledgling entertainment industry could not compete with its burgeoning US counterpart, putting Canadian bands, both swing and sweet, at a severe disadvantage when vying for the attention of Canadian fans.

The Canadian recording and film sectors remained effectively non-ex-istent. CBC radio, meanwhile, was more likely to relay US network broadcasts than to feature bands from local dance halls. Bill Newell, radio columnist for the Vancouver *Sun*, surveyed the CBC's programming in 1938 and noted, "you can hear only about 90 minutes of dance music produced by Canuck outfits in an entire week."[5]

Don McKim, Vancouver correspondent for *Down Beat*, identified the same problem the following year. "The [CBC] carries approximately five American dance periods to every one Canadian."[6] The latter, McKim added, usually featured orchestras broadcasting from CNR or CPR hotels, venues far too proper to have a swing band in their employ.

"In Canada," Newell concluded, "there are no 'name' bands known to the country as a whole. Regions have their own favorite outfit, but that's as far as it goes. Although there are plenty of good dance crews in Canada, few listeners know it and, as a result, our younger set has an ear for only American orchestras."

A US band could further enhance its standing in Canada with personal appearances. There too — no less ironically — it had the advantage of its Canadian counterparts. An American orchestra on the road departed at various points from its stateside itinerary and crossed into Canada, touring here only for as long or as far as economic factors advised. Those same economic factors — specifically the distance, lack of work and difficulty of travel between the major urban centres along the country's east-west axis — limited most Canadian bands to their own regions.

Canadian bands were put at yet another disadvantage by the country's immediate entry into the Second World War in September 1939. Young musicians enlisted or were called up in great number for military duty, the most skilled among them seconded to entertainment units and service bands, including *Meet the Navy*, *The Army Show*, and such dance orchestras as the Royal Canadian Air Force's Westernaires, Modernaires and Streamliners. As a result, bandleaders back home were left scrambling to maintain some semblance of stability in their orchestras.

George Fairfield of Regina, for one, saw his nine-man band at the Trianon Ballroom undergo 28 changes in personnel before the war ended in 1945.[7] Dal Richards, who took over the orchestra at the Hotel Vancouver's Panorama Roof in 1940, recalls, "Starting in 1941, I guess, I had [either] 17-year-olds or 65-year-olds." The loss of musicians to the services also gave rise to women's bands, among them les Belles du swing at Regina's Arcadia Ballroom and the Melody Maids with trumpeter Polly Dadson at Winnipeg's Beacon Theatre. The American dance band scene, meanwhile, was not similarly affected until the United States entered the war in December 1941.

By the time the Swing Era began to wind down at war's end, only two Canadian bandleaders had developed something approaching a national profile. Both were based in Toronto: Mart Kenney, originally from Vancouver, and Bert Niosi, who began his career in London. The Kenney and Niosi orchestras were heard nationally on the CBC and toured the same circuit of dance halls and auditoriums frequented by the name US bands that made regular Canadian stops. Kenney, whose Western Gentlemen generally played in a sweet style, also recorded extensively. Niosi, whose orchestra played swing, did not.

The regionalism that characterized the Canadian scene in fact allowed at least three bandleaders to proclaim themselves — or be proclaimed — Canada's King of Swing. Niosi was the first, early in 1936. Sandy De Santis in Vancouver followed suit in May 1937, and Irving Laing in Montreal in the summer of 1938.

Niosi alone made good on the claim.

Bartolo Niosi (1909-1987) was born and raised in London, Ontario, home of Guy Lombardo and his Royal Canadians, now based in New York and regarded as the epitome of American sweet bands. Niosi studied with the Lombardo brothers' teacher, Pasquale Venuta, and joined the Lombardos themselves in Cleveland at the age of 14, setting a precedent for several other precocious, young Canadian jazz musicians of the Swing Era.

"In those days the Lombardos played some jazz," Niosi recalled 22 years later. "I was hired to play the hot clarinet solos. It was a lot of fun, but only lasted six months. My family naturally thought a boy of 14 should be in school. So they made me come home."[8]

Niosi was nevertheless still in his teens when he returned to the United States with a second London band, the McPhillips Buescher Boys' Orchestra, sponsored by the Buescher Band Instrument Company of Indiana; his brother

Joe was the group's bassist and Tony Briglia, later of the Casa Loma Orchestra, its drummer.

These early experiences seem to have satisfied any ambition Niosi may have had to seek his fortune stateside. Despite offers of employment in later years from several US bandleaders — Jimmy Dorsey, Glen Gray, Gene Krupa and Bob Chester reportedly among them by 1945[9] — he spent the rest of his career in Canada.

Niosi's potential value to Dorsey *et al.* lay in his unprecedented versatility, catalogued for *Down Beat* in 1939 by a Toronto writer, Len R. Smith. "Bert plays piano like [Bob] Zurke," Smith wrote, "blasts a trumpet like [Louis] Armstrong, clarinets [sic] like Goodman and rambles on alto sax like

Advertisement, *Toronto Star*,
16 Apr 1936.
[Metropolitan Toronto
Reference Library]

[Jimmy] Dorsey..."[10] At that, Smith left Niosi's flute and trombone playing unremarked.

It was Bert Niosi, in fact, who served as an inspiration in the early 1930s for the younger multi-instrumentalist Murray McEachern. "A Toronto fellow got me mixed up," he told journalist Helen McNamara in 1974. "Bert Niosi. I was originally a violinist at 13, at 14 I played clarinet, then tenor sax, then trombone and trumpet. A teacher told me: 'You can't play all those.' Being a stubborn Scot, I said, 'If Bert can do it, I can do it.'"[11] And indeed McEachern could: after working in his teens with as many as a dozen bands in Toronto and Montreal, including the Rex Battle, Ronnie Hart, Roy Locksley, Luigi Romanelli, George Sims and Gilbert Watson orchestras, he joined Benny Goodman in the United States as a trombonist in 1936 and moved to the Casa Loma Orchestra as both a trombonist and alto saxophonist — a most unlikely double — in 1938.

Bert Niosi, undated. [Gene Miller Collection]

An even younger Georgie Auld (born John Altwerger) was equally precocious. "I got left back at year [at school] because I got a saxophone on my 10th birthday," Auld recalled in 1981. "Before I knew it, I was making money blowing at weddings and bar mitzvahs, and playing for the drunks who came to our house — we were bootleggers on Sullivan Street [in Toronto]. I lost all interest in school; I just wanted to blow the horn."

"I started listening to the radio... We had a Majestic radio and I just sat and listened and started playing along with the bands on the radio. The next thing I knew, I was making more money playing saxophone for all these drunks than my dad did pressing ladies' coasts for T. Eaton and Company all week long. He'd make $18 a week and come home with hands full of blisters, and I'd pick up $20 in a night playing for the drunks. They'd shove those big dollar bills down the bell of my horn."

Auld left for New York in 1932, the day after his 13th birthday. He became a member of trumpeter Bunny Berigan's orchestra at 17, drawing notice for his youthful exuberance as a tenor saxophonist, and played with both Artie Shaw and Benny Goodman by the age of 21. Maturing into a dashing soloist whose playing embraced a wide range of influences, Auld led his own orchestra from 1943 to 1946, and was one of the first Swing Era bandleaders to embrace elements of bebop, the style that would follow swing in the ongoing evolution of jazz.

The Bert Niosi Orchestra made its initial appearance in Toronto at the Embassy in 1931 and during the same year as far afield as Wong's Café in London and Lanin's Dance Pavilion on the St. Lawrence River near Cornwall. In January 1933 it took the first of many engagements, through 1949, at the Palais Royale in Toronto; Niosi also performed with some frequency at Burlington's Brant Inn during the 1930s, toured western Canada in the fall of 1945 and 1946 and appeared regularly at Crystal Beach in the late 1940s.

When not in residence at the Palais, the Brant Inn or Crystal Beach, Niosi kept his musicians busy with an itinerary of one-nighters that criss-crossed southern Ontario. Teddy Davidson, who played tenor saxophone and sang ballads with Niosi from 1938 until 1942, remembered, "We kept going from Kingston to London, London to Belleville. It was the craziest thing I ever saw in my life: Ottawa to London, the next night in Kingston, and the next night in Brantford. We were going through Toronto like it was a stop sign!"

The Palais Royale was Niosi's castle, as it were, from 1937 to 1949, save for a period in 1943 and 1944 when he and the hall's operators, George Deller and W.E. (Bill) Cuthbert, apparently differed on monetary issues. The clapboard and stucco Palais, which opened in 1922, was one of several dance spots in operation through the Swing Era along the Sunnyside stretch of Toronto's western waterfront. The Club Esquire (Club Top Hat as of 1941) lay to the north, just across Lakeshore Boulevard, while the open-air Sea Breeze, the Queensway Ballroom (Palace Pier as of 1946) and the Silver Slipper (Club Kingsway as of 1942) were a pleasant summer evening's walk west along the shore of Humber Bay.

In Niosi's absence during the mid-1940s, the Palais brought in other

Canadian swing outfits, among them the Morgan Thomas band from Hamilton and the Stan Wood and Maynard Ferguson orchestras from Montreal. American bands also made regular stops: Count Basie, Artie Shaw, Bunny Berigan, Glen Gray, Gene Krupa, Jack Teagarden and Bob Crosby, for example, all appeared with their orchestras at the Palais in 1939.

The hall in fact enjoyed enough success with its swing policy to underwrite a variety of selective admission practices, including the exclusion of patrons that management deemed undesirable — namely blacks and zoot-suiters — as well as the automatic expulsion of dancers who "broke" from each other's arms to jitterbug.

"We had anywhere from 1300 to 1500 people on a Monday," remembered Teddy Davidson. "On a Saturday, they had 3300 in there one night. It was really a way of life for a lot of people. One fellow they had barred used to come down and sit on the bench outside. He didn't know where else to go, because everybody he knew was inside."

Bert Niosi ran a tight, disciplined orchestra; his own virtuosity was its only real flamboyance. Personnel remained steady at 11 musicians through the 1930s, growing to 16 in the 1940s. Lead trumpeter Tony Furanna, pianist Harold Gray and guitarist/vocalist Doug Hurley were long-time members. Niosi's brother Johnnie was the band's drummer for many years, spelled by Sonny Hart, and Joe Niosi its bassist for shorter periods.

Following the common practice of the day, Niosi drew a small group from the ranks of his big band. The septet, which performed at the Palais on a small stage built in the shape of a drum, had its own CBC broadcasts in the mid-1940s and recorded for Victor and Musicana in 1947. Niosi limited himself to the clarinet and alto saxophone with the small band, as was consistent with a style that, according to Dillon O'Leary, combined "the subtlety of arrangements and voicings that were the trademark of the former small group of John Kirby, plus some of the vigor and élan of the Benny Goodman sextets."[12]

Tenor saxophonist Phil Antonacci, who joined Niosi in 1941 at the age of 17, was second only to the leader himself as a featured soloist with both the big band and sextet. Antonacci had heard jazz for the first time at 15 on

Bert Niosi Septet, Palais Royale, circa 1945. From left: Harold Gray, Phil Antonacci, Johnny
Dobson, Doug Hurley, Sonny Hart, Niosi, Tony Furanna.
[Gene Miller Collection]

a juke box; the record was Count Basie's version of *Twelfth Street Rag*,
featuring an extended Lester Young solo. "All of a sudden, something turned
in my head," he remembers. "I said to my brother, *I* can do that." Showing
the same precocity as Niosi, Murray McEachern and Georgie Auld before
him, he began playing professionally before his 16th birthday, signing on with
a local swing band known as the Modernaires.

Like Niosi, Antonacci declined several offers of employment stateside,
among them a last-minute call to replace Don Byas beside Coleman Hawkins
at a club engagement in New York; the young Canadian had jammed with
the two American tenor saxophonists during a Coleman engagement in 1944
at the Club Top Hat. Antonacci was making a good living in Toronto,
drawing $78 a week with Niosi — $20 above union scale and $18 more than
his bandmates — plus $15 for each of Niosi's CBC broadcasts. He was also
something of a celebrity in a town that had no shortage of fine tenormen
during the 1940s, not the least of them Lew Lewis, Mitch Melnick, Benny

Winestone, Bob Burns and Hart Wheeler. He was, moreover, still young. "I had people here," he explains. "I had my mother and father. I come from an Italian family. You can't just up and go. They worry about you."

Antonacci remained with the band through the 1940s. Other musicians of note worked with Niosi for shorter periods during the decade as their service obligations allowed. Teddy Davidson was a member of the band for four years before going into the navy in 1942. Trumpeter Paul Grosney spent two years with Niosi after a tour of duty overseas in the RCAF's *Swingtime* variety show and a short stint early in 1946 in New York with Georgie Auld. In fact, when Niosi made a 29-city tour of western Canada in the fall of 1946, fully half of his musicians were veterans, alto saxophonist Pat Riccio (leader of the RCAF Streamliners) and trombonist Ross Culley prominent among them.

At the outset of Bert Niosi's 12-year run at the Palais Royale in 1937, a Toronto radio personality, Dick MacDougal, wrote in *Down Beat*, "The band swings out in the best Goodman tradition and is easily one of the two or three best swing bands in the country." But MacDougal could not resist adding a parenthetical sneer: "(If there are that many.)"[13]

By then, in fact, there were at least a dozen "swing bands" across Canada.[14] As had been the case with the new music known as jazz 20 years earlier, though, some bandleaders may have turned to "swing" in name only. Indeed Rudy Spratt, so quick to identify himself with swing in 1935, took some time to catch up with the style itself, according his quartet's bassist, Sam Levine. "As we went along, we started to get a swing feel; we'd take pop tunes and make them sound a little bit like [the John] Kirby [band] and the others."

Even fewer Canadian bands were recorded during the 1930s and 1940s than in the 1920s; once again the exact nature of their music remains open to question, however fashionable the term they used to describe it. In truth, sweet bands would outnumber swing bands in Canada throughout the Swing Era.

Nevertheless, at least one other Sunnyside outfit enjoyed Dick MacDougal's favour in 1937. He took note in the same *Down Beat* column of the "swell jazz" played by the Trump Davidson Orchestra at the Club Esquire. "It's hard to realize it," he wrote, again taunting swing musicians and their fans across the country, "but all the *good* swing in Canada is to be heard on the same street [Lakeshore Boulevard], within a half mile radius."

Jimmy (Trump) Davidson (1908-78), a singer and self-taught cornetist from Sudbury, Ontario, started his career with Toronto dance bands in 1929. While a member of the Luigi Romanelli Orchestra at the King Edward Hotel, he came under the influence of the American trombonist and arranger Red Ginzler, who had remained in the city after an engagement during the winter of 1927-8 with the future Casa Loma Orchestra. "Now there was a musician," Davidson marvelled, in an interview with Patrick Scott in 1964, "[Ginzler] could work out an arrangement while playing bridge, doing a crossword puzzle and listening to the radio, all at the same time."[15]

Though hired as a singer, a hopeful Davidson always carried his cornet to the bandstand. One night, simply as a lark, Romanelli let him take a solo. "I stood up there," Davidson told Scott, "and played the first thing that came into my head — probably some of the stuff that was still floating around there off the Mound City Blue Blowers records that had first opened my ears to jazz in Sudbury. Anyway, the minute I finished that solo, Red Ginzler threw his arms around me; he'd recognized a kindred spirit, I guess — and from that night we always hung out together."

Davidson left Romanelli for Rex Battle's Maple Leaf Orchestra in 1935, then freelanced through 1936. He organized his own band in 1937 for the Club Esquire and spent most of that year at the Sunnyside nightspot, backing shows and playing for dancers. "We patterned our approach on the old Red Norvo style," he explained to Scott, "sort of softer and more subtle than the usual thing in those days, but with plenty of swing." Davidson sang in what he called his Broderick Crawford style — others were reminded of Jack Teagarden — and played straighforward cornet in the balanced, melodic tradition that ran from Bix Beiderbecke to Bobby Hackett.

Through the good graces of the British bandleader and songwriter Ray Noble, who was touring North America in early 1937 with an orchestra of US musicians, Davidson's Club Esquire band twice enjoyed a degree of international exposure that would elude all other Canadian bands of the day. Davidson invited Noble to visit the Esquire during the Toronto stop on his tour and prepared a medley of the Englishman's songs for the occasion. It was a hospitable gesture, to be sure, but Davidson must also have been mindful of the fact that Noble would not be allowed by the British musicians' union to tour with his American orchestra in England. A Canadian band, on the other hand, was under no such ban.

The ploy worked: Noble was impressed enough to have an NBC wire put into the Esquire, supplementing the band's local broadcasts on CRCT. The airtime in the United States brought Davidson a distant, 45th-place showing in the swing category of the *Metronome* readers' poll for 1937. The Canadians received five votes; Benny Goodman's orchestra stood first that year with 3174.[16]

After wintering at the Gatineau Country Club and taking a two-week spring warm-up at the Palais Royale, Davidson and his musicians — Teddy Davidson among them — toured Great Britain under Noble's leadership during the summer of 1938, travelling where Noble's Americans could not. The tour was a triumph for Noble, less so for the Canadians who laboured both in his shadow and under the resentful gaze of the British musicians who felt perfectly qualified to play Noble's music themselves.

Moreover, Davidson found on his return home that his association with Noble meant little to Canadian swing fans. After four years of miscellaneous engagements — the Brant Inn in Burlington, the Dardanella Ballroom at Wasaga Beach, Standish Hall in Hull, a weekly *Sweet and Hot* broadcast on CKCL from the Arcadian Ballroom in Toronto — he joined Horace Lapp's Royal York Hotel orchestra in 1942. Two years later, he introduced a new, 14-piece orchestra at the Queensway Ballroom, opening September 16, 1944 opposite no less than Louis Armstrong.

The Queensway was an impressive, Art Deco structure built — as its later name, Palace Pier, suggests — out from the shore of Lake Ontario, near the mouth of the Humber River. It remained Davidson's base until its destruction by fire in 1963. Like the Palais Royale nearby, it brought in American bands on a regular basis during the 1940s. The visitors normally alternated with their Toronto hosts, but on one occasion — just six months after Louis Armstrong's appearance — the rising trumpet star Dizzy Gillespie was a guest soloist with the Davidson band itself. According to legend, the evening was not a success, as Gillespie's neoteric bebop style proved incompatible with the Canadians' older-fashioned approach.

Gone by now from Davidson's music was the refined Red Norvo influence of 1937; in its place the cornetist had adapted the colour and spontaneity of dixieland jazz to swing, looking to the example of Bob Crosby's recently disbanded big band (with its component small ensemble, the Bob Cats) and also harking in his own arrangements back to the sound that Johnny Burris had created in 1935 for Rex Battle's Maple Leaf Orchestra. Moreover, Davidson employed saxophonist Morris Zene, and in later years Teddy Davidson, both ardent admirers of the vigorous tenor style that had made Eddie Miller one of the Crosby band's star soloists.

Toronto swing fans now enjoyed a clear choice: the Goodman-styled Niosi orchestra or the Crosby-styled Davidson band. From their respective dance halls on opposite sides of Humber Bay, Niosi and Davidson were themselves the friendliest of rivals. Teddy Davidson bore witness to both the amicable relationship and the stylistic disparity between his former employer, on one hand, and his brother, on the other.

"Bert was always after Jimmy to bring an arrangement [to the Palais Royale]. He finally did, an arrangement of *Wait Till the Sun Shines, Nellie.* It was awful, because nobody in Bert's band [played] like that. The tempo was wrong, *everything* was wrong. Bert was *so* disappointed. But I played it [later] with Jimmy's band and it sounded great. Dixieland was just not a part of Bert, and that always bothered him, because he wanted to [be able to] play everything."

Trumpeter Ellis McLintock, just 13 when Benny Goodman arrived in California in 1935, offered Toronto swing fans a third, still more modern alternative by the mid-1940s. Already a veteran of both the Niosi band and the Toronto Symphony Orchestra when he took his new big band into Casa Loma in 1944, McLintock patterned himself after the American trumpeter Charlie Spivak; though not a jazz soloist as such, Spivak was widely admired for the technical assurance and tonal purity of his playing.

So, too, McLintock. Writing in *Ad Lib*, a short-lived Toronto music publication patterned after *Down Beat*, James Buller described him in 1946 as "an agreeable front man," and continued, "Not the gushing, showman type, Ellis is nevertheless extremely popular with the crowds. After all, he does play a beautifully mellow trumpet, which is not too different from Spivak's trumpet style, only much richer in tone."[17]

Like Spivak, McLintock surrounded himself with a strong contingent of jazz musicians, many of them young beboppers. When *Ad Lib* organized an "all-Canadian" jazz concert at Eaton Auditorium in January 1947, seven of the 11 participants were members of the McLintock band — trumpeter Moe Miller, tenormen Hart Wheeler and Bob Burns, alto saxophonist Gordie Evans, pianist Jimmy Coxson, bassist Murray Lauder and drummer Mickey Shannon. At that, two other soloists of note had left McLintock just months before, Tommy Cronin, a trumpeter with the energy and drive of a Roy Eldridge, and Mitch Melnick, an easy-blowing tenor saxophonst who would spend 1947 in the United States with drummer Gene Krupa's orchestra.

The Spivak influence aside, McLintock and his young musicians were inevitably drawn to the newest developments of the 1940s, in particular to the work of the Elliot Lawrence Orchestra, heard on radio from Philadelphia. Lawrence, along with Claude Thornhill and Boyd Raeburn, was in the vanguard of modern jazz orchestration. For his influence, the McLintock band was surely ahead of its time in Canada. Steady engagements — like those held by Niosi at the Palais and Davidson at the Pier — proved elusive, but the trumpeter kept his band together until 1950, taking a variety of jobs in the Toronto area and working as far afield as Belmont Park in Montreal.

Lawrence (Sandy) De Santis (1910?-57) was leading a six-piece band in Vancouver at the Venice Café, a converted brothel on Main Street, when the Benny Goodman Orchestra kicked off the Swing Era 1750 kilometres down the west coast. The New Jersey-born trumpeter and his brother Carl (known to all as Beaky), a tenor saxophonist, may well have heard Goodman's CBS broadcasts from Los Angeles in August and September of 1935.

Unlike their contemporaries elsewhere in Canada, Vancouver musicians

Sandy De Santis Orchestra, Palomar Ballroom, 22 May 1937. Sandy De Santis, third from left; Carl De Santis, far right; other unknown.
[Photograph 16239, Vancouver Public Library]

relied entirely on radio and recordings to keep up with the new trend. An edict set out by local 145 of the American Federation of Musicians prohibited American dance bands from performing anywhere in Vancouver during the 1930s save on the theatrical stage.[18] Not until Duke Ellington appeared in concert at the Forum in April 1940, followed by Benny Goodman in May, did the city become a regular stop on the west coast big band circuit.

In the absence of US orchestras — and in face of the popularity enjoyed by Mart Kenney and his Western Gentlemen with the aptly named CBC program *Sweet and Low* from the Hotel Vancouver — the entrepreneurial Sandy De Santis formed a 14-piece swing band in 1936. His brother, Carl, emerging as one of the city's finest jazz musicians, took a prominent role. "The guys before Carl," remembers a younger Vancouver tenor saxophonist, Lance Harrison, "all sounded as though they wanted to play like Pat Davis from the Casa Loma Orchestra, who wasn't a very good player... Carl was the first guy who sort of got into a Coleman Hawkins or Lester Young influence."

The new De Santis orchestra caught the ear of a Canadian living in Los Angeles, promoter Hymie Singer, who had decided that Vancouver should have a Palomar Ballroom of its own. When the hall, with its elaborate lighting effects and spring-supported maple dance floor, opened at the downtown corner of Burrard and Georgia in May 1937, De Santis — billed as Canada's King of Swing[19] — was in place on the bandstand. His only potential rival in Vancouver, trumpeter Bobby Reid, had conveniently left town a month earlier with a 10-piece swing band of local and US musicians; as the Americanadians they spent the next three years working in Australia and New Zealand.

With no reason to fear contradition, Hymie Singer took the hyperbole a step further, hailing De Santis as "The Benny Goodman of Canada" in 1938.[20] In truth, De Santis owed his success in emulating the Goodman style to the expert guidance of alto saxophonist and clarinetist Gordie Edwards and trumpeter Johnny Murdie. Lance Harrison remembers Edwards as "the first guy [in Vancouver] who used Goodman as a role model." Edwards wrote arrangements for the orchestra and was a prominent member of Carl De Santis' Jam Band, a featured attraction at the Palomar.

Sandy De Santis' initial engagement at the Palomar lasted until March 1938, at which point he took his musicians across the country for a summer engagement at the Gatineau Country Club. His replacement at the Palomar was the bassist Trevor Page, whose dance band included Lance Harrison; Page gave way in January 1939 to a new swing orchestra led by Dal Richards, formerly of the De Santis band.

Having already had the Canadian Benny Goodman in his employ, Hymie Singer introduced Richards as the Canadian Artie Shaw; Singer had heard the saxophonist and his musicians rehearsing arrangements of *Indian Love Call* and *Begin the Beguine* "lifted" from Shaw's Blue Bird recordings of the previous year. Carl De Santis stayed on at the Palomar with the Richards band, which also featured trumpeter Gordon Delamont's "Dixieland Six."

Sandy De Santis returned to the Palomar as both bandleader and manager at the end of 1939, by which time the ballroom had been converted into a supper club. His orchestra, down to 10 men including Carl De Santis, Gordie Edwards and trumpeter Bobby Gimby, now played for floor shows and only secondarily for dancing. In the latter capacity, it was deemed "an okay outfit" by Don McKim, writing for *Down Beat* late in 1940, "much better on the swing than the sweet."[21]

By then, Mart Kenney had moved east and Dal Richards had started what would be a 25-year association with the Hotel Vancouver's Panorama Roof. De Santis, meanwhile, led the house orchestra at the Palomar until 1949. Now the Palomar's owner, he replaced himself on the bandstand with a trumpeter originally from Winnipeg, Chuck Barber, and Barber in turn with Bobby Reid, long since returned from Down Under.

Irving Laing had an advantage over other dance-band leaders in Montreal. His father, Sam, ran the Auditorium, the Ontario Street ballroom that had introduced jazz to the city in 1917. With both history and nepotism on his side, the trumpeter and arranger was able in the late 1930s to sustain what *Down Beat* correspondent Gordon Richardson described as "the tops in swing bands around Montreal."[22]

Irving Laing Orchestra, Montreal, undated. Front row: Irving Laing, centre; others unknown.
Back row: Adrien Gaboury, far left; Rolland David, centre; others unknown.
[Joe Bell Fonds, P010/P39, Concordia University Archives]

The Laing orchestra appeared at the Auditorium from 1936 to 1940, taking summers off to work at the Terrace Gardens in the Laurentians resort community of Ste. Agathe in 1937 and at the Verdun Boardwalk Dancing Pavilion on the south shore of Montreal Island in 1938, 1939 and 1940.

Laing was just beginning his first season in Verdun when the Benny Goodman Orchestra made its Montreal debut, June 28, 1938, at the Forum in a concert that was broadcast across North America on CBS radio's *Camel Caravan*. (Goodman offered one of his rare versions of *Canadian Capers* to mark the occasion.[23]) Some 7000 fans attended, a clear indication of the potential market for swing music in the city. Laing scarcely missed a beat in capitalizing on Goodman's success: he proclaimed himself Canada's King of Swing in a Montreal *Star* ad for the Verdun Pavilion two days later.[24]

Laing's promotional rhetoric grew bolder still. "What have the Americans got that we haven't got,"[25] asked a second ad, not long after the Laing band had returned in September 1938 to the Auditorium. A Montreal writer, Irv Mauer, narrowed the terms of reference slightly the following March, when he noted approvingly in *Down Beat*, "Many local cats think Laing and his boys can outswing Niosi of the Queen City."[26]

In time, Laing sent a letter to the Palais Royale challenging Bert Niosi to what *Down Beat* described in suitably courtly terms as "a duel of jazz"[27] early in 1940. Laing, however, was called into the Canadian army before the two Canadian Kings of Swing could arrange a suitable time and place — indeed, even before his own band could finish its summer engagement in Verdun that year. One of Laing's star soloists, tenor saxophonist Rolland David, praised in *Metronome* for "slay[ing] the gates with his tasty licks and powerhouse tone,"[28] took over the band for its final weeks on the boardwalk.

The sudden demise of the Laing orchestra left the local swing crown in the hands of alto saxophonist Stan Wood, whose band was in the middle of an 11-year affiliation, 1935-46, with Belmont Park, a summer amusement centre in Cartierville, on the north shore of Montreal island. The Wood band wintered downtown at the Palais d'Or in 1939 and 1940 and moved into the Auditorium in 1941.

Wood, described by the *Star* as "[a] quiet, unassuming Montreal maes-

Stan Wood Orchestra, Montreal, early 1940s. Herb Johnson (tenor saxophone) far left, front row; Russ Meredith (trumpet) standing in front row; Donat Gariépy (drums) rear; others unknown. [John Gilmore Fonds, P004/P09, Concordia University Archives]

tro,"[29] lacked Irving Laing's flair for promotion, although he twice did "battle" with Bert Niosi, first in May 1943 during a foray to the Palais Royale in Toronto, and again the following October, when Niosi visited the Auditorium. The outcome of these encounters may well be reflected in Wood's decision to describe himself thereafter only as Montreal's King of Swing.[30] He subsequently put his "title" on the line locally in battles with the bands of Jimmy King, Hal Hartley and Jimmy Jones.

Jones, in fact, had been a featured soloist briefly with the Wood band at the Auditorium in early 1942. Billed as "Harlem's Crown Prince of the Trumpet,"[31] he played Cootie Williams to Wood's Benny Goodman — or Roy Eldridge to his Gene Krupa — parallelling an important trend in the United States that saw white swing bands employing black soloists in what would be the first step toward the racial integration of jazz.

Wood's other featured musicians at various points during his band's five winters at the Auditorium included the saxophonists Adrien Robichaud and

Teddy Davidson, trumpeter Russ Meredith and the drummers Ray Cook and Donat Gariépy. As always, promotional material used American terms of reference: Robichaud was described as either the Artie Shaw or Charlie Barnet of Montreal, depending on the instrument the instrument that he played — clarinet or tenor saxophone — while Gariépy was hailed as the Gene Krupa of Canada.[32] Wood also had a succession of fine pianists that in 1943 alone included Johnny Gallant, Reid McLeod and Paul Schnobb. The turnover was, of course, a direct result of military call-ups.

Rolland David, meanwhile, returned to Verdun with his own orchestra in 1943 for the first of two summers on the boardwalk. He spent the following winters at the Chez Maurice Danceland, a refurbished Ste. Catherine Street nightspot that had passed through several hands since it opened in 1919 as the Venetian Gardens. Like Sandy De Santis at the Palomar in Vancouver before him, David assumed both managerial and musical roles in Danceland. He made a point of presenting American bands whenever they were available; Duke Ellington, Cab Calloway, Count Basie and Jimmie Lunceford all appeared opposite the David band in the course of 1944 and 1945.

David regarded these one-night stands as something more than just a means of boosting the room's business. "I want to have an orchestra of note," he told Duke Delory of *Down Beat*. "But first I must educate the city to what good Jazz is, and is not. That is my reason for bringing into Danceland all of the biggest names in the American dance biz to-day."[33]

That David also presented the Bert Niosi and Mart Kenney orchestras from Toronto is a measure of their national profile in the mid-1940s. David's own band, meanwhile, developed only a local following during its two seasons at Danceland, despite a strong line-up of Montreal musicians. Duke Delory pointed to the saxophone and rhythm sections as the David band's strengths in late 1943, singling out for praise the leader himself, as well as drummer Donat Gariépy (who moved between the David and Wood bands in this period), alto saxophonist Adrien Gaboury, trumpeter Al Kane, pianist Joey Burton and bassist Bert Brown.

By now, however, swing's popularity was beginning to wane. David turned the Danceland stage over to other bandleaders in 1946, while Stan Wood put both Belmont Park and the Auditorium behind him the same year and began playing for shows at the Palm Café. Montreal would see the rise of just one more significant big band before the Swing Era passed altogether.

Maynard Ferguson played trumpet with both the Stan Wood and Rolland David bands in his youth. Born in Montreal in 1928,[34] he was just 14 when he joined Wood at the Auditorium early in 1943, replacing Russ Meredith, a musician nearly 21 years his senior.

Meredith, nicknamed "Oakie" for his resemblance to the Hollywood actor Jack Oakie, had been taken on by Jack Teagarden after the American trombonist's orchestra had played opposite the Wood band at the Auditorium in February 1943. Meredith specialized in high notes and volume: "One has only to pass within a few miles of [Belmont] park," Bob Redmond wrote in *Down Beat* in 1942, with more than a hint of exaggeration, "to dig an ear full of powerhouse Meredith's trumpet solos."[35] Meredith, who also sang, remained with Teagarden for the rest of the trombonist's Canadian engagements. In the absence of a work permit, however, he was left behind in Windsor when the band crossed back into the United States. By the fall of 1943 he was working with Morgan Thomas at the Palais Royale in Toronto and in the later 1940s led his own band in alternation with Ferguson's orchestra at Danceland.

"He must have had some range," Ferguson suggests. "I didn't hear him that much, but I know, for instance, that he used to do *I Can't Get Started*, which I also did — imitating Bunny Berigan — so he had to have the [high] E-flats and Fs."

As young as Ferguson was, he had little trouble filling Meredith's shoes with the Wood band. Indeed, the older trumpeter's strengths — range and power — would also become trademarks of Ferguson's solos, routinely suprising the Americans who played in Montreal dance halls opposite Wood, Rolland David and, soon enough, the boy wonder's own orchestra. Years later, though, Ferguson qualified the striking first impressions he had made in his youth. "There's freedom in being the leader when you're 16 [sic] and look 13; you're lucky because you can make all kinds of mistakes and everyone thinks you're absolutely adorable."[36]

Rolland David Orchestra, Chez Maurice Danceland, Montreal, 26 Feb 1944. From left, back row: Norm Calvert, Maynard Ferguson, Joe Christie, Sr., Al Kane, Jimmy Malone. Middle row: Frank Taplitsky, Joe Bell, Rita Gail, Armand Samson. Front row: Frank DiStaulo, Tony Mazza, Adrien Gaboury, Frank Costi (Constantini), Rolland David (standing), Bert Brown, Joe Stroble (Burton). [Joe Bell Fonds, P010/P46, Concordia University Archives]

Ferguson and his older brother Percy, sons of a school principal and a teacher, played violin and piano as children, then switched to cornet and clarinet, respectively, as members of the Kiwanis Boys' Band. Still in his youth, Ferguson studied at the Conservatoire de musique du Québec à Montréal with former NBC Symphony Orchestra trumpeter Bernard Baker, who would travel from New York every second week to meet with his Montreal pupils.

Ferguson was taken aside and advised that his growing love of jazz should remain unspoken in the conservatory's halls. "When I went there, they told me never to mention jazz or blues. *'Don't even mention it!'*" No matter: he had already decided where his future lay. "When I was about 11 years of age I looked around at the guys in the symphony and at the jazz guys. The guys having the most fun were the jazz guys."

His instincts proved correct. He was soon playing in Percy's semi-professional dance band, the Victory Serenaders, with several fellow High School of Montreal pupils, among them a pianist three years his elder, Oscar Peterson. The Ferguson brothers also took casual work in fully professional settings.

"Much to the amusement and sometimes the worry of my parents," Percy Ferguson recalls, "Maynard and I both substituted in the bands at Rockhead's and the Café St-Michel, because we'd had good training and we could read the shows... So here we were, really young teenagers, and of course they had strippers and everything. But my parents were pretty good that way, for teachers and school principals. They figured it was all part of the experience."

Ferguson himself remembers playing the black clubs in St. Antoine clearly. "I think they were a little nervous — the owners, I mean — about this little kid walking in."

After moving between the Wood and David orchestras for two years, Ferguson, a week past his 17th birthday and already billed as King of the Trumpet, took David's place at the Verdun Pavilion with his own band in the summer of 1945. The hall, however, had fallen into disrepute as one site, among several around Montreal, of running battles in June 1944 between servicemen and zoot-suiters. The two groups were openly contemptuous of one another during the war years, their animosity no doubt fueled by the widespread aversion in Quebec to Canada's involvement in a European conflict, and particularly to talk of making military service compulsory. Set against the backdrop of this "Conscription Crisis," the so-called "zoot-suit riots" in Montreal drew the attention in Parliament of the minister of justice and future prime minister, Louis St. Laurent.

The Verdun Pavilion engagement proved an inauspicious, but not unsuccessful debut for the teenaged bandleader. "We used to start the job without one single customer in the place," Ferguson remembered in 1959, "but the band had a ball. Gradually the word got around, and the crowds started flocking in."[37]

Not surprisingly, Ferguson played more jazz than either of his former employers. "After all," he notes, "Stan Wood was not an improvising jazz soloist himself. Rolland David was, but he was also a businessman and wanted to pack [Danceland]. So I would have to say yes, I wanted more of a jazz

Maynard Ferguson, mid-1940s.
[Courtesy *The Gazette*]

band than they did, but as I've grown more mature I understand what their reasoning was."

Still, Ferguson's orchestra was ultimately "a dance–jazz band," as he described it in 1979. "We certainly played a lot of ballrooms. We did a lot of ballads in a jazz way. I know that older people were always wishing I would play the ballads a little faster and the fast tunes a little slower."[38]

In his role as the band's featured soloist, Ferguson took his lead from the era's greatest players. "I was copying *everybody*," he explains, "whether it was Roy Eldridge's *After You've Gone* — I'd get someone to do a chart on that for me — or *Struttin' with Some Barbeque*, which was my Louis Armstrong feature. And I had a few Harry James things..."

Whatever its models, Ferguson's bravura style was already fully formed. He was 17 when an unnamed reviewer in the Montreal *Herald* formulated what would become the standard critical line: "A tendancy to sacrifice tone for flashiness and to outblow Gabriel in the upper register marred the young musician's work."[39] Ferguson would sustain this showy virtuosity for more than 50 years as the leader of a succession of powerful, US-based groups, from the Birdland Dreamband of 1956 to Big Bop Nouveau of the 1990s.

During the time that Ferguson led what he has come to call his "teenage band" in Canada, from 1945 to 1948, he also became a familiar figure in southern Ontario at the Palais Royale and at Crystal Beach. In each case, at the Palais and the Beach, he would either precede or follow Bert Niosi, whose jazz leanings — Ferguson remembers — were even stronger than his own. "I think he had his act together a little better than I did in the sense that he had been at the Palais Royale for years and knew what he could get away with [in terms of playing jazz] and still have the people dancing."

In Montreal, Ferguson worked at the Auditorium early in 1946 and spent the following two winters at Danceland. American orchestras continued to pass through Danceland a night or two at a time, including the Gene Krupa, Stan Kenton, Cab Calloway and Dizzy Gillespie bands. "Maynard would always open the show," remembered another Montreal musician, pianist Paul Bley. "He played three octaves higher on trumpet than anyone else, and you ought to have seen the jaws drop on the visiting musicians."[40]

Kenton, then in the process of developing his progressive, brass-domi-nated sound, was sufficiently impressed to make Ferguson a standing offer: a place in the Kenton trumpet section, simply for the asking. Ferguson disbanded his orchestra in the spring of 1948 to pursue the opportunity.

"Whatever was going on with the Canadian scene had taken a bit of a nose-dive. I thought, 'Now's the time.' I told my folks and they said, 'Okay.' We went through all the immigration things. It took a long time in those

Maynard Ferguson Orchestra, Montreal, circa 1947. From left, front row: unknown pianist,
Ferguson standing, Bennie Winestone, Adrien Gaboury, Percy Ferguson, unknown tenor
saxophonist, Johnny Reno. Back row, Gus Bélisle, Elder Léger; others unknown.
[John Gilmore Fonds, P004/P116, Concordia University Archives]

days. For one thing, they had all kinds of immigration rules. When I got
through all that, I found out Kenton no longer had a band. That was when
he took a year off and went to South America."

Ferguson instead made his US debut in July 1948 with the Boyd Raeburn
orchestra and travelled in turn with Jimmy Dorsey and Charlie Barnet in
1949 before joining the revitalized Kenton band at the beginning of 1950.
His recordings with Kenton brought immediate recognition: the trumpeter
won the first of three consecutive *Down Beat* readers' polls later that year.

Paul Perry (1916-1992) was just one of the many other Canadian bandleaders
to embrace swing during the 1930s and 1940s. Perry, who grew up in rural
Saskatchewan, first heard big band jazz on radio. "That was a wonderful era,"
he remembered in 1980, "because on the prairies you could sit all night long
and listen to one big band broadcast after another — from The Terrace in
Chicago on west." Perry also saw the black Kansas City orchestras that

travelled as far afield as Kenosee Lake and Estevan in southern Saskatchewan during the years around 1940; Buck Douglas, star soloist with the Tommy Douglas Orchestra, gave the young Canadian tenor saxophonist some pointers.

The sound of the Kansas City bands must still have been ringing in Perry's ears in 1941 when he went into Penley's Pavilion in Calgary. "I got the axe at that job; they said we were playing too much jazz." Undaunted, Perry used a Kansas City classic, Count Basie's moody *Blue and Sentimental*, as his theme song, and hired pianist Chris Gage, trumpeter Herbie Spanier and drummer Jimmy Wightman — bright, young Regina jazz musicians all — when his band was featured regularly at the Trianon Ballroom from 1946 to 1948. "We played a lot of jazz, more than we should have," Perry noted, acknowledging the swing musician's dilemma. "Otherwise, we'd have made more money — if we had been more commercial."

To be more commercial was — in the terminology of the day — to be sweeter, smoother, schmaltzier, cornier. There was little enthusiasm among jazz musicians for sweet music, and even less for actually playing in what they derisively referred to as "Mickey Mouse bands." Teddy Davidson remembered the Montreal tenor saxophonist Adrien Paradis, his bandmate in the Stan Wood orchestra of the mid-1930s. "All he wanted to play was jazz, and if we did any of the sweet tunes, he wouldn't play."

Herbie Spanier took a different, though no less headstrong tact. "Every time I played — lead or solos — I just played jazz. They'd say, 'Play more *melody*.' I always got that from all kinds of leaders I played with." According to Spanier, at least some of his contemporaries had the same attitiude. "We were just full of piss 'n' vinegar, playing what[ever] the hell we wanted, getting away with what we wanted. We weren't [so] tenacious about [keeping] our jobs that we wouldn't have some fun at it."

Most bandleaders nevertheless tried to maintain a practical balance between swing and sweet. In Winnipeg, trumpeter Herbie Brittain, bandleader at the Auditorium from 1940 to 1945, styled his music "subtle swing."[41] Trombonist and singer Gar Gillis, who followed Brittain at the downtown hall, saw his 13-piece orchestra advertised as a "hot sweet band" in 1946.[42]

Inevitably, a swing band had some sweet numbers in its repertoire; no less than Irving Laing promised "popular dance tunes, including waltzes and slow numbers, as well as jitterbug music,"[43] when he opened his final season at the Verdun Pavilion in 1940. In turn, a sweet band would have a few swing tunes to offer its dancers. The Cape Breton trumpeter Emilio Pace, an Italian musician who had somehow found his way to this most Scottish of Canada's regions, included at least one identifiable jazz medley, concluding with Count Basie's *One O'Clock Jump*, in a program of fox trots and waltzes advertised for a dance at St. Mary's Hall in Sydney Mines in 1945.[44]

The dichotomy between swing and sweet was underlined by the presence in sweet bands of swing musicians, no doubt attracted by the prospect of steady employment. Emilio Pace's eight-piece band, for example, included one of Cape Breton's finest jazz musicians, the ill-fated tenor saxophonist Alex Jones, who also worked for Pace's Sydney rival, drummer Charlie Hillcoat. Neither Pace nor Hillcoat allowed Jones much leeway as a soloist and he played instead whenever possible with a smaller group of the city's black jazz musicians, led by sometime Pace pianist Alf Coward. "He liked what we did," Coward recalls. "We were making peanuts, but he came with us all the time." Jones, who had worked briefly in the United States in 1943, was en route back to New York by train just days after the Sydney Mines dance when he fell — or jumped — to his death near Trois Rivières, Quebec. He was 35.

Mart Kenny's commercial style was apparently no less inhibiting to the jazz musicians in the Western Gentlemen. Reviewing the band for *Down Beat* in 1942, Don McKim dismissed its music as "academic schmaltz" and observed, "several of the musicians who long to blow their tops are permanently under wraps." McKim cited as examples Bobby Gimby, "who plays a [Harry] James-style trumpet and never fails to bring the house down on solos," and Arnie Moller, "who handles one of the finest tenor saxophones in Canada."[45] Ironically, when Gimby formed his own band in Toronto during the mid-1940s, he exercised similar restraint.

Of course not every Canadian bandleader worried about offending his patrons' more delicate sensibilities. The Halifax pianist Chaucy Power, a Fats Waller devotee, led a swing band during the early war years at the Bucket of

Blood, a dance hall that took its name from the frequency of fights among its clientele — members of the Canadian, British and French navies on shore leave. The Power band, whose soloists included the black tenor saxophonist Charlie Adams and a powerful, Cat Anderson-styled trumpeter, Andy McManus, played behind wire nets as protection against the flying bottles.

And it was precisely to the country's finest young jazz musicians, some still teenagers, that Jerry Gage looked when he assembled an all-star band in March 1948 for a trip to Britian as part of a cultural exchange that would see trombonist Ted Heath's London orchestra tour in Canada. With private backing in place, Gage — "a promoter [who] played better than average tenor saxophone," according to his prairie rival Paul Perry — summoned to Winnipeg musicians from as far east as Montreal and as far west as Victoria. His younger brother, Chris, was the band's pianist. Another brother, Tony, played trumpet alongside Stewart Barnett, Moe Miller and Carse Sneddon. Trombonist Jack Fulton, late of the Gar Gillis Orchestra, wrote most of the arrangements and was effectively Gage's music director.

The 16-piece band made its debut on March 29 at the Winnipeg Auditorium and immediately embarked on an ambitious "farewell tour" that was to take the musicians west to Vancouver and then east to Halifax, whence they would sail for England. In fact they got no further than Saskatoon. "We were surprised that the bottom dropped out, whatever the reason," Fulton remembers, "because it seemed like the people were there, and enjoying it. The disaster became apparent in Saskatoon. I remember going to the [hotel front desk] to talk to one of the backers who was travelling with us about getting some money. The clerk said, 'Oh, he's checked out...'"

Thus stranded in early May, the Gage band made its way to Vancouver, where it spent part of the summer at the Alexandra Ballroom. The British tour was cancelled, but Moe Miller went to London on his own in November and within two weeks of his arrival took over the solo chair recently vacated in the same Ted Heath Orchestra by Britain's foremost jazz trumpeter, Kenny Baker. Several of the Gage band's other members, including Stewart Barnett, Jack Fulton, Chris Gage and Carse Sneddon, chose to settle in Vancouver; like many of their Swing Era contemporaries across Canada, they would become stalwarts of local CBC and nightclub orchestras during the 1950s and 1960s.

Bert Niosi was ready to renounce his title as Canada's King of Swing by 1945. It was, wrote Trent Frayne in *Liberty*, "a name he'd be very happy to sell to the lowest bidder."[46] Niosi elaborated further in an interview with Dillon O'Leary for *Maclean's Magazine*. "I wish I had never been called 'King of Swing'... It types me as a jitterbug band. That's not my idea of music or of what a band should be. Of course I want music with a beat — to be good an orchestra must have a rhythm section that will lift the band. But there must be good arrangements, harmonies with lots of tone color."[47]

An aircheck of a CBC broadcast from the Palais Royale in 1946 reveals a well-rehearsed band that was now at least as much sweet in style as swing. Just three of the half-hour program's eight selections could be categorized as swing performances — *Dark Eyes, Blue Skies* and *In the Hall of the Mountain King*. Three others featured singer Pat Barry, while a fourth included a vocal by Doug Hurley.

Niosi had toyed with the idea of adding a small string section after the war. "You can get so much more variety and tone with strings added," he told O'Leary. "Then we could play everything — the old jazz standards, modern instrumentals and beautifully scored ballads."

Was Niosi seeking new challenges, or had he simply realized that swing was running its course? To an observant bandleader, the signs of swing's demise would have been clear by 1945. For one, the American Federation of Musicians had introduced a motion in 1942 prohibiting its members from recording. The ban was designed to support the union's position that recording companies should pay a royalty on record sales in order to compensate musicians for the use of said recordings on radio and, more specifically, for the negative effect that such use was having on the demand for live music.

The ban's impact on Canadian jazz musicians would be negligible — the country's swing bands were not recording commercially anyway — but it had the effect in the United States of weakening swing's hold on the recording and broadcasting industries and thus diminishing its presence before the public. Of course any trend in the United States soon resonated in Canada.

The recording ban did not, however, affect singers. Every dance band, swing or sweet, featured at least one vocalist. Led by Frank Sinatra, late of the Tommy Dorsey Orchestra, singers had already started to compete in popularity with their employers. Now they had the recording market to themselves; co-incidentally the sentimentalism of many a pop-song lyric spoke eloquently to listeners caught up in the emotional strain of the war years.

When the recording ban was lifted in 1944, swing bands found that the public's tastes had shifted. Jazz fans remained loyal — those not drawn to the revival of traditional New Orleans music and the rise of bebop now concurrently underway — but swing itself had ceased to be the popular music of the day. The fate of the Bert Niosi orchestra was telling: when it finally recorded commercially in 1949, the last year of its 19-year existence, it was asked simply to provide non-descript backing for a pop singer.

CHAPTER FOURTEEN
The small bands

Toronto now has its musicians' club — the Onyx — formed from a vacant but competely equipped cabaret by Lou Snitman and Sam Levine and their swing ork. The proposition seems to be going over very nicely and will provide a livelihood for the musicians and a congenial place for the boys to hang around and talk shop.

Metronome, November 1938[1]

Tenor saxophonist Lou Snitman, also known as Lew Lewis, and bassist Sam Levine had been working together around Toronto in 1937 and 1938 with guitarist Rudy Spratt's swing-styled quintet. "We were talking about having a spot where we could play," Levine remembers, "and we saw this place on Church Street, just north of Dundas. It was sitting empty; it had been a restaurant. We took a look at it and we thought we could manage it. Lew sold his car, I sold a banjo..."

Thus rather precariously refinanced, the former Grotto Italian Restaurant opened in the fall of 1938 as the Onyx Club, "Haven of Swing,"[2] with a capacity of about 50 and a name taken from a famous 52nd Street jazz room in New York. The Lewis "ork" was the Hungry Five — a quartet. ("We ate one," was the musicians' standard reply to questions about the discrepancy.) Lewis and Levine were, of course, constants, with Bill Isbister and later Wilf Mellor at the piano, and either Sonny Hart or Sid Shore on drums.

Jam sessions were the order of the night at the Onyx. According to Levine, the US bands that worked a week at a time at Shea's Theatre, a 10-minute walk away, "made it their second home, a hang-out between shows." Other musicians, including members of the Andy Kirk band that stopped for a night at the Palais Royale in November 1938, found their way to the Onyx after hours.

No less a figure than Duke Ellington, in town for a concert at Maple Leaf Gardens, dropped by with friends. "He had dinner and we played," Levine recalls. "He said he'd like to sit in, which floored us, and he played for the better part of an hour — mostly with Sonny Hart and myself. If there's any claim to fame that I have, I guess that's it."

Lew Lewis also played with Ellington at the Onyx and apparently made a favourable impression. "He may not be out of this world," the pianist is reported to have said of Lewis, with characteristic Ducal diplomacy, "but he sure is out of this town."[3]

Despite its popularity, the Onyx lasted less than a year. "We were a huge success musically," Lewis suggests, "but a great disaster financially. I think we charged 25 cents admission. Of course the musicians who'd want to come in — they never had 25 cents. So they'd get in, and of course they'd get thirsty and want a Coke or something like that, and I'd give them a drink. Our business partner — Mitchell, Frank Mitchell — would be screaming that we were giving everything away, and not selling anything. We weren't great businessmen."

Moreover, Onyx received complaints from the neighbouring St. John's GWCS Spiritualist Church about the noise and encountered licensing problems with the city. By the summer of 1939, the room was dark. Its example nevertheless inspired another Toronto musician, vibraphone and marimba player Jimmy Namaro, to front a similar venture in Hogg's Hollow, beyond the city limits on north Yonge Street. Though rather more comfortably appointed than the Onyx, Namaro's Café Marimba was equally short-lived. "He had money," Lewis explains. "We didn't have anything. We used to get orange crates, put a dish towel over them; you'd sit on that."

Advertisement, *Toronto Star*, 3 Oct 1938. [Metropolitan Toronto Reference Library]

215

The Onyx and Café Marimba were the first jazz clubs in Toronto, and very likely in Canada. There were, to be sure, other places across the country in the late 1930s where small bands played jazz and musicians jammed informally, among them the Terminal Club, Rockhead's Paradise and the Café St. Michel in Montreal, the Shanghai Tea Gardens in Winnipeg and the Mandarin Gardens in Vancouver. The three St. Antoine cabarets presented floor shows, however, as did the Mandarin. The bands that worked at the Shanghai played for dancing.

The Mandarin was touted in 1939 by *Down Beat* correspondent Don McKim as "the only spot [in Vancouver] drawing a crowd that wants its music hot."[4] Drummer Jackie Williamson was in place when the club opened in 1935; other bandleaders there through the 1940s included pianist Bill Sinclair, drummer Al Ferris and the saxophonists Al Darby and Carl De Santis.

Ferris worked at the Mandarin in 1944 and 1945. "We had everybody come down there — from the CBC, from the Belmont [Cabaret], from north, east, south and west. It seemed to be the hot spot, bottles flying, smoke so thick that... well, think about the fog in Vancouver... the smoke was that bad. When you walked out of there in Chinatown, the air smelled fresh and pure."

According to Ferris, the club operated with some impunity from the law. Liquor was freely available — "the bootlegger was the bouncer" — and police raids were seldom a surprise. "We knew when they were coming, so half an hour before we'd tell everybody to put their crocks under the table and smile. The cops would come in, walk all around, and walk out again."

The East Pender Street establishment was generally the best place to hear tenor saxophonist Carl De Santis, either in the club's employ — he worked there in 1939 with Bill Sinclair and returned with his own quartet in 1946 — or just sitting in. Stewart Barnett, late of the Gar Gillis and Jerry Gage bands in Winnipeg, played trumpet with De Santis at the Mandarin on occasion in 1948. He describes the saxophonist's style as a composite of all the leading tenormen of the Swing Era.

"He'd listen to some record and the next night he'd sound like that guy. Basically, he had his own rollicking, rolling style of playing, sometimes a bit like Lester [Young], although he had a bigger sound... For a guy who was relatively untrained — just a natural musician — he'd play *Body and Soul* and break your heart. He sounded as good as anybody you ever heard. Different solo every time. Real character, too. Funny guy: he used to disappear for days playing fan tan in Chinatown. He loved to gamble."

The advent of the Onyx Club and the parallel activities of musicians in other nightspots across the country in the late 1930s marked the break of jazz in Canada from both the dance hall and the regimentation of the big band. Small bands were on the rise — swing "combos" at first, usually patterned after the most successful US groups of the day.

The John Kirby Sextet, based in New York and popular on both records and radio, was especially influential, its mellifluous, deftly arranged style echoing during the early 1940s in the music of bassist Jack Norton's sextet in Montreal and the RCAF Western Command's Jo-Boys in Vancouver. Kirby's example also shaped two bands heard on CBC radio during the mid-1940s, the Bert Niosi Septet in Toronto — as has been noted in Chapter 13 — and the Johnny Holmes Sextet, with Oscar Peterson at the piano, in Montreal. Similarly, the Nat (King) Cole Trio in Los Angeles was an early model for the Ray Norris Quintet, whose weekly CBC radio show, *Serenade in Rhythm*, went on the air from Vancouver in 1941.

In due course, the worldwide revival of interest in the traditional jazz styles of New Orleans and Chicago also reached Canada, followed from New York by the startling new sounds of bebop.

The traditional jazz revival — sometimes called the New Orleans revival or the dixieland revival, descriptions that reflected different aspects of the same phenomenon — started around 1939 as the result of several overlapping events. The return to notice of important New Orleans musicians like Jelly Roll Morton and soprano saxophonist Sidney Bechet was one; their careers had gone into eclipse during the early 1930s. The discovery of other Crescent City musicians like trumpeter Bunk Johnson and clarinetist George Lewis was another; neither man had known celebrity outside New Orleans and was therefore thought to play the music in something close to unadulterated form. The rejuvenation in New York of the veteran, white Chicago jazzmen of the 1920s was a third, concurrent to a new wave of younger white musicians like the Californian Lu Watters, England's George Webb and Australia's Graeme Bell, all of whom established bands faithful to jazz in its classic forms.

Bebop, by comparison, developed on a single front: New York's 52nd Street jazz clubs and Harlem nightspots. There, in the years around 1940, a new generation of black musicians — trumpeter Dizzy Gillespie, alto saxophonist Charlie Parker, pianist Thelonious Monk, guitarist Charlie Christian and others born during, or soon after, the Great War and already young veterans of the Swing Era — began to advance the harmonies, reshape the melodies, streamline the rhythms and pick up the tempos of jazz.

Bop was typically played by one or two horns — saxophone and/or trumpet, more rarely clarinet and trombone — supported by piano, occasionally guitar, bass and drums. In its urgency and assertion, it eschewed the pre-arrangement of swing in favour of short themes, usually voiced in unison for the horn(s) and piano, leading to and from a round of solos. The themes themselves were given to asymmetry, or at the very least to unpredictability; the solos that followed mirrored these same qualities and drew further complexity from the sharply accented rhythms and the extended and compounded harmonies that bop used as its improvisational substructure. It was a daring music, both for its many intrinsic challenges and for its willingness to reject to the formulas of swing, and with them the likelihood of wide popular acceptance.

The "trad" revival and bebop could not have been more at odds, one reactionary, the other revolutionary. Where traditional jazz stood as a reaffirmation of the music's original values in face of what its proponents saw as the commercialism of swing, bebop turned those same values on end. Where traditional jazz was forgiving of its adherents' failings — as indeed it had to be with the aging Bunk Johnson, who became the revival's figurehead — bebop demanded virtuosity of those musicians who would play it. Where traditionalists espoused a simplicity that welcomed one and all, boppers strived for an improvisational complexity that, intentionally or not, excluded both players and listeners alike.

Traditional jazz and bebop had this much in common: each challenged the status quo of swing and thus developed outside the mainstream of popular culture. The rise of bop in particular was accompanied by the advent of a counterculture that promoted berets and horn-rimmed glasses as its fashion statement, a hipper-than-thou disdain for the uninitiated as its prevalent attitude, and heroin as its narcotic of choice.

As a result, the influence of traditional jazz and bebop on Canadian musicians would be less immediate and widespread than that of swing just a few years earlier. Where swing had been pervasive, the new sounds were elusive, ignored initially by American network radio and championed only by Blue Note, Commodore, Dial and Savoy and other small, independent record labels whose Canadian distribution was often limited to the import services of specialist stores like the Promenade Music Centre and Campus Record Bar in Toronto, the Music Box Record Shop in Montreal and the J.W. Kelly Piano Company and Western Music in Vancouver.

Isolated in Winnipeg during the early war years, trumpeter Paul Grosney ordered new releases by mail directly from Milt Gabler's Commodore Music Shop in New York. "I would write and tell him my story: 'Please send me the good ones.' It would be up to his tastes [and] his tastes were excellent. You'd expect all Commodores, and there were a few of them, but he also sent me other labels like Blue Note. All that was available in Winnipeg was Victor, Columbia and Decca. That was it. Later on we got some Capitol."

And not until 1947 or 1948 did the Regina teenager Herbie Spanier chance upon recordings of Charlie Parker and Dizzy Gillespie while browsing in Eaton's department store. "I was looking for records of jazz and I heard Bird [Parker] doing these things. I thought, 'Jesus Christ, *what?*' and I bought the records, 12-inch 78s, took them home and listened. So I started playing this shit — bebop, or whatever they called it. As far as I know I was the only person in town who dug that." Significantly, one of the first 78s that the trumpeter discovered in this manner, Red Norvo's Dial recording of *Congo Blues* with Parker and Gillespie, was already at least two years old.

Canadian appearances by leading revivalists and beboppers were equally rare. The jazz concert, as a formal event, came to Canada in October 1944, when the Crelinsten brothers, Abe and Ed, owners of the Music Bar in Montreal, presented the first of several jam sessions with small, all-star bands of traditional and swing musicians from New York at His Majesty's

Theatre. A Toronto promoter, Dave Gillman, followed suit at Eaton Auditorium in October 1945.

Among beboppers, Charlie Parker was still largely unknown when he made his Toronto debut at Massey Hall in November 1945 as a member of a hybrid swing-bop quintet that included pianist Erroll Garner and trombonist Trummy Young. He also performed with the moveable jam session known as Jazz at the Philharmonic at Massey Hall in April 1948 and at the Verdun Auditorium in September 1949.

Interaction between Canadian and American musicians on these occasions was at best fleeting. Oscar Peterson appeared as a guest soloist at some of the concerts held at His Majesty's Theatre and participated in jam sessions with members of the US bands that stopped at the Chez Maurice Danceland. Meanwhile, several Toronto musicians, including Bert Niosi and guitarist Stan Wilson, played informally with Charlie Parker at a local radio station before his first Massey Hall concert. Peterson invariably made a strong impression on the visitors, garnering several offers of employment in the United States. Stan Wilson drew a similarly favourable response from Parker.

"Charlie Parker, who leads a group of his own in Manhattan," wrote *Globe and Mail* columnist Dillon O'Leary, "got the address of Stan Wilson soon after he heard Stan knock off the first few chords on his guitar — said he could use a sideman like that in any New York swing outfit."[5] Wilson, remembered as a guitarist of extraordinary skill, spent much of his career working in Toronto radio orchestras. He had apparently raised eyebrows in this manner before. "As usual," noted the Toronto tabloid *Hush* after the same sesssion, "Stan Wilson had the American boys talking to themselves."[6]

Clyde Clark was a chemical engineer with Ontario Hydro. Michael Snow, studying at the Ontario College of Art, would become one of Canada's most celebrated visual artists. Ken Dean and Art Schawlow were attending the University of Toronto; Dean's future lay in corporate law, while Schawlow went on to win the Nobel Prize for his work in developing the laser. Such were the backgrounds of just four of the young Canadians caught up in the traditional jazz movement of the 1940s. Amateurs in the best sense of the word, Clark and Snow were pianists, and Dean a trumpeter. Schawlow played clarinet, although not — to anyone's recollection — very well.

Clark emerged as the key figure. He wasn't the best musician of the 20 or so Torontonians who had organized themselves into three bands by 1948. That distinction perhaps belonged to Dean. Or to clarinetist Johnny Philips, who played in Chicagoan Johnny Dodds' earthy style with Clark's Queen City Jazz Band. Or to another Queen City musician, trombonist Bud Hill.

No, Clark's role was unique. A little older than the

Clyde Clark & Harvey Hurlbut, Centre Island Association Club House, 1950.
[Courtesy Clyde Clark]

rest, he served as a mentor to the local traditional jazz scene through his involvement with CJBC's *1010 Swing Club*. Each week, beginning in December 1944, he selected and scripted a half hour of New Orleans and Chicago music for the 90-minute Saturday afternoon broadcast. His segment, *The Jazz Band Ball*, immediately became a rallying point for the growing number of like-minded jazz fans in the city. Indeed, it was probably the major reason why Toronto, virtually alone among Canadian cities at the time, embraced the revivalist movement.

At that, Clark's Queen City band, Dean's Hot Seven and trombonist Ron Sullivan's Delta Jazz Band were formed relatively late, compared to George Webb and his Dixielanders (who included the Vancouver-born

The Ken Dean Jazz Band, Toronto, circa 1948. From left: Ken Glandfield, Michael Snow, unknown drummer, Don Priestman, Ken Dean, Roy Glandfield.
[Courtesy Michael Snow]

clarinetist Wally Fawkes) in England and Graeme Bell's Dixieland Band in Australia. But England and Australia had strong brass band traditions that produced trained musicians capable of making a ready transition to jazz. "When *we* started," Clark notes, by way of contrast, "most of the fellows just picked up instruments and started to play them."

The Queen City Jazz Band was the first of the three Toronto groups. Its members met informally as early as 1943 but did not make their public debut until September 1946, when they appeared at the Circle "M" Ranch in Kleinburg, north of the city, earning seven dollars a man — a typical sum — for their efforts. The Delta Jazz Band followed in 1947 and Ken Dean, who had played in the Toronto Youth Symphony and was briefly a member of the Queen City band, introduced his Hot Seven in August 1948. Both the Clark and Dean bands played for summer dances at the Centre Island Association Club House; the Hot Seven were also regulars at the east-end Balmy Beach Canoe Club and at a similar hall in Oakville, west of Toronto.

Of the three groups, the Delta band — with Ron Sullivan, trumpeter

Bob Donnelly and, briefly, Art Schawlow on the front line — adhered most closely to the revivalist model, taking its lead from the recordings made by Bunk Johnson, George Lewis and Kid "Shots" Madison for the American Music label. The Dean band, on the other hand, was influenced by the more progressive Chicago veterans who were now based in New York, in particular those heard weekly in the mid-1940s on the so-called Blue Network's *Eddie Condon's Jazz Concert* — Wild Bill Davison, Muggsy Spanier and others.

"We weren't a revival band that specialized in one set style, like the Lu Watters or Turk Murphy bands did," Dean's pianist, Michael Snow, explained in 1991. "With us it was more mixed up, and there used to be lots of arguments about that. The real New Orleans purists thought Louis Armstrong was an impostor, that everything after Bunk Johnson was a negation of the music. But we didn't feel that way. We liked Louis and Wild Bill Davison both. Our style depended on the tunes, but the repertoire was basic Dixieland."[7]

The Queen City musicians, resplendent in orange sports jackets, took the middle ground between the Dean and Delta bands, tending —in the words of visiting Montreal writer Henry F. Whiston — "more to the accent-on-melody found in the New Orleans style than to emphasis on beat and excitement."[8] In retrospect, Clark supports the observation. "Dean's band played very hot, with everybody in the band stomping their feet like mad. [It had] a very driving style. Queen City tended to play more slow tunes and blues."

The three bands were not, of course, alone in championing the traditional repertoire. Other musicians across Canada led dixieland bands in more commercial, swing-influenced styles during the 1940s and early 1950s, among them trumpeter Peter Power in Halifax, trumpeters Russ Meredith and Johnny DiStaulo in Montreal, trombonist Jerry Bourgeault in Ottawa and cornetist Trump Davidson in Toronto.

In some cases, though, their dedication to traditional ideals was tempered by more practical considerations. Power's experience with his sextet, formed in 1945, was a case in point. "We got into the big band business because we wanted more work. People were hiring the dixieland band for lobster fests,

Oktoberfests, those kinds of things. But for dances, no. So that's why we put the big band together, and then we'd have a dixieland group come out and do some sets."

Ken Dean draws another distinction between his own band, for example, and the small ensemble modelled on Bob Crosby's Bob Cats that Trump Davidson culled from his Palace Pier orchestra for summer engagements at the Centre Island Casino and for radio work on the CBC. "They were professional musicians trying to make a living at it," Dean admits freely. "We were just guys playing by the seat of our pants, trying to have a good time and blowing our heads off if we could."

Of Canada's two major dance-band leaders during the 1940s, Mart Kenney was — perhaps surprisingly — more sympathetic to bebop than Bert Niosi. Of course Kenney's sweet style would have been less directly threatened than Niosi's swing by the advent of a new style of jazz.

"Bebop," a prescient Kenney told Toronto *Telegram* columnist Helen McNamara early in 1949, "is a natural progression in the evolution of jazz... While it may not gain complete public acceptance, it will certainly leave its mark in various ways on modern popular music as time goes on."

Niosi, meanwhile, could not hide his disdain. "Ninety per cent of bop should be played behind closed doors," he informed McNamara. "It impresses no one. The other 10 per cent [is] for [the] amazement of trained ears only."[9] Ironically, Niosi's own septet had shown a boppish influence with its 1947 recording of *Blues in B-Flat.*

By 1949, however, bebop — now four years in circulation on disc — had only a precarious footing in Canada. Individual musicians were mastering its challenges but organized bands devoted in whole or in part to the new music remained rare — Louis Metcalf's International Band in Montreal and short-lived "boptets" led late in the decade by Herbie Spanier in Regina and his fellow trumpeter Kenny Almond in Vancouver. Tellingly, when the teenaged Toronto alto saxophonist Moe Koffman made his first recordings in 1948 — *Main Stem's Bopportunity, Boppin' for Sid, Bop Lop* and *Rockin' with the Bop* — he did so in Buffalo, and with musicians from that city.

Louis Metcalf and His International Band, Café St. Michel, Montreal, 1947.
From left, Steep Wade, Willy Girard, Louis Metcalf, Al King, Herb Johnson,
Wilkie Wilkinson, Butch Watanabe.
[Photographer: Louis Jaques. Herb Johnson Fonds, P088/P03, Concordia University Archives]

There was nothing in Louis Metcalf's background that would have made him a likely candidate to lead the first putative bebop group in Canada. The best years of the St. Louis-born trumpeter's career appeared to be behind him when, in January 1947, a month shy of 42, he took six musicians into the Café St. Michel. He had worked in New York with Duke Ellington, Jelly Roll Morton and Luis Russell in the late 1920s and, after an initial Montreal sojourn at the Terminal Club during the early 1930s, played with Fletcher Henderson in 1935. By bop standards, Metcalf was old-fashioned. Indeed, when he visited Montreal in 1945 for a jam session at His Majesty's Theatre, he appeared in the company of traditionalists like trombonist Wilbur de Paris and pianist Sammy Price.

But Metcalf was a shrewd musician. "When I first came to Montreal to form my International Band," he noted in 1962, "I already found a dixieland band and some swing and commercial outfits, to[o]. In order to bring something different into town, I organized a modern band which in those days was called Bebop. That attracted the attention of the young people."[10]

But more than its style of music, which also encompassed swing and dixieland, the band itself would become Metcalf's major selling point. When both Canadian immigration and Montreal union officials protested his plan to use New York musicians on an extended basis in Canada, he looked instead locally for his sidemen and opened at the St. Michel with saxophonist Benny Winestone, trombonist Jiro (Butch) Watanabe, guitarist Gilbert (Buck) Lacombe, pianist Steep Wade, bassist Al King and drummer Mark (Wilkie) Wilkinson. Winestone and Lacombe were soon replaced by Herb Johnson and violinist Willy Girard, respectively, and the personnel thereafter remained constant until August 1949.

Metcalf was quick to identify the band's novelty: each musician could, in a stretch, claim a different nationality or ethnic background. "I think he just lucked into the idea of the 'International Band,'" Watanabe suggests, "because of me, and Willy Girard, and Benny Winestone... It was different. Who ever heard of a Japanese jazz trombone player? Or a French-Canadian jazz violinist?"

Or, for that matter, a Scotsman — Winestone — who presented himself as the ultimate hipster with his brogue-inflected bop slang, picked up during a year recently spent on 52nd Street in New York? Steep Wade, meanwhile, was of West Indian background and King, a black American from Chicago, had some Mexican blood. Wilkinson's parents were Swedish. Metcalf himself was part Cherokee. The band was organized on a co-operative basis and took "Democracy in Music" as its slogan, drawing favourable comment for its constitution from the Montreal *Standard* in April 1947 and *Down Beat* the following month.[11]

Metcalf's sudden rise in profile did not change the fact that he was basically leading a showband. Like Lou Hooper, Bill and Andy Shorter, Eddie Perkins, Irving Pall, Lloyd Duncan and Bill Wade before him at the St. Michel, he co-ordinated the music for the singers, tap dancers, shake dancers, comics, acrobats, ventriloquists and roller skaters who arrived, three or four acts at a time, from New York.

Not that there weren't opportunities to play jazz in the course of a night's work. "Most of the acts that came into the St. Michel had quite a bit of jazz as their [backing] music," notes Watanabe. "But not bebop, more like swing." The International Band also played for dancing between shows. Girard, the band's shyest musician but its most daring soloist, was featured on the up-tempo tunes that invariably concluded the dance set — *Cherokee*, for example, or *Air Mail Special*. Herb Johnson, a model of sobriety compared to the colourful Winestone, could be heard emulating Coleman Hawkins in *Body and Soul* and other ballads like *Harlem Nocturne* and *Yesterdays*.

Surely more to the musicians' satisfaction, though, were the jam sessions at the St. Michel, held in the early morning after the 1 a.m. show or on Sunday afternoons. Wade and Wilkinson would take great sport in testing the mettle of visiting Americans and off-duty locals who dropped by to play.

"When you arrived in Montreal," explains the Winnipeg drummer Billy Graham, who did so late in 1949, "the first place you went was the St. Michel. The next thing you did was sit in there. And I did... We were into *Cherokee*. Steep took an introduction and, I mean, the *janitor* could have played drums, it felt so good. He just *had* it. I put more of an edge on it, because I was a little scared, and he loved it, man. He was standing at the piano, yelling my name — 'Billy Graham, Billy Graham' — and the piano was *shaking*."

Wade and Wilkinson were in fact the only truly competent modernists in a band that was essentially caught in the transition between swing and bebop. Wade had studied Bud Powell's style closely, without ever matching the American pianist's facility. Wilkinson, who had made extended visits to New York earlier in the decade, made no secret of his admiration for Powell's colleague, Max Roach.

Metcalf stood at the opposite end of the spectrum. "He wasn't a bebop player himself," suggests fellow trumpeter Allan Wellman, who worked across Mountain Street with the Sealey Brothers at Rockhead's Paradise during the late 1940s. "He knew how to read all the charts, so he used to play them, but when he took a solo, he was no bebopper."

Watanabe remembers Metcalf in similar terms. "Louis to me was a businessman. He wasn't a bad musician — he wasn't the best — but he was a good leader, a good front man. He had this air that he'd been around the block. As a trumpeter, for what he knew, he was okay. He was more or less a blues player."

Metcalf's success as a bandleader was not so much a matter of democracy in music as diplomacy in music: drawing on his experience playing for revues in Harlem nightspots, he was able to balance the competing interests of his employer and his musicians. Indeed, the International Band's first engagement at the St. Michel came to an end in August 1949 when those interests could no longer be reconciled.

Bruce Taylor of the *Herald* described the chain of events that led up to the band's departure. "Metcalf's crew, Canada's top jazz organization, had been at the Mountain st. bopera house for three years, and LM's unusual arrangements had helped make the club one of the village's leading niteries. When shows failed, Louie still drew customers. Some time ago, Café St. Michel changed hands, and almost before the boys knew it, they were being urged to drop jazz and be-bop and stick mostly to rhumba and other Latin American stylings. The band balked at the proposition. One word led to another..."[12]

With trumpeter Russ Meredith taking over at the St. Michel, Metcalf moved immediately to the former Rendez-Vous, now the El Patio, on St. Lawrence Boulevard below Ste. Catherine. Herb Johnson declined to follow, however, and Wilkinson, Wade and Al King left the band almost immediately, returning briefly to The Corner, where they took over the St. Michel's street-level lounge, known familiarly as the Snake Pit, for several weeks.

The departures left the International Band in some disarray. Metcalf's consternation was surely compounded by the fact that his efforts to take the band on tour stateside in its heyday had been unsuccessful, thwarted by US immigration. And he now looked on as Wilkinson entered a Montreal studio in September 1949 with his Boptet of seven musicians — four from the International Band — to record for a new Toronto company, Monogram.[13]

While the International Band had broadcast at various times from the St. Michel over CHLP, the CBC's Eastern Network and CKVL, it did not record commercially. Thus the results of the Monogram session must stand for both the Metcalf and Wilkinson groups. In truth, *Wilk's Bop* and *All The Things You Are* do not reflect especially well on the development of bebop

Sealey Brothers, Rockhead's Paradise, Montreal, 1947-9. From left, back row: Milton Sealey,
Hugh Sealey, George Sealey. Front row: Willie Wade, Allan Wellman.
[Photographer: Lew McAllister. John Gilmore Fonds, P004/P33,
Concordia University Archives]

in Montreal before 1950: both are stilted performances with only Girard's
deft, fanciful violin solos to recommend them.

Metcalf regrouped over the next several months at the El Patio and, with
Benny Winestone again a member of the band,[14] returned to the Café St.

Michel in May 1950, only to run afoul of the RCMP. The Mounties had long kept a watchful eye on the St. Michel musicians, and probably on denizens of The Corner more generally. Wilkinson and Wade were, or would soon be, heroin addicts, and marijuana was popular with some, though not all, of Metcalf's other musicians. "The Mounties used to come to our dressing room," Watanabe remembers. "I knew they'd been there. They were searching for pot. I used to leave my trombone there, and they'd put it [back in its case] backwards."

On a night off from the St. Michel in November 1950, Metcalf, Winestone and King set out to hear Louis Armstrong at Standishall in Hull. Stopped en route by the RCMP, the trio was searched and arrested for possession of marijuana. Metcalf's pianist, Sadik Hakim, recently arrived from New York, was similarly charged at his Montreal apartment the same night. All four were found guilty; the Americans, whether by choice or by order, left Canada as soon as their prison sentences were up.

The Sealey Brothers — George, Hugh and the teenaged Milton — worked opposite the International Band for two of its three years on The Corner. George played tenor saxophone, Hughie alto, and Milton piano; Allan Wellman and drummer Willie Wade rounded out the quintet.

Rockhead's Paradise, like the St. Michel, presented all manner of black entertainers from New York and the Sealeys' duties, as Milton remembers them, parallelled those of the Metcalf band closely. "We played music for people to dance to. When the show came out, sometimes we'd feature the band during a particular number and we'd all just get off [improvise]. Then we'd [play for] one act after another. After the show we'd take a little break and then we'd play for dancing and do another show. There were two, sometimes three shows a night."

Here, too, bebop was at least in the air. "It wasn't out and out jazz. You were playing for the customers [but] you had a chance to grow a little bit, to develop, from playing John Kirby arrangements, Tadd Dameron arrangements, Charlie Parker things... [You'd] get into it that way."

Of the five musicians in the band, Milton alone eventually became proficient in the new idiom, pursuing his career during the 1950s in Europe

— he recorded with the expatriate American bop tenorman Don Byas in Holland in 1956 — and later in the United States. His brothers, like Allan Wellman, played in a swing style, while Willie Wade is remember largely as a fine showband drummer. "George was more of an improviser [than Hughie]," their younger brother suggests. "He could improvise well, maybe in the style of Coleman Hawkins. He used to play *Body and Soul* note for note. I would say he was a better improviser in a sense; Hughie was laid-back and straightahead, more so than George. George was a little more avant-garde."

Sonny Rollins, not yet 20, was probably the youngest of the New York beboppers who were drawn to Montreal in the late 1940s. The tall, soft-spoken tenor saxophonist made his first trip north on a family holiday, and returned several times by himself for longer periods, frequenting the St. Michel and associating with Louis Metcalf's musicians.

In another few years, Rollins would emerge as one of the most commanding improvisers of the modern era. For the moment, though, he was simply another impressionable musician at a formative stage in his career. "As a young kid," he says, "it was just great to be away from home. It was sort of a big adventure for me to get out, be with musicians, play my horn, and pick up whatever gigs I could."

More significant to the development of bebop locally were the Brooklyn musicians a few years Rollins' senior who first visited Montreal as members of Al Cowans' Tramp Band and then, in 1949, made the city their home.

The Tramp Band, which began in the early 1930s as a novelty act on Chicago street corners, had travelled internationally from 1936 to 1938 with Cab Calloway's Cotton Club Revue. In 1943 it appeared as the Musical Madcaps in several film shorts and was seen — again as the Tramp Band — backing the renowned dancer Bill (Bojangles) Robinson in the successful Hollywood celebration of black popular culture, *Stormy Weather*.

Such wide exposure should have promised even greater things, but the late 1940s in fact found Cowan and his musicians, now based in New York, working on a circuit of theatres and nightclubs in the US northeast, Ontario and Quebec. They performed on several occasions throughout the decade

MARK MILLER

in Montreal at the Val d'Or (formerly Connie's Inn), the Gayety Theatre and the Café St. Michel before taking an extended engagement over the winter of 1949–50 at the Alberta Lounge.

Initially, the Tramp Band featured kazoos with a rhythm section of washboard (Cowans), piano (Nick Aldrich), guitar and drums. The musicians, dressed as hobos in battered derby hats and tuxedos cut a little short in the leg, were "conducted" to comic effect by a dancer and pantomimist known as Pinky (Lester Johnson) in a manner reminiscent of Slow Kid Thompson's antics with the Tennessee Ten 20 years earlier.

In time, Cowans replaced the kazoos with horns. Now capable of taking both theatrical and dance engagements, the band that travelled in Quebec and Ontario in 1948 and 1949 variously included trumpeter Henry (Buddy) Jordan, tenor saxophonists Benjamin (B.T.) Lundy and Leroy Mason, and drummer Walter Bacon, boppers all. Soon enough, the Tramp Band — with Pinky still "conducting" — could be heard playing the odd Parker, Gillespie or Tadd Dameron theme, along with the pop tunes of the day.

Buddy Jordan had a particular impact locally. "He came into Montreal with a lot of new tunes, a lot of ideas," remembers the pianist Oliver Jones, who was in his mid-teens when the Tramp Band musicians began to make their presence felt. "He was a very inventive, wonderful player. He lacked reading skills, so that kind of limited him, but he was a good showman... People like Allan Wellman, although they were good trumpet players, didn't have Buddy's experience as far as playing bebop. Buddy had all that down. He was just a real natural musician. Great sense of phrasing. When he first came in, I would have put him up with anyone."

The Americans' influence was felt in Montreal less through their work with the Tramp Band, though, than informally at jam sessions. Indeed, for Butch Watanabe of the International Band, they were a revelation. "When I first heard them, I said, 'Yeah, that's it.' When B.T. and Buddy used to get together and play those [bop] lines, I said, 'Yeah.'"

Moe Koffman had just turned 19 when he came to the attention of Barry Ulanov in January 1948. The New York critic, an early champion of bebop, was visiting Toronto — "this new and thriving jazz town by the lake" — to

1010 Swing Club, 27 Dec 1947. From left: Hart Wheeler, Gordie Evans, Bernie Piltch, Graham Topping. [Courtesy Hart Wheeler]

participate in the presentation of awards to an all-star band chosen by *1010 Swing Club* listeners. He and Koffman crossed paths at Fantasy Farm, a Don Valley inn that was the site of regular Sunday night jam sessions held under the radio show's aegis.

Writing about his Toronto trip for *Metronome*, Ulanov described Koffman as "young, inexperienced, still in the imitative stage but Toronto's best, it appears, and maybe a lot more than that." Noting the inevitable influence of Charlie Parker on the young alto saxophonist, Ulanov continued: "He has added an original touch: he plays with astonishing lung power... he plays with continuity, carrying his melodic line, in the best bop tradition, across choruses, from one to another, to still another, and sometimes another, with little apparent pause for breath, with almost none of the fragmentary staccato phrasing which makes so much mince of so much of the meat of the school of Bird and Diz."[15]

Koffman had taken up the saxophone at 13 and was already playing in

Jam Session, Toronto, 1947. From left: Moe Koffman, Bill Goddard and Moe Miller.
[Photographer: Hart Wheeler. Courtesy Hart Wheeler]

local dance bands when the first Parker and Gillespie recordings began to show up at the Campus Record Bar ("Let us put good wax in your ears") near the University of Toronto. His immediate enthusiasm for bebop was shared by several other Toronto musicians, among them two teenaged trumpeters, Moe Miller and Graham Topping, as well as tenormen Bob Burns, Bill Goddard and Hart Wheeler.

Miller, who had moved east from Winnipeg by 1946, was especially precocious — "a very hip guy," in the estimation of his fellow Winnipegger, trombonist Jack Fulton, who called the trumpeter home in 1948 to play in Jerry Gage's all-star band. "He knew what was going to happen tomorrow by noon today."

In the absence of clubs, Toronto's boppers played together informally during the late 1940s. "It was mainly jam sessions," Koffman recalls. "Moe Miller, Bill Goddard, myself — we used to jam at the old House of Hambourg... and we used to go on Saturday afternoons and play jazz at beer parlours, just for the sake of being able to blow."

The House of Hambourg, run by Clement Hambourg, flourished at four different addresses between 1947 and 1963. Initially it was nothing more than a cluttered music studio above a Bay Street dress shop; Hambourg, the eccentric scion of a distinguished family of Russian classical musicians, taught piano there and made private recordings.

"We used to go up," Koffman explains, "because Clem had a recording machine. He used to record, his wife Ruth would be sewing, and she'd make sandwiches. And then he started to charge for these jam sessions." In time, the House of Hambourg became a popular nightspot, a coffeehouse of sorts, and served many Toronto jazz musicians of Koffman's generation as an early proving ground.

It was typical of Koffman's determination that by 1947 he was also looking to Buffalo for kindred spirits, drawn by the romance of playing in the United States — "in those days anything in the USA was hip; of course we realize now that's not necessarily true" — and in particular with black musicians. "We used to go over to the black Musicians' Club to play a bit on the weekend, because that was the place to jam, and to meet people. I remember meeting Frankie Dunlop, a drummer who went on Maynard Ferguson's [New York] band for a while, and Elvin Shepherd, who was an incredible Dizzy-like trumpet player."

Indeed, when Barry Ulanov's praise in *Metronome* brought Koffman an invitation to record for a small New York label, Main Stem, later in 1948, he hired Dunlop, Shepherd and two other Buffalo musicians for the session. If these first efforts were not a notable success, Koffman's next recording most certainly was. After spending the early 1950s working out of New

Ray Norris Quintet, caricature. CBC *Times*, 27 May 1945.

York with several post-Swing Era big bands, he returned home and in 1957 made the LP *Cool and Hot Sax*. One of its eight tracks, the innocuous flute feature *Swinging Shepherd Blues*, became an international hit the following year and launched Koffman on a long and successful career in Toronto studio and jazz circles.

There were, of course, kindred spirits across Canada, unbeknownst to each other save perhaps by word-of-mouth or the occasional, brief notice that appeared in *Down Beat*. On the east coast, for example, the black alto saxophonist Les Bryan, originally from Sydney, was a fixture at the Gerrish Street Hall in Halifax. As remembered by Bucky Adams, a younger Halifax saxophonist who started his career in 1948 as a trumpeter at Bryan's side, "He played in the style of Charlie Parker. He had such speed it was unbelievable. And accuracy..."[16]

In Winnipeg, according to Paul Grosney, who was sympathetic to bop himself, George Andrews "was the guy who would lift all the [melodic] lines off the Diz/Bird records, and we got to play them." Adds Andrews' friend, Billy Graham, "He played wonderful trumpet, but he never developed an embouchure. Blew his lip playing bugle, I think, when he was a kid. [He had the] most gorgeous sound you ever heard — but he just couldn't sustain notes. That's why bebop was great for him, because you can do all that fast [tonguing]. He wouldn't have to hold notes long."

On the west coast, guitarist Ray Norris (1916-58, of Saskatoon) also drew on bop's ideas, although as only one of many influences on the pleasantly progressive style that made his quintet, and its guest vocalist Eleanor Collins, so popular during the 1940s on the CBC's *Serenade in Rhythm*. His use of a clarinetist — Phil Nimmons at first, spelled by Art Lintott and Cliff Binyon — and his addition in 1947 of an accordionist, Vic Centro, had several popular American precedents, among them the small swing bands of accordionists Ernie Felice, Joe Mooney and Art Van Damme.

Nimmons, then just starting a long and distinguished career as a bandleader, composer and educator, also brought his own, formative influences to the quintet both as a player and as a composer — John Kirby, Artie

Shaw's Gramercy Five, Raymond Scott and the Benny Goodman Sextet with Charlie Christian. Norris was receptive.

"Deep down in his musical psyche," Nimmons observes, "Ray really dug being a supporter of new thoughts and innovations. He was pretty well self-taught; I've thought about my involvement with the group, because I was like really avant garde for those days, when I came out with eight chord changes to a bar... He was not the best reader, the best technician. I'd bring these parts in, and he'd *slave* over them. He was really committed to learning them. [Pianist] Bud Henderson was a much better player, in terms of technique, as well as other things, and he didn't have too much trouble, but Jackie Williamson used to cringe at the vibraphone parts."

Ray Norris & J.P. (Doc) Hamilton, Vancouver, 1940s.
[Courtesy Stewart Barnett, Vancouver Musicians' Association]

The guitarist's sympathy for new ideas, bop among them, did not, however, interfere with his quintet's commercial success. He sustained *Serenade in Rhythm* even after he moved to Toronto in late 1948. There, with Nimmons, Centro, pianist Jimmy Coxson and bassist Bob Weir he recorded four tunes for Monogram in 1949. *That's My Bop!*, *Bop Off!*, *Billboard Bop* and *Billboard Bounce* each touch lightly but quite creditably on the idiom.

Herbert Spanier was a slight, bookish kid during his student days at Central Collegiate in Regina. Born in nearby Cupar, in 1928, he played harmonica and guitar as a boy, took up bugle with the Sea Cadets during his early teens

237

and switched to trumpet in high school. He was still a student at Central Collegiate when he began working with Paul Perry at the Trianon Ballroom.

By all accounts, Spanier's exposure to bebop at 18 or 19 changed his personality completely. "He was a straight-arrow sort of guy," remembers Jim Moffatt, then a drummer in Regina, "and he became a real eccentric when he started to play jazz." Indeed, Spanier would become a figure of some legend in the course of his adventures in New York and Los Angeles during the 1950s and his capers, as he once called them, in Toronto and Montreal in later years.[17]

"Herby Spanier and his Boptette" — berets and floppy, plaid bow ties all around — were quite busy during the last months of 1948, appearing at the Trianon and Saskatchewan Hotel ballrooms, among various other venues, and even taking a Christmas Eve engagement at a senior citizens' home. Ted Franklin was the Boptette's alto saxophonist and Bob Moyer its tenorman. Geoff Hall played piano, Harold Grills bass, and Jimmy Wightman drums.

"We had to play for dancing because there were no [jazz] clubs," explains Franklin, who had the unenviable task of serving as Charlie Parker to Spanier's Dizzy Gillespie. "But people danced to 'up' tempos... We would do *Ornithology* [based] on *How High the Moon*, things [based] on *I Got Rhythm*, standards like *Out of Nowhere*. It was primarily bebop — at least that's what we thought. We played ballads for slow dancing."

Spanier was also constantly organizing jam sessions and, with the bravado that would characterize his career, sought out any American musicians who might be passing through the city. Franklin recounts one incident that reveals something about both the young Reginans and their guests.

"We found out that there were these black guys staying at the Regina Hotel, which was a dollar-a-night hotel. Of course in those days, we thought that any black guy was a jazz musician. We went over to the hotel, and they *were* musicians — from Kansas City. The older guys were pretty standoff-ish for a while; the younger guys warmed up sooner.

"We had a gig the next night. Herbie said, well, let's get this guy [to play] piano. Turned out he was a terrible piano player, a kind of boogie-woogie pianist. But the other guys in the band — we jammed with them —

they were great. We went up to CKCK. The guy who had the night show — I think he recorded us. We had another session at somebody's home, and the guys told me that was the first time they'd ever been in a white person's house... I remember them telling me about the black union and the white union [in Kansas City]. They knew about Charlie Parker; they didn't live that far away from his house. They were good players."

After four eventful months, the Boptette played its final engagement on New Year's Eve, 1948. Spanier made his first trip stateside weeks later. "Geoff Hall was going to Los Angeles during a cold February and I figured, 'Great, I'd like to go along, for a change, get the hell out of town.' I heard a lot of jazz: Harry James at the Palladium, and Howard McGhee at some club. I heard a lot of groups. And I should have gone and sat in, because I knew I played as well as they did, even then — I was about 19 [sic]. I knew that I could play, but I was shy."

Spanier returned from Los Angeles in time to join several other like-minded prairie musicians for concerts in the spring of 1949 at Regina's Darke Hall and Saskatoon's Club 400. Participants in one or both of the events included Geoff Hall, Harold Grills, Jimmy Wightman and tenor saxophonist Glen Acorn from Regina, pianist Len Barber and guitarist Gordie Brandt from Saskatoon, and Jack Fulton, trumpeter John Frosk, tenor saxophonist John Kelsey and drummer Al Johnson from Winnipeg.

Spanier composed two of the tunes played at the Saskatoon concert, *Monad* and *Dynapulsion*, and also contributed an essay, "The Art of Jazz," to the program notes. At a time when Canadian musicians were just beginning to master bebop, Spanier, already in character, was looking beyond it. "'Ragtime,' 'dixieland,' 'swing' and 'bebop,'" he wrote, "have provided the stepping stones to a larger musical expression — a mature art form."

Clearly caught up in the very latest developments, he praised "such geniuses" as pianist Lennie Tristano, trumpeter Miles Davis and alto saxophonist Lee Konitz, with implicit reference to the innovative recordings that Tristano had made for New Jazz, and Davis for Capitol, four months earlier in New York, each with Konitz a participant.

"In its battle to educate the masses," Spanier continued, "jazz has encountered our stagnant social status quo with its usual interferences: the putrefying effect of commercialism, gross social ignorance and those retro-gressive individuals whose inability to understand and refusal to investigate jazz, forces them to cling violently to old familiar patterns. Let them cling. Time will vindicate the pioneers of modern art."

Time proved Spanier correct: once established belatedly in Canada during the 1950s, bebop would remain the dominant language among the country's jazz musicians for the next 40 years.

CHAPTER FIFTEEN
Oscar Peterson

The Alberta Lounge, located on the ground floor of the Alberta Hotel at the southeast corner of Windsor and Osborne streets in downtown Montreal,[1] was a small, intimate room furnished in red leather. "The atmosphere is such," wrote Al Palmer in *Herald* in 1948, "that you immediately lower your voice as you enter."[2] In keeping with its name, the walls of the lounge were hung with Rocky Mountain scenes — large, colour photographs made from transparencies supplied by the public relations department of the CPR, whose Windsor Station loomed directly across the street from the hotel.

Oscar Peterson called the Alberta Lounge home from October 1947 through October 1949, a Canadian wonder among Canadian wonders. For all intents and purposes, he was still part of the St. Antoine scene: The Corner was just a five-minute walk away, down Windsor Street to St. Antoine, and three short blocks west — past the old Terminal Club and the former Clef Club headquarters — to Rockhead's Paradise and the Café St. Michel. Peterson routinely finished his last set at the lounge in time to visit and sometimes sit in with the Sealey Brothers or Louis Metcalf's International Band.

Figuratively speaking, though, he was moving uptown. He had already reached national celebrity by 1947, with a burgeoning recording, radio and touring career to his credit. His first boogie-woogie performances for Victor, now two years in release, "sold thousands," according to the company's director of recording, A. Hugh Joseph.[3] Regular CBC appearances further piqued the country's interest: the pianist's Winnipeg debut in March 1946 at the Auditorium drew a reported 4000 fans.[4]

Peterson's rags-to-riches story — "born poor, in a rented parsonage on Delisle Street in St. Henry Ward" in 1925 and now "the most commercially successful pianist of his age in Canada, and perhaps anywhere"[5] — was celebrated in mass-circulation publications like *Maclean's* and *Liberty*. Indeed, his ascendancy was without precedent in Canada; among the country's jazz

Advertisement, *Montreal Herald*, I Jun 1948.

musicians, only Bert Niosi, 16 years Peterson's senior and now very near the pinnacle of his career, enjoyed a similar profile in the 1940s.

The higher Oscar Peterson's star rose, first nationally and then internationally, the longer the shadow it cast over the achievements of other Canadian jazz pianists active in the 1940s, among them Dave Bowman, then working in New York, Wilf Wylie and Chris Gage, both important figures in the west, Al McLeod in Toronto, and Joe Stroble and Steep Wade in Montreal.

Dave Bowman (1914–1964) was born to Canadian parents in Buffalo, a twist of fate that surely facilitated his career stateside. Raised in the town of Dundas, west of Hamilton, he began to work locally at 18 with a dance orchestra led in turn by guitarist Ken Steele and saxophonist Duart Maclean. Under Maclean's direction, the band worked as far afield as the Old Mill in Toronto and Crystal Beach on Lake Erie, showcasing its young pianist at every opportunity. Although Bowman was unable to read music, his improvising — in Maclean's words — "was out of this world. Some of the work he did with me was so colourful, you'd just want the band to be playing melody, with Dave doing the colour work on top. It was pretty, but rhythmically so."

Bowman spent three years with Maclean and a shorter period with Hamilton saxophonist Morgan Thomas before leaving for England in 1936 to join Canadian Billy Bissett's orchestra at the Savoy Hotel in London. He subsequently toured Europe with noted

Dave Bowman, Old Mill, Toronto, 1934.
[Courtesy Duart Maclean]

British bandleader Jack Hylton. By 1938, Bowman was in New York, where his adaptably modern style, influenced by Jess Stacy — Stacy was Benny Goodman's pianist at the time — attracted the attention of several leading traditional and dixieland musicians.

In the next five years — until he became a staff musician at NBC — Bowman took club or recording work with cornetist Bobby Hackett, soprano saxophonist Sidney Bechet, tenor saxophonist Bud Freeman, trombonist Jack Teagarden, clarinetist Joe Marsala, cornetist Muggsy Spanier and others. His impact on the New York scene was reflected in his 12th-place showing among pianists in the 1940 *Down Beat* readers' poll.[6]

At least three other Canadian pianists were also active in New York during this same period. Bill Clifton, a veteran of the Cliff McKay and Rudy Spratt bands in Toronto, followed Bowman stateside around 1939, finding employment with Paul Whiteman and Bud Freeman, and also playing briefly for Woody Herman and Benny Goodman. A second Toronto pianist, Lionel Prouting, spent time with the Bob Chester and Charlie Spivak orchestras. Meanwhile, Max Chamitov of Montreal worked intermittently with Joe Marsala during a nine-year period, 1937-46, in the United States.

Wilf Wylie (1913?-1985) waited until the war's end before leaving Vancouver for Los Angeles. Accounts of his activities there vary: he may have played for one or all of Ray Bauduc, Bob Crosby and Tommy Dorsey before returning home in the summer of 1947.

Wylie is remembered as a somewhat eccentric and rather temperamental character, initially a drummer, most notably a pianist, eventually also a tenor saxophonist and, parenthetically, a plumber. He led bands at a succession of dance halls during the early 1940s — Alma Academy, the White Rose Ballroom, Happyland, the Embassy and up the coast at Horseshoe Bay — and also taught piano at the Rex School of Popular Music.

Wylie, who went unrecorded during his career, was identified in 1943 by *Down Beat* correspondent Bud Herman as a pianist in the style of Teddy Wilson,[7] whose clarity of thought and unassuming melodic grace departed from the darker and more vigorous approach of the pianists who preceded him in the 1930s. The attribution is supported by a recollection from the Vancouver saxophonist Lance Harrison: "I remember being at a jam session with him and saying how much I admired Fats Waller. He said, 'Well, there's a better piano player than him now — Teddy Wilson.'"

Doug Parker, a younger Vancouver pianist, speaks admiringly of Wylie's "control over the whole piano," which is also consistent with the Wilson influence. "He had wonderful hands, very large hands," Parker adds. "Until Chris Gage came to town, there was no one like him."

By the time that Chris Gage — born Christian Giesinger in Regina in 1927 — made Vancouver his home in 1949, he had been playing publicly for more than a dozen years. As the star attraction in bands led by one or another of his brothers — Jerry, a tenor saxophonist, and Tony, who played trumpet and sang — he was a teenaged sensation throughout the west, known especially for his boogie-woogie style, much as Oscar Peterson had been in the east.

Indeed, Gage was Oscar Peterson's only true rival among pianists in Canada during the 1940s. And yet when he died in 1964, a suicide, Gage left no commercial recordings. Only a few CBC transcriptions and airchecks remain as evidence of the skill, imagination and power of his playing.

"It was totally his own style," observes Doug Parker. "He was a shortish guy, with short arms, so he had to sit very close to the piano. He had very strong hands and he played *loud*, but he was extremely accurate... He was in the great tradition of strong players. Anything he heard, he could do."

Though two years younger than Peterson, Gage was active professionally at an earlier date, appearing first on Regina radio and then in local nightclubs. He was 13 when he started working with Xavier and the Swing Aces at the Silver Dell in 1941. Fes Fairley, reporting for *Down Beat*, described Gage there as a "vest-pocket edition of Count Basie, who plays with an eight-to-the-bar beat."[8]

Gage turned 16 as the bandleader at the same South Railway Street nightspot during the winter of 1943-4. He subsequently worked for Jerry Gage, summering in Alberta at Sylvan Lake in 1945 and at the Waterton Lakes Provincial Park in 1946, and wintering at the Trianon in Regina. Drummer Jimmy Wightman, later a member of Gage's Vancouver trio, first heard the pianist at this time. "Jerry's band was playing at the Trianon Ballroom then and this curly haired, baby-faced kid was playing piano like I'd never heard before. Boogie-woogie, locked hands, Erroll Garner style, you name it, he did it."[9]

Oscar Peterson also made Gage's acquaintance during this period, probably during a guest appearance with the Jerry Gage Orchestra at the Trianon in October 1946. "He had an uncanny sense of the unexpected," Peterson has said. "The first impression I got of him, from him, was that he had no qualms, certainly no problems with the keyboard. Some pianists have a natural affinity for the instrument. It comes across in the things they just naturally do; other pianists would have to rev up to those kinds of things. Chris did it naturally. He could almost be reading a book — it was that natural. I found him to be a person who generated a wealth of musical ideas, beautiful rhythmic conception, as I remember, and certainly no harmonic hassles. He had *everything* at the time."

Everything, it seems, but opportunity. Isolated on the prairies, Gage — unlike Peterson — had neither the chance to record nor the occasion to associate freely with the American musicians who might have encouraged him to broaden his horizons. He remained instead under his brothers' sway, leaving Regina in the spring of 1947 for Winnipeg, where he appeared — this time with Tony — at The Flame, the Don Carlos Casino and the 15 Stairs.

In March 1948, the three Gage brothers were reunited in Jerry's new all-star orchestra. The venture, as has been seen in Chapter 13, was ill-fated, stranding the band first in Saskatoon and again in Vancouver. By now, Gage had been a musician for more than half of his 20 years, much of that time spent on the road. He returned to Regina for another winter and then, seeking some measure of stability in his life, spent his last 16 years as Vancouver's premier jazz pianist.[10]

Al McLeod was known in Toronto during the 1940s as "the white Tatum"[11] and "The 10 Hottest Fingers on Radio."[12] Duke Delory, who suggested the comparison to the virtuoso Art Tatum in *Down Beat*, followed with a brief though revealing portrait of McLeod at 20, newly arrived from Kingston, Ontario, in 1942.

"For the last seven years Al, who has marvelous technique and a sharp ear, has made a study of all the different styles of the big time Yankee 88-ists [pianists], and can do a carbon job on anyone from [Eddie] Duchin to [Teddy] Wilson. These last three years Al has concentrated mostly on his fave stomp-box artist, Art Tatum, whose style he claims is the toughest, and whose ivory work there is more to than any other pianist, for his dough."

The opportunities in Toronto for a solo or trio pianist — à la Tatum — were limited until a change in local liquor laws led to the advent of the cocktail lounge in 1947. Several of the city's finest players, Jimmy Coxson, Bob

Chris Gage, Varsity Hall, Sylvan Lake, 1945.
[Courtesy Glen Acorn]

Fenton, Wally Gurd, Gordon Hahn and Bill Isbister among them, worked instead in the relative anonymity of the city's dance bands. Isbister, another highly regarded pianist in the Jess Stacy style, at least had the opportunity to play regularly with the small swing band led by clarinetist Cliff McKay, throughout the 1940s.

McLeod, meanwhile, worked as a staff pianist at CKEY before he joined Coxson, Fenton, Bernie Black, Billy O'Connor and others on the new lounge circuit and in later years travelled as a novelty act under the name Gloves McGinty.

Joe Stroble, known also as Joey Burton and remembered for his stubby fingers and cheap cologne, was in Montreal by early 1943, arriving either directly or indirectly from Winnipeg. He joined Rolland David's swing band almost immediately.

Trumpeter Paul Grosney, who participated in after-hour sessions with Stroble at the Shanghai Tea Gardens in Winnipeg during the late 1930s, adds him to the list of pianists inspired by Jess Stacy. "He was one of the very few piano players that didn't play full [accompaniment] all the time. Most piano players, they'd feed you [chords] continually, they'd keep playing, and playing, and playing. *He'd* let the rhythm come through. He knew every tune there was and he was very lyrical. He played beautifully."

Montreal proved to be little more than a stopover for Stroble on his way to the United States and, in time, a position as music director to the actress Jane Russell. He moved from the David band at the Chez Maurice Danceland to Stan Wood's orchestra in 1944 and left the city in 1945. His bandmate with David, Maynard Ferguson, remembers Stroble as "a very aggressive pianist," adding facetiously, "I could tell he was a *real* professional, as I look back, because he was always arguing with the bass player."

Steep Wade seldom left St. Antoine during the 1940s. He spent four months at Standishall in Hull with trumpeter Jimmy Jones in 1943 and worked uptown in Montreal at the Auditorium with Maynard Ferguson's big band briefly in 1946, but was otherwise found with Jones and then Lloyd Duncan at Rockhead's Paradise and, later, with Willie Wade and then Louis Metcalf at the Café St. Michel.

Steep Wade was the dominant pianist on The Corner during the 1940s, rivalled only by the older Art Davis, an American remembered as a fine blues and boogie-woogie player, as well as a handy arranger. A third St. Antoine pianist, Ilene Bourne, was also well-respected, particularly for her abilities as an accompanist. According to Oliver Jones, who played "trick" piano at the Café St. Michel as a boy in the mid-1940s, "Anytime anyone wanted to know the verse to a tune — some obscure tune — [they'd] get in touch with Ilene." Bourne, Jones suggests, consciously played like the American Mary Lou Williams. "Her solos were very exact. She was one of those pianists who didn't have tremendous technique, but she always played *right*... She knew what she was doing, like a classical player who would make the transition [to jazz] and knew exactly what she wanted to play. A very controlled pianist."

It was Steep Wade, however, who captured the imagination of impressionable younger St. Antoine pianists like Peterson, Jones and Milton Sealey. A physically imposing man, severe in temperament and uncompromising in matters of music, Wade was known by word of mouth far beyond Montreal as a judicious accompanist, rhythmically and harmonically incisive in a way that reminded his contemporaries of Bud Powell. His work as an alto saxophonist with Mynie Sutton's Canadian Ambassadors in the 1930s and with Lloyd Duncan's Seven Sharp Swingsters as late as 1946 gave him rare insight into the ways in which a pianist might best serve a soloist's purposes.

"In that period, an awful lot of musicians around town would rather [Steep] accompany them than even Oscar," Oliver Jones notes. "He was really 'way ahead of his time, very intense when he played, and another one who had a good command of the piano. He seemed to know a lot of different styles, a lot of tunes... We talk a lot about Oscar, but I think back to Steep. Oscar got a lot from Steep — that same driving force. Milt had it, too, and another fellow, Gene Cooper."

Sealey, for his part, acknowledges Peterson as "the kingpin," but adds, "Steep Wade was also a very fine pianist. He didn't have the dexterity that Oscar had, but he was a very tasty pianist. Nice ideas, *good* ideas. What he played was *there*... When he sat at the piano to play, you knew it was Steep Wade.

"At that time, he had [his own] style, and at that time Oscar and all the younger pianists, they used to listen to him. I know personally I would listen to him — sit up there and watch him play... He struck me as the type of player who didn't practise much. He didn't run over the piano, or really get over the piano, like Oscar or some of them. He wasn't a Teddy Wilson. Not quite as fluent. But [he was] precise in what he played."

Peterson himself has said: "He had one thing — I know because I was very close to him — he had the same sense of time as Nat Cole: impeccable. He could not sit down at the piano unless it swung... If I learned nothing else from anyone, that's one thing I learned from Steep... Technically, he was certainly not a great pianist, but he had a way of playing things and making them work musically, of making them *his* statement. He spoke in a certain dialect, let's put it that way — you could always recognize Steep...

"He was always sort of a gruff man in a loving way towards me, like

'Don't get out of line, little brother.' He'd always look for me. I'd walk into the Café St. Michel where he played with Hugh Sealey's orchestra [sic] and later with Louis Metcalf — when I was old enough to get in, I'd *always* go to hear him — he'd give me a nod and as I walked over, he'd get up, walk away from the piano, and say, 'You got it.'"

This public rite of succession was both figurative and literal. As Peterson's career soared, Wade's prospects — now captive to his use of drugs and alcohol — declined. Largely inactive during the early 1950s, Wade made his last appearance of note one February afternoon in 1953 at the Chez Paree, where he was recorded in a jam session with no one less than Charlie Parker.[13] By December, Wade was dead of heart failure, a month shy of 36.

The 1940s were a decade of transition as swing evolved into bebop against the backdrop of the older styles that were enjoying renewed popularity as part of the traditional jazz revival. A Canadian pianist maturing in this period had his or her pick of influences. Just as Wilf Wylie was apparently drawn to Teddy Wilson, and Chris Gage at least initially to boogie-woogie, Al McLeod was taken with Art Tatum, Bill Isbister and Joe Stroble with Jess Stacy, Ilene Bourne with Mary Lou Williams and Steep Wade with bebop and Bud Powell.

Oscar Peterson, as documented on record beginning in 1945, was clearly also in thrall to some of these same styles and stylists. From his base in Montreal, he was close enough to New York to be aware almost immediately of the latest developments but remained at some remove from the pressures to conform to any one of them. He stood still further apart from many of his American contemporaries on the strength of his background and active interest in classical music, evident — for example — in his use of Chopin's *Prelude in A Major* as a basis for improvisation in his concert programs throughout the 1940s.

Peterson was the fourth of five children, all of whom played piano, each assisting the next with the lessons initiated by their father, Daniel, a CPR porter and self-taught musician. So it was that Peterson's sister Daisy, five years his senior, effectively served as his first instructor; she would also guide

Milton Sealey, Oliver Jones, Reg Wilson and Joe Sealy during a long and distinguished career as a piano teacher in Montreal.

Not yet a teenager, Peterson studied with once and future Canadian Ambassador Lou Hooper, whose own career in jazz — dating back to the 1920s in Harlem — was supported by solid classical training acquired at conservatories in Detroit and New York. Peterson, now in his teens, looked for further guidance to the Hungarian-born concert pianist Paul de Marky, whom he described in 1945 as an adviser rather than a teacher and credited with refining his keyboard technique through a variety of classical exercises.[14] Their relationship was significant, as Peterson biographer Gene Lees has observed: de Marky was himself a pupil, once removed, of the 19th-century virtuoso Franz Liszt, whose bravura playing is surely one antecedent of the mature Peterson's extravagant style.[15]

Hooper was undoubtedly sympathetic to his young charge's love of jazz. So, too — perhaps more surprisingly — was de Marky. And rightly so. It was already bringing the teenager some notice outside of St. Antoine in the early 1940s — a $250 first prize in an amateur talent contest, broadcasts on CKAC and work with saxophonist Percy Ferguson's High School of Montreal dance band, the Victory Serenaders. It was also a more realistic career choice than classical music might have been for a young black Canadian pianist at the time.

By 1943, Peterson had left school and moved from the Victory Serenaders to the Johnny Holmes Orchestra, a white, semi-professional swing band that appeared at Victoria Hall in the fashionable neighbourhood of Westmount on Saturday nights and also took engagements elsewhere in the upper echelons of Montreal society. Holmes, a trumpet player and arranger, was known for the gifted young players who passed through his band during the 1940s. Peterson, the only black musician among them, was the most gifted of all.

Shirley Oliver, Tommy Thompson, Frankie Nelson, Ollie Wagner, Charlie Adams, Alf Coward and Jimmy Jones preceded Peterson across the colour line in Canada — Oliver almost 20 years earlier with Graydon Tipp in Edmonton, Thompson with Sandy De Santis in Vancouver, Nelson with

Joey Jampol and Wagner with Eddie Franks in Winnipeg, Adams with Chaucy Power in Halifax, Coward with Charlie Hillcoat and Emilio Pace in Sydney, Nova Scotia, and Jones with Stan Wood in Montreal.

While such opportunities generally offered more and higher paying work than would otherwise be available to a black musician, they also brought the close and often unforgiving scrutiny of white employers and patrons. Harold Karr, one of Frankie Nelson's bandmates with Joey Jampol's 10-piece swing band at the Canadian Legion in the fall of 1938, remembers clearly the trumpeter's discomfort.

"Frankie was very aware that he stood out like a sore thumb. But he played great trumpet and we insisted that he stay with the band. In order to keep the Legion job, we had to join the union. Some of us were already members; Frankie had to join. Fortunately at that time, an uncle of mine, Joe Karr, was on the board of the union... I spoke to Joe, and he assured me that the board wouldn't have any objection to Frankie. So Frankie joined the union with our blessing. We were all delighted. We played that job for just a few weeks and then there was some static from the management that we had a black musician in the band. One day, Frankie just sort of disappeared on us."

Alf Coward was similarly wary in the early 1940s. Like Peterson, he had studied the classics but was drawn to jazz, playing piano in the Sydney area with his own band, sometimes known as the Royal Sizzlers, and appearing on many occasions with Sydney's leading white bands. "Every time I went out with Emilio Pace — to Glace Bay or New Waterford — I was watched very carefully. I guess if I had moved the wrong way, there'd have been a punch or something. I *suspect* that's what would have happened. There were certain people in the audience who were watching me very carefully, because I was the only black."

In Montreal, meanwhile, Oscar Peterson's growing following was in the majority white, if only as a function of the city's racial demographics. Nevertheless, his prominent role in the Johnny Holmes Orchestra was not universally accepted. In late 1945, by which time trombonist Frank Johnson, tenor saxophonist Herb Johnson and trumpeter Ted Brock had all played for Stan Wood, and other black musicians were working for white leaders in cabarets outside St. Antoine, the Holmes band found itself unwelcome at the swanky Ritz-Carlton Hotel.

The Montreal *Herald* reported the story: "The Johnny Holmes Orchestra, booked for several dos at The Ritz, among them a deb dance and the IODE [Imperial Order Daughters of the Empire] Blue Orchid Ball, may not carry through with their chores. Seems the Ritz is objecting to their colored pianist, that brilliant virtuoso Oscar Peterson, and Johnny and the boys consider the issue more important than a few bookings."[16]

Holmes, according to Gene Lees, threatened to take out newspaper ads in the *Herald*, *Star* and *Gazette* announcing that the band would never again play the Ritz-Carlton because of its apparent policy of racial discrimination. In the event, the IODE intervened on the band's behalf and the evening went ahead as planned, Holmes exacting a measure of satisfaction by featuring Peterson even more extensively than usual.[17]

Oscar Peterson remained associated with Johnny Holmes until 1947, all the while determinedly advancing his own career. Holmes in turn played various roles in Peterson's development — one as his employer, one for a time as his manager and a third as a kind of mentor. "He is responsible for building up my technique," Peterson explained in 1946. "He really broke me all apart when I started with him. I was overdoing boogie-woogie and was completely at a loss for slow music. He showed me the style I'm using today."[18]

Peterson made a particular point of seeking out and playing with American musicians during their visits to Montreal. An early-morning jam session in January 1944 found the pianist, now 18, sitting in at the Café St. Michel with members of the Count Basie Orchestra after their engagement uptown at the Chez Maurice Danceland. No less than Basie himself was subsequently quoted in the New York publication *Music Dial* as saying, rather awkwardly, "I've never heard the Ivory-box played that way, by a youngster."[19] The Basie endorsement was refined with further use to a more succinct assertion: "The best ivory box player I've ever heard."[20]

Peterson made a similarly favourable impression three months later on another Danceland attraction, Jimmie Lunceford. Indeed Basie, Lunceford, Frankie Newton, Mezz Mezzrow, Coleman Hawkins and several other

Oscar Peterson, Home Service Community Centre, Toronto, 6 Mar 1946.
[Globe and Mail Collection, photograph 102548, City of Toronto Archives]

American visitors during the 1940s all encouraged the pianist to leave Montreal for the United States. Peterson himself voiced his ambition to do exactly that as early as the summer of 1944,[21] but would in fact resist such overtures for another five years.

In truth, he barely had his professional career underway in 1944; only now was he starting to lead his own bands. One, the Tophatters, worked occasionally at Wood Hall in Verdun. Another, a trio with bassist Brian McCarthy and drummer Frank Gariépy, appeared on local radio. At the same time, though, his popularity was growing quickly through his national appearances on CBC radio. He was a guest on *The Little Review* in the summer of 1944, starred with Johnny Holmes' sextet on Bovril's *Recipe Tunes* during the winter of 1944–5 and performed regularly on Sweet Caporal's *Light Up and Listen* over the winter of 1945–6.

His rising national profile was further boosted by the release in June 1945 of his first trio recordings for Victor, beginning with a triumphant *I Got Rhythm* and a vivacious version of *The Sheik of Araby*. Each captured an as-yet unrefined virtuosity, driven by the energy and impatience of youth. Peterson's impressive command of boogie-woogie was a feature of both performances; the rumbling bass figures that carry the final choruses of *I Got Rhythm* are particularly electrifying.[22]

Peterson's second release, pairing *Louise* and *My Blue Heaven* from the same April session, was comparatively sedate — *Louise* eschewed boogie-woogie altogether — but still prompted Gorman Kennedy of the Montreal *Herald* to praise the pianist for "just about the greatest left hand since [Robert] Grove used to do a pitching chore for [Philadelphia Athletics' manager] Connie Mack."[23]

In this, Peterson was very much in the tradition of St. Antoine pianists like Steep Wade, Art Davis and Ilene Bourne, whose powerful left hands routinely compensated for the absence of bass players in St. Antoine show-bands. According to Allan Wellman, who took over at Rockhead's Paradise from the Sealey Brothers in July 1949, "Club owners figured, 'Why should I hire a bass? He don't do nothing but keep time. You got a drummer to keep time.'"

Peterson recorded a total of 16 tunes between April 1945 and July 1946 accompanied by bassist Bert Brown and a succession of drummers — Frank Gariépy, Roland Verdon and Russ Dufort. Armand Samson played guitar on one of the four sessions. Six of Peterson's eight sides from 1945 were in whole or in part boogie-woogie pieces. He would return to the idiom in 1946 with *Honeydripper* and again in late 1947 with *Oscar's Boogie*, but his playing on his early Canadian releases otherwise stands as an informal, though enthusiastic survey of the many influences then in circulation — Nat Cole, Art Tatum and Teddy Wilson among stylists, Harlem stride and "locked-hands" among styles.

Taken together, the 1945 and 1946 recordings reveal a young musician looking for his own identity and, equally, a popular artist contending with pressures to sustain his early success. "My first two boogie records seem to have typed me," he told the Vancouver *Sun* in October 1946. "But even if it's good commercially, I can't play boogie all my life. We had a big argument about it at Victor. They said — Peterson, do you want to be a good

Oscar Peterson Trio, 1947-9. From left: Austin (Ozzie) Roberts,
Oscar Peterson, Clarence Jones.
[Oscar Peterson Fonds, photograph NL 19363, Music Division, National Library of Canada]

commercial musician or do you want to be a collector's item[?] I said collector's item!"[24]

Nevertheless, there could be no denying Peterson's commercial success in 1946. He made his first forays outside of Quebec in March — to the Auditorium in Winnipeg and Massey Hall in Toronto — and was finally heard during the summer on his own weekly, 15-minute national CBC radio show. As interest continued to increase across the country, he embarked in late September on a five-city tour of the west that saw him featured at each new stop with a local dance band — with Gar Gillis at the Auditorium in Winnipeg, Jerry Gage at the Trianon in Regina, Bob McMullin at the Drill Hall in Edmonton, Bruce Bristowe at the Mewata Armouries in Calgary and Dal Richards at the Exhibition Gardens in Vancouver.

Such was Peterson's impact nationally that by year's end, with his US debut still more than 30 months away, he was able to garner enough votes — presumably in Canada alone — to place 28th among pianists in the 1946 *Down Beat* readers' poll.[25] *Metronome* also took notice. "For a country reputedly as unhip as Canada in the creation of musicians," wrote Jim Buller in January 1947, "a miracle has occurred. His name is Oscar Peterson."[26]

The Oscar Peterson Trio, with bassist Austin or Ozzie (formerly Vivian) Roberts and drummer Clarence Jones, opened at the Alberta Lounge on October 8, 1947. Roberts, a veteran of the Cy McLean Orchestra, hailed from Toronto. Jones was a Montreal musician.

Peterson had outstripped the Johnny Holmes Orchestra long before he finally put it behind him. But as a jazz musician on the rise, he was breaking new ground in Canada; the opportunities available to him would be severely limited as long as he remained in the country. Typically, his recording activities continued apace in 1947 — he employed bassist Al King and drummer Wilkie Wilkinson from Louis Metcalf's new International Band for his fifth session in April — but his concert work that year was restricted to a return appearance at Massey Hall, where he was accompanied in May by three Toronto musicians, among them Stan Wilson, the guitarist who had so impressed Charlie Parker 18 months earlier.

With Roberts and Jones as a working trio, and the Alberta Lounge as its base of operations, Peterson was at least able to settle into a routine that allowed him to focus his energies and interests as the final step before testing the US market. Ironically, the first tune that the new trio recorded together in December 1947, *Oscar's Boogie*, was a throwback to the very style that

Peterson had expressly hoped to put behind him — no doubt over Victor's objections.

The trio did not record again for another 15 months, the longest hiatus in the four-and-a-half years that Peterson was associated with the Canadian company. His initial effort on his return to the studio in March 1949 was a version of Dizzy Gillespie's *Oop-Bop-Sha-Bam*, a departure from previous Peterson's recordings on two counts: it marked his debut as a singer in the manner of Nat Cole and signalled his growing interest in bebop. The foundation of the mature Peterson style was now fully in place.

In the spring of 1949, Peterson replaced Clarence Jones with guitarist Ben Johnson, bringing the trio in line with the instrumental format used so successfully by Cole and Art Tatum. He was now talking openly about going to the United States. "We've been booked into a number of spots starting in September," he told the *Herald* in May. "We've been after this for some time."[27]

Came September, Peterson did indeed go to the United States. But when he went, he went alone. The details of his first trip to New York are the stuff of legend.[28]

The story has been told many times over.

How Jazz at the Philharmonic producer Norman Granz, visiting Montreal on business and en route by taxi to the airport, was impressed by a pianist he heard on the cab's radio. How the driver identified the source of the music not as a recording but as a live broadcast — Oscar Peterson at the Alberta Lounge. How Granz, who knew of Peterson by reputation, immediately headed back downtown in order to hear the pianist for himself.

How Peterson agreed to be planted in the audience for a Jazz at the Philharmonic concert at Carnegie Hall in New York. How Granz brought him to the stage as a "surprise guest" on a bill headlined by Coleman Hawkins, Lester Young and Charlie Parker.

How, at some point after 9:30 p.m. on September 18, 1949, a Canadian pianist made one of the most remarkable debuts in the history of jazz.

APPENDIX

The following individuals have been quoted in *Such Melodious Racket* from interviews done by the author on the dates indicated.

Phil Antonacci — 19 Nov 1996
Georgie Auld — 24 Nov 1981
Ed Bailey — 20 Dec 1994, 6 Jan 1995
Harvey Bailey — 6 Jan 1995
Stewart Barnett — 17 Oct 1994
Syd Blackwood — 15 Feb 1995
Don Carrington — 10 Feb 1995
Clyde Clark — 14 Mar 1997
Alf Coward — 19 Dec 1996
Edwin Culley — 17 May 1991, 20 May 1993
Teddy Davidson — 2 May 1980
Trump Davidson — 26 Jan 1976
Ken Dean — 20 Mar 1997
Maynard Ferguson — 19 Jan 1996
Percy Ferguson — 4 Feb 1996
Al Ferris — 11 Jan 1997
Ted Franklin — 31 Aug 1994
Jack Fulton — 18 Dec 1996
Bill Graham — 18 Apr 1995
Paul Grosney — 12 Apr 1994, 2 Mar 1995
Lance Harrison — 24 Oct 1994
Bill Hayes — 1 Dec 1994
Oliver Jones — 21 Nov 1996
Harold Karr — 17 Jan 1997
Ernest King — 18 Oct 1994
Moe Koffman — 31 Mar 1997
Sam Levine — 6 Mar 1997, 7 Mar 1997
Lew Lewis — 24 Apr 1997
Cecil Lewsey — 18 Dec 1994
Duart Maclean — 26 Sep 1995
Elliott Mitchell — 25 Jan 1995, 18 Feb 1995
Les Mitchell — 22 Jan 1995
Jim Moffatt — 1 Oct 1994
Phil Nimmons — 25 Mar 1997
Doug Parker — 14 Apr 1997
Paul Perry — 27 Aug 1980
Oscar Peterson — 27 Feb 1980
Peter Power — 3 Mar 1997
Dal Richards — 19 Dec 1996

Sonny Rollins — 2 Feb 1996
Milton Sealey — 29 Dec 1987, 5 Jan 1996
Frank Sklove — 18 Dec 1993
Herbie Spanier — 1 Mar 1976, 19 May 1995
Alice Wagner — 21 Jan 1995
Del Wagner — 24 Aug 1994
Butch Watanabe — 7 Nov 1995
Allan Wellman — 12 Jul 1995, 27 Aug 1995
Everett Williams — 14 Dec 1994

The following individuals were also interviewed in the course of researching *Such Melodious Racket*: Bucky Adams, Ken Almond, Walter Bacon, Tommy Banks, Ed Bickert, Adolphus (Doc) Cheatham, Melvin Crump, Gordon Evans, Jerry Fuller (Sr.), Jack Harrison, Albert Johnson, Mart Kenney, Leroy Mason, Billy O'Connor, Don Palmer, Gordie Phillips, Sonny Rollins, Lloyd Salmon, Ron Sullivan, Alan Symonds, Clark Terry, Bryan Wagner, Douglas Watson, Hart Wheeler, Lloyd Williams, Phil Williams and Wilfred Williams.

NOTES

AUTHOR'S NOTES

1 Unless otherwise cited, all first-person quotes in *Such Melodious Racket* have been drawn from interviews conducted by the author between 1976 and 1997, as listed in the Appendix.

2 An effort has been made to maintain quoted material in its original form, however archaic— or incorrect— the spelling of some words.

3 As a matter of convenience, these abbreviated references have been used in the notes that follow:

AFM for American Federation of Musicians

Chilton, *Who's Who of Jazz* for John Chilton, *Who's Who of Jazz* (New York 1985)

Gilmore, *Swinging in Paradise* for John Gilmore, *Swinging in Paradise: The Story of Jazz in Montreal* (Montreal 1988)

Gilmore, *Who's Who of Jazz in Montreal* for John Gilmore, *Who's Who of Jazz in Montreal: Ragtime to 1970* (Montreal 1989)

Litchfield, *Canadian Jazz Discography* for Jack Litchfield, *The Canadian Jazz Discography 1916-1950* (Toronto 1982)

Rust, *American Dance Band Discography* for Brian Rust, *The American Dance Band Discography 1917-1942* (New Rochelle, NY 1975)

Rust, *Jazz Records* for Brian Rust, *Jazz Records 1897-1942* (New Rochelle, NY 1978)

PREFACE

1 Duke Ellington, *Music Is My Mistress* (New York 1973), 138

INTRODUCTION

1 Transcribed from the two-CD compilation *The Will to Swing*, Verve 847 703-2

2 Michael Levin, "Mix thinks concert was a dandy — for a change," *Down Beat*, 21 Oct 1949, 3

3 Richard Palmer, *Oscar Peterson* (Tunbridge Wells, Kent 1984), 15

4 See Marshal Stearns, *The Story of Jazz* (New York 1958), 11-110; James Lincoln Collier, *The Making of Jazz* (New York 1978), 3-71

5 See Donald Marquis, *In Search of Buddy Bolden: First Man of Jazz* (New Orleans 1978)

6 See James Lincoln Collier, "The rise of individualism and the jazz solo," *Jazz: The American Theme Song* (New York 1993), 25-47

CHAPTER ONE

1 "'Just Kids,' winner," Winnipeg *Tribune*, 22 Sep 1914, 3

2 For further discussion of the Creole Band's "prehistory," see Lawrence Gushee, "How the Creole Band came to be," *Black Music Research Journal*, vol 8, no 1, 1988, 83-100.

3 G. Ten Wright, "Theatres and Music: Clever artists this week at Pantages," Edmonton *Bulletin*, 29 Sep 1914, 3

4 Marmaduke, "In the footlights glow," Edmonton *Journal*, 29 Sep 1914, 3

5 G. Ten Wright, "Theatres and Music: Reminding you of this week's Pantages bill," Edmonton *Bulletin*, 1 Oct 1914, 3

6 Quiller, Carl, "Echoes of wartime at Pantages Theatre," Calgary *Herald*, 6 Oct 1914, 9

7 "Music is at Pantages show for the week," Vancouver *Sun*, 2 Nov 1914, 8

8 Frederic Ramsey and Charles Edward Smith, *Jazzmen* (New York 1939), 21

9 "News and reviews of things theatrical," Winnipeg *Tribune*, 19 Sep 1914, second section, 2

10 By late 20th-century standards a wholly ignoble profession, minstrelsy put white performers in blackface (using burnt cork) to present songs, dances, skits and speeches in the purported manner of American blacks. It had its greatest popularity in the mid-1800s. Black minstrel companies emerged following the Civil War and both white and black minstrelsy continued well into the 20th century. Several white, Canadian-born performers had successful US careers as minstrels. The most famous was George Primrose (1852-1919, of London, Ont.) who led or co-led a succession of companies from 1877 until his death. Other popular figures included Lew Benedict and Tommy Granger of Kingston, Ont., Colin ("Cool") Burgess and Charley Gardner of Toronto, G. Washington ("Slim Jim") Dukelan of Smith's Falls, Ont. and John Hogan of Montreal. See Edw. Le Roy Rice, *Monarchs of Minstrelsy, from Daddy Rice to Date* (New York 1911).

11 As heard in this period by Sid LeProtti, whose description of Johnson's bass playing is quoted by Tom Stoddard in *Jazz on the Barbary Coast* (Chigwell, Essex 1982), 31

12 Alan Lomax, *Mister Jelly Roll* (Berkeley and Los Angeles 1973), 126

13 Listed among new releases for May in *Canadian Music Trades Journal*, April 1917, 44

14 One other event merits acknowledgement: the lone Canadian stop on the so-called "whirlwind tour" undertaken in the spring of 1914 by the dancers Vernon and Irene Castle, accompanied by James Reese Europe's 18-man orchestra. Europe's recordings for Victor over the previous five months — *Castle House Rag* in particular — offer rare evidence of the exuberant orchestral ragtime played by New York's black musicians in this period. Europe's Tango Orchestra, as it was billed for the Castles' matinee and evening concerts in Toronto at Massey Hall on May 19, would have included the novelty percussionist Buddy Gilmore. It was Vernon Castle, however, whose drumming drew notice in the Toronto *Globe*. "Mr. Castle's dancing, of course, was a joy to the beholder, but its fascination was as nothing to his work with the big drum, the little drum, the cymbals and the motor horn in the 'Danse Furore' by the orchestra." ("The Castles in Motion," Toronto *Globe*, 20 May 1914, 4)

15 H.W.M., "Real French life shown at Pantages," Manitoba *Free Press*, 18 Jul 1916, 3

16 "Theatreland," Vancouver *Sun*, 7 Sep 1916, 3

17 "Much cleverness seen at Pantages," Victoria *Daily Colonist*, 12 Sep 1916, 8

CHAPTER TWO

1 Thompson and Mills, who eventually married, each left the troupe at least once during its five-year history, and thus may not have been present for all of the troupe's Canadian engagements. Thompson, for example, was in the US army from May 1918 to August 1919. Both were performing in *Shuffle Along* by late 1921.

2 Personnel has been drawn from contemporary references in the Chicago *Defender*, interviews during the 1960s with U.S. Thompson by Jean and Marshall Stearns (*Jazz Dance: The Story of American Vernacular Dance*, New York 1968) and entries in Chilton, *Who's Who of Jazz*. Paul Barbarin refers to Shea's and the Lyric Theatre in "Paul Barbarin — his story as told to John Norris," *Eureka*, vol 1, no 1, January-February 1960, 23-27.

3 "First night at theatres: Orpheum has a great show," Winnipeg *Tribune*, 19 Aug 1919, 7

4 "Clever dancers on Orpheum circuit," Victoria *Times*, 30 Aug 1919, 8

5 Stearns, *Jazz Dance*, 178-179

6 E.R. Parkhurst, "Music and the drama," Toronto *Globe*, 27 Nov 1917, 8

7 "Vaudeville bill at Empire gets by very nicely," Saskatoon *Star*, 12 Mar 1918, 15

8 "Strong vaudeville bill is presented at Regina Theatre," Regina *Leader*, 15 Mar 1918, 10

9 "Music in the home: What is a jazz band," Regina *Leader*, 13 Apr 1918, 10

10 R.J., "First night theatre reviews," Vancouver *Sun*, 26 Mar 1918, 7

11 Advertisement, Hamilton *Spectator*, 1 Nov 1919, second section, 1

12 Source unknown, quoted in "The Musical Spillers: an examination by Rainer Lotz," *Storyville*, 152, 1 Dec 1992, 63

13 E.R. Parkhurst, "Music and the drama," Toronto *Globe*, 5 Sep 1911, 9

14 "Band leader cornetist dies in 89th year," Toronto *Telegram*, 18 Oct 1947, 11

15 Rust, *American Dance Band Discography*, 1708-1710, identifies the non-Browns on recordings made by the group during the years 1914-20 as, variously, Harry Cook, Harry Finkelstein, Guy Shrigley, Sonny Clapp and, improbably, James "Slap Rags" White. (See also Chapter 5, footnote 21.)

16 "Minstrels delight crowded audience," Ottawa *Citizen*, 29 Mar 1913, 15

17 Program notes, Tivoli Theatre, Sydney, Australia, undated [early 1925]

18 "Vaudeville bill of unusual merit at Regina Theatre," Regina *Leader*, 31 Jan 1919, 12

19 *The International Musician*, September 1929, 6

20 Listed in Rust, *American Dance Band Discography*, 1708-1710

21 John Chilton, *Sidney Bechet: The Wizard of Jazz* (New York 1987), 31-32

22 "Wilbur Mack's comedy big draw at Orpheum," Vancouver *World*, 23 Mar 1920, 7

23 Robert Kimball and William Bolcolm, *Reminiscing with Sissle and Blake* (New York 1973), 82

24 "Wrecked," Chicago *Defender*, 24 May 1919, 8

25 "The Firing Line," Chicago *Defender*, 13 Dec 1919, 8

26 "All-stars win from minstrels by 6-4 score," Saskatoon *Star*, 14 Aug 1919, 6

CHAPTER THREE

1 Advertisements, Montreal *Star*, 31 Dec 1916, 2; 2 May 1917, 2; 11 Sep 1917, 2

2 Quoted in Samuel Charters and Leonard Kunstadt, *Jazz: A History of the New York Scene* (New York 1962, 1981), 77

3 Wallace's five titles are not listed in Rust, *Jazz Records*. They do, however, appear in Rust, *American Dance Band Discography*, 1872-1873.

4 An early black Canadian newspaper, the *Observer*, makes reference to "Teasley's Orchestra" in connection with black social functions in 1917 — eg., "West Indian Cricket Club 3rd annual reception," 23 Jun 1917, 1

5 Advertisement, Edmonton *Bulletin*, 29 Jan 1917, 4

6 Advertisement, Edmonton *Bulletin*, 1 Feb 1917, 4

7 Advertisement, Edmonton *Bulletin*, 17 Feb 1917, 2

8 Advertisement, Calgary *Herald*, 3 Feb 1917, 12

9 File NA-625-20, Glenbow Archives, Calgary

10 Advertisement, Calgary *Herald*, 18 Oct 1919, 22

11 "Big time," Chicago *Defender*, 2 Aug 1919, 6

12 "Letters," Chicago *Defender*, 10 Jun 1922, 8

13 "Jass band," Hamilton *Spectator*, 31 Aug 1917, 14

14 "Royal re-opened," Hamilton *Times*, 3 Sep 1917 [unpaginated clipping in the collection of Hamilton Public Library]

15 "A big night," Hamilton *Spectator*, 27 Sep 1917, 11

16 "Canada," Chicago *Defender*, 27 Nov 1917, 7

17 Charles Stone may have been a Canadian by birth; he was the brother of pianist-songwriter Fred Stone (1873-1912, of Chatham, Ont.), who wrote *Bos'n Rag* and *Ma Rag Time Baby* in the 1890s. The Stone family moved to Detroit when Fred was a child. (Eileen Southern, *Biographical Dictionary of Afro-American and African Musicians*, Westport, Conn. 1982, 361)

18 Advertisement, Ottawa *Citizen*, 3 May 1919, 19

19 Advertisement, Ottawa *Citizen*, 3 Aug 1920, 13

20 Advertisement, Ottawa *Citizen*, 16 Aug 1920, 11

21 "Letters," Chicago *Defender*, 3 Sep 1921, 6

22 Edward B. Moogk, *Roll Back the Years: History of Canadian Recorded Sound and Its Legacy (Genesis to 1930)* (Ottawa 1975), 85

23 In addition to the Novelty and Jazz Orchestra and the Novelty Entertainers, Yerkes also sent bands to the Bustanoby and Castellani Restaurant. The Metropolitan Dance Players (led by pianist Victor Rodriguez) opened the Crescent Street cabaret in December 1921 and Yerkes' Happy Six followed in March 1922.

24 Advertisement, Montreal *Star*, 29 May 1920, 38

25 According to Rust, *Jazz Records*, 1748, Yerkes' Blue Bird Orchestra included Brown, Oliver, Green, violinist Ed Violinsky, possibly Gorman, and others unknown. Brown, in an interview with Rust (*Needle Time*, 7, November 1986, 14) confirmed that he recorded in Canada with the Blue Bird Orchestra and also with (Simone) Martucci's [Venetian Gardens] Orchestra. (Brown, Violinsky, Green and sometime Yerkes pianist Ted Fiorito are credited individually as composer or co-composer of pieces recorded in Montreal by Martucci, suggesting that most or all of Yerkes' Blue Bird musicians recorded under Martucci's name as well.) It cannot be assumed, however, that these musicians were necessarily present at the Blue Bird Cafe for all — or even any — of the engagement, in view of their ongoing recording activities in New York studios during this period (also documented in *Jazz Records*). Brown *et al* may have instead travelled to Montreal solely to participate in the HMV sessions, designed to capitalize on the Blue Bird engagement's success, but left the nightclub work itself in other (and presumably lesser) hands.

CHAPTER FOUR

1 Sources include: "City athletes' friend, George Paris, dies at 78," Vancouver *Province*, 2 Sep 1947, 24; "Death at 79 halts career of George Paris, Negro Sportsman," Vancouver *Sun*, 2 Sep 1947, 9; Alf Cottrell, "On the Sunbeam: memories of George Paris," Vancouver *Sun*, 3 Sep 1947, 11.

2 "Tribute paid George Paris; Rites Thursday," Vancouver Sun, 3 Sep 1947, 2

3 "A note or two," Chicago *Defender*, 22 Dec 1917, 9

4 "A note or two," Chicago *Defender*, 2 Nov 1918, 6

5 "Letters," Chicago *Defender*, 10 Dec 1921, 7

6 "Sheftell letter," Chicago *Defender*, 21 Jun 1924, 6

7 Advertisement, Edmonton *Journal*, 1 Nov 1919, 6

8 "Westmount Jazz Band very active," Montreal *Star*, 15 Nov 1919, 19

9 Advertisement, Montreal *Star*, 24 Jan 1920, 38

10 Advertisement, Winnipeg *Tribune*, 1 Oct 1918, 8

11 "Winnipeg Jazz Babies concert for soldiers," Manitoba *Free Press*, 13 June 1919, 8

12 Obituary, Winnipeg *Tribune*, 6 Dec 1978, 40

13 Advertisement, Saskatoon *Daily Star*, 2 Aug 1919, 14

14 "Jazz Babies draw crowds; Star fund up," Saskatoon *Star*, 28 Nov 1919, 7

15 "No Jazz players wanted at 'Peg," Vancouver *World*, 16 Oct 1920, 9

16 S. Morgan Powell, "Variety keynote of an interesting bill at Princess," Montreal *Star*, 24 Jun 1919, 2

17 Rhynd Jamieson, "Music: in the house, the studio and the concert hall," Vancouver *Sun*, 28 Sep 1919, 38

18 Rhynd Jamieson, "Music: in the house, the studio and the concert hall," Vancouver *Sun*, 2 Nov 1919, 28

19 M.F. Sheridan, "Music: in the house, the studio and the concert — Correspondence," Vancouver *Sun*, 25 Apr 1920, 31

20 Vancouver *World*, 5 Jun 1920, 18

21 "Over the footlights," Vancouver *World*, 12 Jun 1920, 21

CHAPTER FIVE

1 "Some letters," Chicago *Defender*, 6 Sep 1919, 9. Edw. T. Rogers was an employee of the Canadian Pacific Railway; his wife was a cashier at the Patricia Cafe.

2 Morton's itinerancy during this period is documented in Lawrence Gushee, "A preliminary chronology of the early career of Ferd 'Jelly Roll' Morton," *American Music*, vol 3, Winter 1985, 389-412.

3 See Lawrence Gushee, "New Orleans-area musicians on the West Coast, 1908-1925," *Black Music Research Journal*, vol 9, Spring 1989, 1-18.

4 All Morton quotes in this chapter have been drawn from Lomax, *Mister Jelly Roll*, 170-171.

5 Holden's Seattle career is discussed in Paul de Barros, *Jackson Street After Hours* (Seattle 1993). According to the dues ledgers of AFM/Vancouver local 145, Holden maintained his affiliation until 1927.

6 As per Patio's entry in the AFM/Vancouver local 145 dues ledger. Elsewhere spelled Pattio or Padeo (Padéo), Patio was thought by the songwriter and publisher Reb Spikes (as quoted in Stoddard, *Jazz on the Barbary Coast*, 57) to have died in Vancouver. Mamie Johnson, wife of the Creole Band's Bill Johnson, suggests that Padio went insane (Gushee, *Black Music Research Journal*, 1988, 91). This is not inconsistent with Morton's aside to Lomax in 1938, "Poor Padio, he's dead now..."

7 "Winter Garden is dancers' delight," Vancouver *Sun*, 12 Oct 1919, 2

8 Bricktop, with James Haskins, *Bricktop* (New York 1984), 72. Bricktop dates her arrival in Vancouver as 1920 and the broken leg to New Year's Eve of that year. However, according to a Smith letter paraphrased by the *Defender*, ("Brick-Top Smith," 14 Feb 1920, 8), the accident occurred on Christmas Eve, 1919.

9 Ragtime Billy Tucker, "Coast Dope," Chicago *Defender*, 31 Jul 1920, 4

10 Bricktop, *Bricktop*, 71

11 In *Mister Jelly Roll*, Morton implies that the Patricia and Regent were consecutive engagements. However, Edw. Rodgers' letter to the *Defender* clearly puts the former in the late summer of 1919 while the dues ledgers of AFM/Vancouver local 145 establish the latter toward the end of 1920. Morton, Eubanks and

Hutchinson were compelled to pay their dues for the first quarter of 1921 to Local 145, and did so December 16 or 17, 1920. Morton withdrew from the local January 7, 1921, Eubanks a week later and Hutchinson in June. This, contrary to Morton's remark to Lomax, "Things went well [at the Regent] until summer, when business slacked and I began gambling again." Morton's whereabouts during the summer of 1921 are well documented. See Gushee, *American Music*, 405-406.

12 Stewart Hall withdrew from local 145 on the same day as Morton, suggesting a circumstantial connection.

13 Lomax, *Mister Jelly Roll*, 178

14 L. Louis Johnson, "A letter," Chicago *Defender*, 8 Jan 1921, 4

15 "All wedded," Chicago *Defender*, 29 Jan 1921, 4

16 Stoddard, *Jazz on the Barbary Coast*, 77, 84

17 "Monte Carlo Cabaret not properly run," Vancouver *Daily World*, 5 Feb 1920, 11

18 Advertisement, Vancouver *Sun*, 31 Dec 1920, 14

19 "Bingie Madison: biography of a career" [oral history given to Bertrand Demeusy], *Jazz Monthly*, September 1964, 7-10. The St. Antoine Club does not appear in the Montreal city directories during this period. The Standard, Utopia and Nemderoloc clubs and the Strathcona Cafe were all in operation on St. Antoine Street in Montreal in the early 1920s. Madison (to Demeusy) dated his Hull, Que., years as 1921-2; references in *Billboard*, however, place him there in 1923, which calls into question the year of his arrival in Montreal. George. B. McEntee is mis-identified in *Jazz Monthly* as Jim McIntyre.

20 "South Hull closes Chelsea Road halls," Ottawa *Citizen*, 8 May 1923, 4

21 Among the inconsistencies, a James Slap Rags White has been listed as a C-melody saxophonist on recordings by the (white) Six Brown Brothers in Rust, *Jazz Records*, 1429-1430, and Rust, *American Dance Band Discography*, 1708. Significantly, White's "presence" corresponds with recording sessions at which the sextet recorded pieces that are known to have been his compositions — *Pussyfoot March* in 1916 and *Jazz Band Blues* in 1920. A James S. White in Boston operated "America's Largest Colored Music Publishing House" (so described in *Woods Directory*, New Orleans, LA, 1913, 72) from ca 1913 to 1927. According to

Boston city directories, however, this White died in 1943.

22 "A note or two," Chicago *Defender*, 3 Mar 1917, 4

23 Perry Bradford, *Born with the Blues* (New York 1965), 95

24 Jelly Roll Morton, "I was first to play jazz," reprinted in *The Jazz Report*, 32, May 1945, 11

25 Dave Peyton, "The Musical Bunch," Chicago *Defender*, 30 Apr 1927, 6

26 Unpublished interview with William Russell in 1959, held at the William Ransom Hogan Jazz Archive, Tulane University, New Orleans

27 Copy held in the Alex Robertson Collection, Concordia University Archives, Montreal

CHAPTER SIX

1 "A note or two," Chicago *Defender*, 9 Jun 1917, 9

2 The Bell Telephone Co. directory published in March 1920, and updated in July, lists Thomas as a music arranger at 20 St. James St. West.

3 Gilmore, *Swinging in Paradise*, 32, incorrectly sites Thomas at the Princess Theatre in Quebec City before his move to Montreal. See *Le Soleil*, Quebec City, 28 Aug 1920, 18; 20 Aug 1921, 10

4 Advertisement, Montreal *Star*, 26 Jul 1919, 2

5 Advertisement, Montreal *Star*, 1 Dec 1920, 26

6 Advertisement, Montreal *Star*, 5 Nov 1921, 6

7 Advertisement, Montreal *Star*, 24 Nov 1921, 6

8 Ted Vincent, *Keep Cool: The Black Activists Who Built the Jazz Age* (London 1995), 124

9 Gilmore, *Swinging in Paradise*, 29

10 Advertisement, Montreal *Star*, 24 Aug 1922, 6

11 Advertisement, Montreal *Star*, 1 Nov 1922, 6

12 Advertisement, Montreal *Star*, 14 Mar 1921, 13

13 "Roses of 'Roseland' drew over 1000," Montreal *Gazette*, 18 Mar 1921, 13

14 Bradford, *Born with the Blues*, 30

15 According to Bell Telephone Co. listings, Wright moved into the St. Antoine neighbourhood late in 1924, living at two successive St. Antoine Street addresses until early 1926. His suspension from Montreal local 406 of the AFM was noted in The *International Musician*, November 1924, 4, and his expulsion in same, December 1925, 5

16 Advertisement, Montreal *Star*, 6 Oct 1923, 6

17 "A note or two," Chicago *Defender*, 7 Aug 1920, 5

18 "Letters," Chicago *Defender*, 14 Jan 1922, 7

19 J.A. Jackson, "Second season in Quebec," *The Billboard*, 11 Feb 1922, 103

20 "A note or two," Chicago *Defender*, 2 Dec 1922, 7

21 Advertisement, *La Presse*, 2 Sep 1922, 12

22 "Le Radio de La Presse," *La Presse*, 14 Jun 1923, 8

23 The Compo recording sessions took place on different weekdays, suggesting that the band was employed in or very near Montreal during the summer of 1924, possibly at King Edward Park, which advertised the Belmont Novelty Orchestra and the New Famous Novelty Orchestra, in turn, as attractions during June and July.

24 According to a survey of the Compo ledgers undertaken by Toronto discographer Jack Litchfield in 1995, the Thomas orchestra made a total of 29 versions of 13 different tunes between June 6, 1924 and January 20, 1925.

25 Harris has been placed in Chicago with Jasper Taylor and others on Jelly Roll "Marton's" first band recordings in June 1923 by various discographers and CD compilers. *Arville* Harris has also been cited in this same connection (eg., Gunther Schuller, *Early Jazz*, New York 1968, 153) but, co-incidentally, the Morton band also includes yet another member of W.C. Handy's 1917 recording orchestra, the clarinetist Wilson Townes, which seems circumstantially to support *Charles* Harris' presence.

26 The personnel of the CNO on record can only be a matter for conjecture. Rust, *Jazz Records*, 1550, suggests that Thomas was accompanied by Charles Harris (cornet, alto saxophone, trombone), E[mmanuel] Cassamore (cornet, trombone) and C[harles] Gordon (drums), a variation on the personnel for the band's CKAC broadcast a year earlier. No drums are present, however, nor is the clarinetist identified. (Gilmore, *Who's Who of Jazz in Montreal*, 304, proffers one Theodore West, who recorded four sides of similarly distressing clarinet blues for Ajax in February 1925, possibly with Thomas at the piano.) The banjo player who appears on *Page Your Puppies* may have been Wiley J. Teasley, Thomas'

neighbour at 198 de Montigny in 1924 (*Lovell's Montreal [1925] Directory*).

CHAPTER SEVEN

1 "Lewis Bros. to provide public [with] long felt want," Edmonton *Journal*, 20 Feb 1920, 6

2 Dave Peyton, "The Musical Bunch: Shirley Oliver In," Chicago *Defender*, 20 Aug 1927, 6

3 Elsewhere, George B. McEntee worked with three white musicians at the Broadway Inn, Hull, briefly in 1923, Hiram Berry sang with several white bands in Hamilton, Ont., from 1923 to 1926, and pianist Bill Moore appears to have employed white musicians from Regina when he expanded his Plantation Orchestra for concerts at nearby Hungry Hollow Park in the summer of 1926. Moore and Bennie Starks both led white bands in Winnipeg during the 1930s (see Chapter 11). In the United States, inter-racial bands were generally confined during the 1920s to the relative privacy of the recording studio and even there were extremely rare. Jelly Roll Morton recorded with the New Orleans Rhythm Kings in 1923, for example, as did Eddie Lang, Joe Sullivan and Eddie Condon variously with Louis Armstrong in 1929.

4 Robin W. Winks, *The Blacks in Canada: a history* (Montreal 1971), 303-307; Stewart Grow, "The Blacks of Amber Valley," *Canadian Ethnic Studies*, VI (1974), 17-38

5 "Our Negro citizens," Edmonton *Journal*, 15 Apr 1922, 7

6 Indianapolis *Freeman*, 22 Apr 1916; 7 Jul 1917. Another black clarinetist of similar background, Robert Leach, owned a farm near Grassy Lake, Alta., during the 1910s and at one point was the orchestra director for the Eureka Theatre in Lethbridge (*Freeman*, 15 Jan 1910).

7 "Doo-Dads will play at 8 p.m.," Edmonton *Journal*, 11 Oct 1922, 1

8 "Gumps Jazz Hounds will play tonight," Edmonton *Journal*, 25 Oct 1922, 1

9 "Syncopation was feature of radio program," Edmonton *Journal*, 26 Oct 1922, 13

10 Tipp's musicians from 1923 to 1929 variously included the saxophonists Tom Goodridge, Frank Parks and Jimmy Horn, the cornetists Len Dear and George Dewhurst, the trombonists Jimmy Southwood and Raoul Esmonde, the banjo players Cecil Lord and Russ Carter, the Sousaphonist A.M. (Milt) Tipp

(an uncle), and the drummers Bernie Stevens, Milt Weber and Murray (Red) Pawling.

11 Examples of the Tipp Orchestra's repertoire have been drawn from "Syncopators headline Igloo Hut," Edmonton *Journal*, 18 Apr 1924, 13, and "Igloo Hut signs off for summer months; fine farewell bill," Edmonton *Journal*, 9 May 1924, 17.

12 Advertisements, Edmonton *Journal*, 1 Jun 1927, 13; 8 Jun 1927, 9

13 H.M.B., "In the footlights glow," Edmonton *Journal*, 31 Jul 1928, 5

14 Advertisement, Calgary *Herald*, 2 Nov 1927, 19. Frank Harvey's Red Tux Boys were Len Dear (cornet), Johnny Van Deelan (trombone), Bill Fraser (piano) and Johnny Corcoran (drums). The band also worked in 1927 at the Sunnydale Pavilion and Haddon Hall in Edmonton and was heard on CKLC, Red Deer.

15 H.M.B., "In the footlights glow," Edmonton *Journal*, 10 Jan 1928, 5

16 Howard Palmer, *Patterns of Prejudice: a history of nativism in Alberta* (Toronto 1982), 35-37, 87-88, 101-102

17 Dutch Lyons, otherwise a car salesman, led bands at Alberta Beach (summer 1923), Seba Beach and the Sylvan Pavilion in St. Albert's (summer 1924) and the Palais de danse (winter 1924-5). Cecil Lord worked with Graydon Tipp (winter 1923-4), led bands at Haddon and Carlton halls at mid-decade and took extended engagements at the Capitol and Rialto theatres later in the 1920s. Both Lyons and Lord played at one time or another during the decade for a third important Edmonton orchestra leader, John Bowman, at the Macdonald Hotel.

CHAPTER EIGHT

1 Advertisement, Winnipeg *Tribune*, 8 Apr 1922, 4

2 For the next 13 years Rignold played in the dance bands of Jack Hylton, Jay Wilbur and others. In 1935 he recorded two titles with a quartet for Parlophone and in 1939 he made some 78s with his own dance orchestra for Columbia. (See Brian Rust and Sandy Forbes, *British Dance Bands on Record 1911 to 1945*, Harrow, Middlesex, England 1987.) In later years he conducted symphony and ballet orchestras in the Middle East and England.

3 "Rehearsing syncopation for Thursday night at Allen," Manitoba *Free Press*, 16 Sep 1922, 23

4 Advertisement, Toronto *Star*, 21 Mar 1922, 9

5 Advertisement, Toronto *Star*, 22 Mar 1922, 21

6 Photo caption, London *Free Press*, 17 Mar 1923, 26

7 Among the other bands to record for HMV's 216000 series, the Champion Jazz Band and Jazzbo Band were in fact no "jazzier" than the Dumbells' Overseas Orchestra. Both bands, according to Litchfield, *Canadian Jazz Discography*, 206, 366, were led by the American saxophonist Simone Martucci during his Montreal sojourns.

8 A few black American artists in the Ajax series were recorded in Montreal, including the vaudeville team of Chris Smith and Henry Troy. Recordings in the Apex, Starr and Ajax series are listed in Moogk, *Roll Back the Years*, 350-355.

9 I.A. (Irving) Matthews of Toronto, for example, advertised himself in *The Dawn of Tomorrow*, 17 Nov 1923, 7, as a music teacher, orchestra leader, piano tuner and "agent and demonstrator for Mammy's Washday Smile [a laundry detergent] and Black Swan Records." Matthews led the Bostonian Orchestra in Toronto in 1925 and 1926 and was later active in Detroit.

10 John Chilton, *The Song of the Hawk* (London 1990), 17

11 S. Morgan Powell, "Loew's present 'Broadway Rose' as featured on the bill," Montreal *Star*, 17 Oct 1922, 6

12 "Daddy of jazz and his band play tonight," Regina *Leader*, 6 Sep 1922, 10

13 Winnipeg, Regina, Saskatoon, Edmonton, Calgary and Vancouver were regular stops for Pantages shows in the mid-1920s; Regina and Saskatoon shared "split-week" bookings. Robinson's Syncopators were also heard in Victoria. George Morrison did not appear in Winnipeg, nor Carroll Dickerson in Calgary. Occasionally the musicians also performed for a local dance — eg, Morrison at the Art Academy in Saskatoon and Dickerson at Sullivan's in Edmonton.

14 "The Grand," Chicago *Defender*, 30 Aug 1924, 6

15 Stanley Dance, *The World of Earl Hines* (New York 1977), 42

16 Advertisement, St. John's *Evening Telegram*, 1 Feb 1924, 4

17 "Messrs. Foster, Hawkes and Zabriskie score an unprecedented success," St. John's *Evening Telegram*, 2 Feb 1924, 9

18 "Trio hits," Chicago *Defender*, 5 Apr 1924, 7

19 "Letters," Chicago *Defender*, 24 Jan 1925, 8

20 Ethel Waters and Charles Samuels, *His Eye Is on the Sparrow* (Garden City, NY 1951), 177.

21 "'Singing Bellboy' loved life," Hamilton *Spectator*, 4 Aug 1983, A10

CHAPTER NINE

1 Duke Ellington, "The most essential instrument," *Jazz Journal*, 18 (December 1965), 14-15

2 Rainer Lotz, "Johnny Dixon — Trumpet," *Storyville*, 99 (February-March 1982), 102

3 Sean Edwin, "The Sound Track," Montreal *Herald*, 23 Apr 1945, 7

4 "CJGC Free Press radio program," London *Free Press*, 14 Nov 1922, 5

5 An advertisement in the Toronto *Star*, 2 Dec 1922, 23, lists Rich's Versatile Canadians as Harold Swain and Leonard Sievert (saxophones), Stanley Allen and Morris London (cornets), Harry Spicer (banjo), Bill Roberts (trombone) and Norman Eldridge (drums). A program for *Ace High* dated 3 Feb 1925, cited in Edward Moogk, *Roll Back the Years* (Ottawa 1975), 257, identifies the band as Rich, London, Roberts, Cy Stark (violin, saxophone), Freddie Treneer (piano, saxophone), Nat Cassells (saxophone, clarinet), Eddie Duche[s]ne (banjo), Al Johnson (saxophone, sousaphone) and Eugene Fritzley (drums).

6 "The Star's radio program today and tomorrow," Toronto *Star*, 3 Apr 1924, 31

7 Peter Goddard, "Jazzman Cliff McKay sparks enthusiasm with his warm style," Toronto *Star*, 10 Jan 1973, 37

8 James A. Cowan, "Swain and saxophone have stormed London," Edmonton *Journal*, 8 May 1926, Magazine section, 3

9 Les Allen, "Our 'Break' into London," *Radio Review*, 7 Dec 1935

10 "Toronto exports an orchestra to play dances in Old London," Toronto *Star*, 26 Feb 1924, 1

11 Litchfield, *Canadian Jazz Discography*, 516-520, lists 54 New Princes' titles, of which Litchfield had auditioned 36 and designated four as "containing jazz."

12 "Syncopation and dance band news," The *Melody Maker*, undated clipping [early 1926]. Reproduced in Jim Godbolt, *The World of Jazz in Printed Ephemera and Collectibles* (London 1990), 61

13 Litchfield, *Canadian Jazz Discography*, 199-201, lists 56 Caplan titles, of which Litchfield had heard seven and identified two as "containing jazz."

14 A translation of Lange's description in *Jazz in Deutschland: Die Deutsche Jazz-Cronik, 1990-1960* (Berlin 1966) was published in Eugene Miller, "Canada Discophile," *IAJRC* [International Association of Jazz Record Collectors] *Journal*, vol 6, no 3, Summer 1973, 13

15 Advertisement, Brockville *Recorder & Times*, 14 Sep 1929, 8

16 Anthony (Tony) Thorpe worked in the mid-1920s with Burton Till and Gilbert Watson; Frenchie Sartell played for Luigi Romanelli in Toronto and Jack Pudney in London, Ont., during the very early 1930s. For their respective discographies in Britain — and those of other Canadians in Britain — see Brian Rust and Sandy Forbes, *British Dance Bands on Record 1911 to 1945* (Harrow, Middlesex, England 1987).

17 Harry Karr played in Winnipeg with Ab Templin in 1923 and in Vancouver with the Columbians, Harry Pryce's Hotel Georgia Orchestra and, from 1929 to 1930, his own Rhythm Ramblers. According to one of his Vancouver pupils, Mart Kenney, Karr had studied with the renowned American saxophone virtuoso Rudy Wiedoft. "Every time Rudy Wiedoft would come through [Vancouver] on vaudeville, Harry would go every day and have a lesson from him, [then] follow him to Seattle." (Interview, 9 Nov 1992.) Karr moved to London in 1933, recording there with the New Mayfair Dance Orchestra, Jack Harris, Brian Lawrence and others. In 1937 he appeared in a concert headlined by Benny Carter at London's Hippodrome; for his solo contributions to the program, Karr was described by Stan Patch in *Down Beat* (February 1937, 5) as "a saxophonist of the Weidoft school with beautiful tone and technique, but rather out of place at a swing concert..."

18 Brian Rust, *The Dance Bands* (New Rochelle, NY 1974), 81

19 "CFCA's great radio night," Toronto *Star*, 3 Sep 1925, 17

20 Litchfield, *Canadian Jazz Discography*, 747, cites the probable personnel for this recording session as Watson, Little, Tony Thorpe or Bob Cawston (trombone), Johnny Millard (clarinet, alto saxophone) and Tommy Gibson (alto saxophone), Charlie Hayward (banjo), Sam Ryle (tuba) and Doc Hollingshead (drums).

21 "Stewart and Goldner, Gilbert Watson, CFCA," Toronto *Star*, 27 May 1926, 16

22 Watson's CFCA broadcasts in 1928 from Old Spain reveal his return to a repertoire exclusively of popular material. Watson continued to lead orchestras in Toronto nightspots, most notably in the 1930s at the Old Mill, and was also heard in popular and light-classical settings on radio, until his retirement from music in 1942.

23 Litchfield, *Canadian Jazz Discography*, 747, cites the personnel for this session as Watson, Little, Hayward (banjo, guitar and vocal), Ryle, Hollingshead, Ed Culley (clarinet, alto saxophone) and Vern Shilling (trombone).

24 "Thompson's Imperial Orchestra broadcasts tonight on CKCK," Regina *Leader*, 22 Aug 1922, 8

25 Advertisement, *B.C. Musician*, 8 Mar 1926

26 Joe Darensbourg, *Jazz Odyssey: The Autobiography of Joe Darensbourg* (Baton Rouge 1988), 74

27 Mart Kenney, *Mart Kenney and His Western Gentlemen* (Saskatoon 1981), 12

28 "Blind, but has made happiness for many," Saskatoon *Phoenix*, 11 Jan 1924, 3

29 "Dancing and air," Saskatoon *Daily Star*, 12 Jul 1919, 17

30 "Melody Men to broadcast from Leader Tuesday," Regina *Leader*, 2 Jan 1923, 2

31 "Announcements," Regina *Leader*, 6 Sep 1923, 8

32 Advertisement, Regina *Leader*, 30 Jun 1925, 6

33 "Announcements," Regina *Leader*, 3 Apr 1926, 4; 1 May 1926, 20

34 "Noisy dance music is going out," Vancouver *Sun*, 29 Jun 1927, 10

CHAPTER TEN

1 Eddie Condon and Hank O'Neal, *Eddie Condon's Scrapbook of Jazz* (New York 1973)

2 Eddie Condon, *We Called It Music: A Generation of Jazz* (New York 1947), 94-5

3 Advertisement, Winnipeg *Tribune*, 22 Dec 1923, 9

4 Condon, *We Called It Music*, 97

5 Advertisement, Regina *Leader*, 23 Jan 1924, 10

6 "Steward's Stewings," Chicago *Defender*, 7 Nov 1925, 8

7 Advertisement, Saskatoon *Phoenix*, 28 Nov 1925, 14

8 Steward identified his musicians as Terry Crawford (saxophone, clarinet, violin), Nathaniel A. Hall (saxophone and trombone), Booker C. Christian (trombone, banjo), Charlie Segar[s] (piano, cornet), Lawrence (Lonnie) Brown (banjo), James (Chick) August (Sousaphone) and Willie A. (Shorty) Stevenson (drums). An entertainer, Slim Marshall, joined the band toward the end of the Zenith engagement. Segar is likely the pianist who made blues recordings in the mid-1930s for Decca and in 1940 for Vocalion. Subsequent to this Canadian trip, Steward led bands in the southern United States until his death in 1935.

9 Dickie Wells and Stanley Dance, *The Night People: The Jazz Life of Dickie Wells* (Washington 1991), 13

10 Bill Coleman, *Trumpet Story* (London 1990), 43

11 "Fine orchestra," Hamilton *Spectator*, 23 Jun 1927, 7

12 A report from AFM/Columbus, Ohio, local 103, in *The International Musician* (September 1927, 8) lists the following musicians as travelling members of Chicago [black] local 208: Fred Jelly, E. Hubbert, Ed Mallory, Chas Tarrier, A. Starke, Jas. McEndree, J. Robinson, M. Hardy, Warren Seals, Henry Clarke, Henry Crowder — ie, Jelly Roll Morton, Elisha Herbert (trumpet), Eddie Mallory (trumpet), Chas. Turner (brass bass), Artie Starks (alto saxophone, clarinet), Jimmy McHendricks (drums), Ikey Robinson (banjo), Marion Hardy (alto saxophone, clarinet), Warner Seals (tenor saxophone), Henry Clarke (trombone) and Henry Crowder (piano).

13 Unpublished interview with Laurie Wright, Chicago, 1974

14 According to Gilmore, *Swinging in Paradise*, 68, the Royal Ambassadors "never made it to Montreal as a band." However, reports in *The International Musician* (March 1929, 14; July 1929, 7) document seven members of the Ambassadors transferring into, and then out of AFM/Montreal local 406.

15 Gilmore, *Swinging in Paradise*, 67

16 As identified in *The International Musician* (March 1929, 14; July 1929, 7; November 1929, 11; September 1930, 6; February 1931, 10) and the Chicago *Defender* ("Orchestral doings," 31 Jan 1931, 5). In addition to Bill and Andy Shorter, Ed (or Fred) Jackson and H. (possibly Herb) Johnson played saxophones with the Ambassadors at one time or another, and Aaron Johnson was latterly the band's

banjo player. Myron Sutton, in Gilmore, *Swinging in Paradise*, adds trumpeter Ted Brock to the Ambassadors' composite personnel.

17 The two titles, master numbers 3588 and 3589, were discovered in the Compo company's recording ledgers by discographer Jack Litchfield in 1995.

18 Gregory Clark, "What is to become of Sir Henry Pellatt's Castle? The empty substance of a gorgeous dream," Toronto *Star Weekly*, 8 Dec 1923, magazine section, 1

19 Gene Gifford's arrangements and, by extension, the Casa Loma Orchestra's place in the evolution of swing, are discussed in Gunther Schuller, *The Swing Era: The Development of Jazz, 1930-1945* (New York 1989), 637-44.

20 Stanley Dance, *The World of Swing* (New York 1979), 148

21 Advertisement, Toronto *Star*, 10 Sep 1927, 8

22 Dance, *The World of Swing*, 178

23 The Trent band's personnel on its transfer into AFM/Buffalo [black] local 533 for the winter of 1929-30 was recorded in *The International Musician* (November 1929, 11) as Trent (piano), Leroy Smith (violin), Chester Clarke (trumpet), Lee Hilliard (trumpet, alto saxophone), Leo Mosely (trombone), James Jeter (alto saxophone), Hayes Pillars (tenor and baritone saxophone), Eugene Crook (banjo), Robert Jackson (bass) and A.G. Godley (drums) — two men shy of the advertised 12 Black Aces. One may have been Peanuts Holland, who seems to have moved freely in and out of the band during this period.

24 Dance, *The World of Swing*, 178

25 Advertisement, Hamilton *Spectator*, 2 Jul 1929, 4

26 "Bill Reinhardt: Jazz Ltd. — And More," *Storyville*, 154, 1 Jun 1993, 137

27 "Broadcasting," Chicago *Defender*, 6 Jul 1929, 6

CHAPTER ELEVEN

1 *Census of Canada*, 1931, vol 13, 512

2 *Census of Canada*, 1931, vol 3, 160

3 Kenny Kersey and Al Lucas eventually pursued their careers in New York. Kersey played piano for Henry (Red) Allen and Andy Kirk in the early 1940s and achieved particular renown through his travels and recordings with Jazz at the Philharmonic during the late 1940s. Lucas played bass for Coleman Hawkins, Eddie Heywood and Mary Lou Williams in the 1940s

and with Illinois Jacquet from 1947 to 1953. (Chilton, *Who's Who of Jazz*, 185, 204)

4 Chilton, *Who's Who of Jazz*, 254. Parham's recordings are listed in Rust, *Jazz Records*, 1208-1210.

5 Advertisement, Hamilton *Spectator*, 10 Dec 1931, 10

6 Held in the Mynie Sutton Fonds, Concordia University Archives

7 Gilmore, *Swinging in Paradise*, 64-89, and Gilmore, *Who's Who of Jazz in Montreal* are the sources for some of the information concerning Mynie Sutton and the Canadian Ambassadors in this chapter.

8 All Sutton quotes in this chapter have been taken from Gilmore, *Swinging in Paradise*, 64-89.

9 *The International Musician*, February 1932, 7. Sutton, Clyde Duncan, Hooper, Rogers, Summers and Waldon are listed by Ottawa local 180 as "transferring members."

10 *The International Musician*, February 1933, 7

11 Gilmore, *Who's Who of Jazz in Montreal*, 52, lists 23 musicians.

12 Lou Hooper, *That Happy Road*, unpublished mss., 53

13 *Census of Canada*, 1931, vol 3, 158

14 Hooper, *That Happy Road*, 54

15 Gilmore, *Swinging in Paradise*, 88. Sutton may have been thinking of the (unreleased) recordings he made with Lester Vactor's Royal Ambassadors for Compo in 1928.

16 Andy Kirk with Amy Lee, *Twenty Years on Wheels* (Ann Arbor, Mich 1989), 57

17 *The International Musician*, February 1933, 7

18 In Winnipeg, trumpeter Frankie Nelson and saxophonist Ollie Wagner joined local 190 in the late 1930s; both men were working for white bandleaders at the time, Nelson for Joey Jampol and Wagner for Eddie Franks.

19 Although not reported in *The International Musician*, saxophonist Herb Johnson has claimed to have been the first black musician accepted by AFM local 406, circa 1940. (Gilmore, *Swinging in Paradise*, 57)

20 Norman Richmond. "The uphill struggle of our black musicians," Toronto *Star*, 14 Apr 1979, H1

21 "Confrontation at the Palais Royale," Toronto *Star*, 9 Apr 1992, E8

22 Listed in Gilmore, *Swinging in Paradise*, 283. The presence on this list of trumpeter Bennie

Starks, who left Winnipeg for Montreal in November 1934, narrows the date range of the revival to late 1934 or early 1935.

23 Listed in Gilmore, *Swinging in Paradise*, 284

24 Gains made by Canadian blacks during the Second World War are discussed in Robin W. Wink's *The Blacks in Canada: a history* (Montreal 1971), 420-427.

25 Billie Holiday with Willie Duffy, *Lady Sings the Blues* (New York 1956), 6. Holiday suggests that her Montreal engagement followed an appearance at the Apollo Theatre in New York. According to biographer Stuart Nicholson (*Billie Holiday* London 1995, 53), however, Holiday made her Apollo debut in November 1934, several months after the Canadian Ambassadors had left Connie's Inn. Nicholson, 71, places Holiday at an unnamed Montreal venue in October 1935. Confusing the issue further, New York trumpeter Louis Metcalf claimed to have had Holiday in a show in Montreal prior to 1934 (*Record Research*, October 1962, 8); Metcalf is known to have been the bandleader at the Terminal Club at some point in the 1930s.

26 Hooper, *That Happy Road*, 55

27 "Canadian Colored Band... [photograph]," *Down Beat*, November 1937, 32

28 Letter, dated 24 Apr 1934, held in the Mynie Sutton Fonds, Concordia University Archives

29 Don McKim, "Canada cats jump; await royal visit," *Down Beat*, May 1939, 27

30 "Canada," *Metronome*, November 1937, 43

31 "Sutton band poses for Beat," *Down Beat*, 14 Jan 1946, 9

32 Noted in a letter dated 1 Feb 1986 from Mark Grimstead to Gene Lees, held in the Gene Lees Fonds, National Library of Canada

CHAPTER TWELVE

1 George Beattie, "This is news — band makes good," *Down Beat*, July 1939, 33

2 Wagner may have travelled even further east in 1938. An Ollie "Wagar" and his 10-piece orchestra offered "Hot swing, novelty and sweet music in rhythmic harmony" during a tour of eastern Ontario that summer. Stops included the Collins Bay and Beaver Lake pavilions on the Labour Day weekend. (Kingston *Whig-Standard*, 31 Aug 1938, 11; 3 Sep 1938, 11).

3 Beattie, George, "Kenora spot is maker of bands," *Down Beat*, August 1939, 28

4 Advertisement, Calgary *Herald*, 29 Jun 1935, 15

5 "Opening Doors: Vancouver's East End," *Sound Heritage*, vol 8, no 1 & 2, 1979, 141

6 Listed in the Chicago *Defender*, 9 Jun 1934, 20

7 Gilmore, *Swinging in Paradise*, 283

8 Brown, Denny. "On the wire," Winnipeg *Tribune*, 28 Mar 1935, 19. The rumour was probably incorrect. Doc Cheatham, lead trumpeter with Cab Calloway in this period, did not remember playing with Starks when interviewed in 1997.

9 "Bill Moore leads all-white band in Winnipeg, Canada," Chicago *Defender*, 31 Jul 1937, 10

10 Novikoff, Philip A., "Canadian upper-crust turn-up nose as Negro leads white band," *Down Beat*, July 1937, 2.

11 Advertisement, Winnipeg *Tribune*, 9 May 1940, 18

12 "Heavy fine for sale of liquor," Regina *Leader-Post*, 16 Mar 1942, 3; "One license cancelled by council," *Leader-Post*, 8 Apr 1942, 3

13 "Toronto's breeze around," *Hush Free Press*, 23 Mar 1946, 7

14 "Toronto notes," *The Dawn of Tomorrow*, 11 Sep 1931, 5

15 As shown in an undated photograph, the Knights were Charlie Winn and Roy Worrell (trumpets), Cliff Howard (trombone), Tony Jimitello, Nevis Rigby and Jimmy Turner (saxophones), Reggie McLean (piano), Chauncey Dawson (guitar), Alvin Crawford (Sousaphone) and Willie Wright (drums). Winn, Worrell, Howard, Rigby, McLean and Wright had also played with the Aces.

16 Willie Wright, interviewed by Judith McIntosh and Archie Alleyne, 24 Jul 1989

17 The alto saxophonist Tony Jimitello played with both Sam Morgan and Cy McLean; the guitarist Dick O'Toole and the trumpeter Nick Sotnick worked with McLean.

18 Unprovenanced newspaper column, "The Swing Reporter," dated 1944, Helen McNamara Fonds, National Library of Canada. "...Roy had the band before he went on his vacation and when he came back, I had it." Other musicians suggest that Reggie McLean played an organizational role in his brother's first band.

19 Jack Batten, "The jazz pianist Toronto ignored," Toronto *Star*, 28 Jun 1969, 43

20 Dillon O'Leary, "Hot platter chatter," Toronto *Globe and Mail*, 26 Jan 1946, 11

21 Helen McNamara, "McNamara's Bandwagon," Toronto *Telegram*, 12 Aug 1950, 7

22 Jim Foster, "Jazz pianist Cy McLean, 70 led Toronto's first black band," Toronto *Star*, 1 Nov 1986, A10

23 Advertisement, Vancouver *Sun*, 9 Mar 1946, 6

CHAPTER THIRTEEN

1 Dillon O'Leary, "Swing king," *Maclean's Magazine*, 1 Jul 1945, 24

2 "Are you listening?" Toronto *Star*, 19 Nov 1934, 16

3 Reported in "Are you listening?" Toronto *Star*, 30 Jul 1934, 29

4 Battle's musicians in the spring of 1935 were Jimmy Davidson and Jimmy Reynolds (trumpets), Bruce Campbell and Jack Madden (trombone), Charlie Green, Cliff McKay, Howard "Cokie" Campbell and Ted Davidson (saxophones), Johnny Burris (piano), Arnold (Red) McGarvey (guitar), Sam "Bozo" Weiner (bass), Reef McGarvey (drums). The Davidsons and McKay sang.

5 Bill Newell, "Tuning in... Radio Highlights," Vancouver *Sun*, 27 Jan 1938, 15

6 Don McKim, "Canadian bands are still in diapers," *Down Beat*, 15 Nov 1939, 15

7 Isabell Goundry, "Band has 28 changes, still going strong," *Down Beat*, 15 Apr 1945, 9

8 O'Leary, *Maclean's*, 16

9 Trent Frayne, "Liberty profile: Bert Niosi," *Liberty*, 26 May 1945, 14-15

10 Len R. Smith, "Niosi boomed as society ork," *Down Beat*, February 1939, 25

11 Unpublished interview with Helen McNamara, 30 May 1974 (Helen McNamara Fonds, Music Division, National Library of Canada)

12 O'Leary, *Maclean's*, 24

13 Dick MacDougal, "Former Lombardo cat opens in Toronto," *Down Beat*, December 1937, 42

14 Among Canadian leaders nominally boasting swing bands in 1936 and 1937: Larry Bates, Irving Laing, Johnny Luciano, Frank Murphy and Paul Richard in Montreal, Archie Cunningham, Jack Evans and Bert Niosi in Toronto, Jerry Fuller in Calgary, Bix Madden, Barney Potts, Doug Raymond, Sandy De Santis, Cam Smith, and Leroy Williams in Vancouver.

15 Patrick Scott, "Canada's Mr. Dixieland," *Globe Magazine*, 31 Oct 1964, 9

16 "Final standings of bands in all divisions," *The Metronome*, June 1937, 14

17 James Buller, "Ellis McLintock — The Greatest, that's all," *Ad Lib*, Oct 1946, 8

18 Several west coast orchestras appeared for a week at a time in Vancouver at the Beacon Theatre — Curtis Mosby's Dixieland Blue Blowers (in *Change Your Luck*) and Buck Clayton's 15 Gentlemen from Harlem in 1933, Mosby again (in *Harlem Rhapsody*) in 1935 and Les Hite in 1938.

19 Advertisement, Vancouver *Sun*, 27 May 1937, 13

20 Advertisement, Vancouver *Sun*, 19 Jan 1938, 9

21 Don McKim, "Action on the up beat in Vancouver," *Down Beat*, 1 Nov 1940, 21

22 Gordon Richardson, "O'Toole Brothers swing on the strings," Down Beat, Jun 1937, 24

23 D. Russell Connor, *The Record of a Legend... Benny Goodman* (New York 1984), 100

24 Advertisement, Montreal *Star*, 30 Jun 1938, 7

25 Advertisement, Montreal *Star*, 21 Sep 1938, 8

26 Irv Mauer, "Local jerks Hartley from Montreal spot," *Down Beat*, Mar 1939, 34.

27 Duke Delory, "Laing challenges Niosi to duel!" *Down Beat*, 1 March 1940, 22. Although the Laing and Niosi bands never met, Laing did engage in a succession of battles of the bands at the Auditorium over the winter of 1939-40 with the Montreal orchestras of Jack Bain, Len Howard, Alex Lajoie, Johnny Luciano, Maurice Meerte, Stan Wood and others.

28 Johnny Root, "Canadian news," *Metronome*, August 1938, 30

29 "Stan Wood at Auditorium," Montreal *Star*, 29 Dec 1941, 8

30 Advertisement, Montreal *Star*, 7 Jan 1944, 9

31 Advertisement, Montreal *Star*, 30 Jan 1942, 15

32 Robichaud: Montreal *Star*, 16 May 1939, 8; *Down Beat*, 1 Apr 1943, 21. Gariépy: Montreal *Herald*, 12 May 1945, 20. The drummers Mack Wein and Johnny Gilbert were also touted as Canadian Gene Krupas.

33 Duke Delory, "Montreal has young dance band on way," *Down Beat*, 15 Jan 1944, 14

34 The standard jazz reference works erroneously cite Ferguson's place of birth as Verdun.

35 Bob Redmond, "Crew of teen age clicks in Montreal," *Down Beat*, 15 Jul 1942, 15

36 James Warrick, "Personal reflections of a jazz great," *The Instrumentalist*, February 1986, 15

37 Maynard Ferguson, "My early days in music," *Coda*, July 1959, 20

38 Scott Yanow, "Record Review Interview: Maynard Ferguson," *Record Review Magazine*, August 1979, 46

39 "Local artists serve up good brand of jazz," Montreal *Herald*, 7 Jan 1946, 12

40 Juan Rodriguez, "Keyboard wizard recalls the days jazz thrived here," Montreal *Gazette*, 28 Oct 1978, 53

41 Advertisement, Winnipeg *Tribune*, 29 Apr 1944, 24

42 Advertisement, Winnipeg *Tribune*, 1 Jul 1946, 14

43 "Verdun Pavilion opens tomorrow," Montreal *Star*, 21 May 1940, 8

44 Advertisement, Sydney *Post-Record*, 1 Sep 1945, 16

45 Don McKim, "Bands dug by the Beat," *Down Beat*, 15 Jul 1942, 27

46 Trent Frayne, *Liberty*, 15

47 O'Leary, *Maclean's*, 24

CHAPTER FOURTEEN

1 Ben Cline, "Toronto now has its Onyx," *Metronome*, November 1938, 40

2 Advertisement, Toronto *Star*, 3 Oct 1938, 16

3 "Toronto," *Metronome*, August 1939, 29

4 Don McKim, "War cuts down Canadian jobs," *Down Beat*, 15 Nov 1939, 20

5 Dillon O'Leary, "Hot Platter Patter," Toronto *Globe and Mail*, 17 Nov 1945, 19

6 "The Breeze Around," *Hush*, 8 Dec 1945, 7

7 David Lancashire, "Blues in the Clock Tower," *Music/Sound* [The Michael Snow Project] (Toronto 1994), 45

8 Henry F. Whiston, "Mostly about jazz," *Lindsay Clef*, May 1949, 8

9 Helen McNamara, "McNamara's Bandwagon," Toronto *Telegram*, 29 Jan 1949, 7

10 Leonard Kunstadt, "The story of Louis Metcalf," *Record Research*, 46, October 1962, 10

11 Ken Johnstone, "Mixed band," Montreal *Standard*, 26 Apr 1947, 16-17; William Brown-Forbes, "New Canadian mixed ork wows hot jazz fans," *Down Beat*, 21 May 1947, 12

12 Bruce Taylor, "Cabaret Circuit..." Montreal *Herald*, 29 Aug 1949, 18

13 There has been some confusion about the place and date of recording for Wilk Wilkinson Boptet's *Wilk's Bop* and *All The Things You Are*. Litchfield, *Canadian Jazz Discography*, 757, suggests Toronto circa 1949, while Gilmore, *Swinging in Paradise*, 140, posits Montreal in 1950. The Café St. Michel advertised Wilkinson's "Recording Orchestra" in the Montreal *Herald* as early as 30 Sep 1949. According to a report in the Toronto tabloid *Hush Free Press*, 1 Oct 1949, "Toronto's Monogram prexy [president] Chuck Darwyn [is] back from his Montreal visit, where he waxed a local 'Bop' group." The other musicians involved were Willy Girard, Butch Watanabe, Herb Johnson and Steep Wade from the International Band, as well as Allan Wellman (trumpet), Fred Nichols (baritone saxophone) and Bob Rudd (bass). Wellman confirms Montreal as the place of recording.

14 In the spring of 1950, the International Band comprised Girard, Winestone, baritone saxophonist Art Pincus, pianist Valdo Williams, bassist Bob Rudd and drummer Al Jennings (Henry F. Whiston, "Metcalf in Montreal," *The Melody Maker*, 13 May 1950, 9). Other musicians known to have worked with Metcalf between September 1949 and November 1950 include tenor saxophonist Leroy Mason, pianist Sadik Hakim and drummers Kenny Edmonds and Bill Graham.

15 Barry Ulanov, "A trip to Toronto," *Metronome*, March 1948, 20

16 Ian Wiseman, "Carrying on," *Cities*, July/August 1988, 23

17 Herbie Spanier's later career is discussed in the author's *Jazz in Canada: Fourteen Lives* (Toronto 1982), 89-105

CHAPTER FIFTEEN

1 Windsor is now Peel Street; Osborne was integrated into a rerouted La Gauchetière.

2 Al Palmer, "Cabaret circuit..." Montreal *Herald*, 20 Oct 1948, 12

3 Paul H. Zemke, "Hot piano," *Maclean's Magazine*, 15 Oct 1945, 39

4 "4000 Winnipeggers agree Peterson is prince of piano," Winnipeg *Tribune*, 9 Mar 1946, 2

5 Harold Dingman, "Liberty Profile: Oscar Peterson," *Liberty*, 12 Jan 1946, 18

6 "Poll Tabulations," *Down Beat*, 15 Dec 1940, 19

7 Bud Herman, "Vancouver has new dance band," *Down Beat*, 15 May 1943, 11

8 Fes Fairley, "Canuck boogie boy a knock-out," *Down Beat*, 1 Aug 1941, 20

9 Bob Smith, "Just jazz," Vancouver *Sun*, 23 Dec 1965, 6A

10 Chris Gage's Vancouver career is detailed in the author's *Jazz in Canada: Fourteen Lives* (Toronto 1982), 65-85

11 Duke Delory, "Toronto player dies a hero in Europe," *Down Beat*, 1 Jul 1942, 13

12 Advertisement, Toronto *Star*, 2 Nov 1945, 13

13 Wade's encounter with Parker is detailed in the author's *Cool Blues: Charlie Parker in Canada, 1953* (London, Ont. 1989), 44-51.

14 CBC radio interview, 22 Nov 1945, quoted in the author's *Boogie, Pete & The Senator* (Toronto 1987), 211-12

15 Gene Lees, *The Will to Swing* (Toronto 1988), 38

16 Sean Edwin, "The Sound Track," Montreal *Herald*, 23 Nov 1945, 6

17 Lees, *The Will to Swing*, 51-52

18 Dingman, *Liberty*, 19

19 Herb Johnson, "Montreal doings," *Music Dial* (August 1944), 15; Basie's appearance at Danceland, and the jam session that followed at the St. Michel were the subject of a photo essay, "Jive," Montreal *Standard*, 15 Jan 1944, 20-23.

20 "Baron of boogie-woogie," Toronto *Star*, 5 Nov 1945, 18

21 Johnson, *Music Dial*, 15

22 All of Peterson's Victor recordings have been reissued in the two-CD compilation *Oscar Peterson: Beginnings 1945-1949*, BMG 74321-35105.

23 Gorman Kennedy, "Listening post," Montreal *Herald*, 3 Aug 1945, 16

24 "Man! That Re-Bop's hep, boogie passe," Vancouver *Sun*, 7 Oct 1946, 5

25 "1946 Band Poll winners," *Down Beat*, 1 Jan 1947, 20

26 Jim Buller, "Oscar Peterson," *Metronome*, January 1947, 56

27 Bruce Taylor, "Cabaret circuit..." Montreal *Herald*, 21 May 1949, 14

28 Lees, *The Will to Swing*, 63-68, examines the mythology and its contraditions.

BIBLIOGRAPHY

BOOKS

Reid Badger, *A Life in Ragtime: A Biography of James Reese Europe* (New York 1995)

Bricktop [Ada Smith Ducongé], with James Haskins, *Bricktop* (New York 1983)

Samuel Charters and Leonard Kunstadt, *Jazz: A History of the New York Scene* (New York 1962, 1981)

John Chilton, *Who's Who of Jazz* (London 1985)

— *McKinney's Music: A Biodiscography of McKinney's Cotton Pickers* (London 1978)

— *Sidney Bechet: The Wizard of Jazz* (New York 1987)

— *The Song of the Hawk* (London 1990)

Bill Coleman, *Trumpet Story* (Boston 1991)

James Lincoln Collier, *The Making of Jazz: A Comprehensive History* (New York 1978)

Eddie Condon, *We Called It Music: A Generation of Jazz* (New York 1947)

— and Hank O'Neal, *Eddie Condon's Scrapbook of Jazz* (New York 1973)

Stanley Dance, *The World of Earl Hines* (New York 1977)

— *The World of Swing* (New York 1974)

Paul de Barros, *Jackson Street After Hours: The Roots of Jazz in Seattle* (Seattle 1993)

Frank Driggs and Harris Lewine, *Black Beauty, White Heat: A Pictorial History of Classic Jazz* (New York 1982)

John Gilmore, *Swinging in Paradise: The Story of Jazz in Montreal* (Montreal 1988)

— *Who's Who of Jazz in Montreal: Ragtime to 1970* (Montreal 1989)

Jim Godbolt, *A History of Jazz in Britain 1919-50* (London 1986)

Robert Kimball and William Bolcom, *Reminiscing with Sissle and Blake* (New York 1973)

Gene Lees, *Oscar Peterson: The Will to Swing* (Toronto 1988)

Jack Litchfield, *The Canadian Jazz Discography 1916-1980* (Toronto 1982)

— *Toronto Jazz 1948-1950* (Toronto 1992)

Alan Lomax, *Mister Jelly Lord* (Berkeley and Los Angeles 1973)

Albert McCarthy, *Big Band Jazz* (London 1974)

Helen McNamara and Jack Lomas, *Bands Canadians Danced To* (Toronto 1973)

Edward B. Moogk, *Roll Back the Years: History of Canadian Recorded Sound and Its Legacy (Genesis to 1930)* (Ottawa 1975)

Brian Rust, *The American Dance Band Discography* (New Rochelle, NY 1975)

— *Jazz Records 1987-1942* (New Rochelle, NY 1978)

— and Sandy Forbes, *British Dance Bands on Record 1911 to 1945* (Harrow, Middlesex, England 1987)

Gunther Schuller, *Early Jazz: Its Roots and Development* (New York 1968)

— *The Swing Era: The Development of Jazz, 1930-1945* (New York 1989)

Michael Snow, ed. *Music/Sound* (Toronto 1994)

Eileen Southern, *Biographical Dictionary of Afro-American and African Musicians* (Westport, Conn. 1982)

Marshall and Jean Stearns, *Jazz Dance: The Story of American Vernacular Dance* (New York 1968)

Tom Stoddard, *Jazz on the Barbary Coast* (Chigwell, Essex 1982)

Ted Vincent, *Keep Cool: The Black Activists Who Built the Jazz Age* (London 1995)

William Weintraub, *City Unique: Montreal Days and Nights in the 1940s and 50s* (Toronto 1996)

Dickie Wells, *The Night People* (Washington, DC 1991)

E. Austin Weir, *The Struggle for National Broadcasting in Canada* (Toronto 1965)

Robin W. Winks, *The Blacks in Canada: a history* (Montreal 1997)

PERIODICALS

Ad Lib (Toronto), 1946-7

Down Beat (Chicago), 1937, 1939-49

International Musician (St. Louis, Newark, NJ), 1920-45

Metronome (New York), 1917-49

Others as cited in the footnotes

NEWSPAPERS

Calgary *Herald*, 1917-29

Canadian *Observer* (Toronto), 1914-19

Chicago *Defender*, 1915-1937

The Dawn of Tomorrow (London, Ont.), 1923-49

Edmonton *Bulletin*, 1917-20

Edmonton *Journal*, 1921-29

Hush (Toronto), 1943-49

Montreal *Star*, 1916-45

Montreal *Herald*, 1945-9

Ottawa *Citizen*, 1917-29

Regina *Leader*, 1917-29

Saskatoon *Star*, 1917-29

Toronto *Star*, 1917-1949

Vancouver *Sun*, 1917-1949

Winnipeg *Tribune*, 1917-1949

Others as cited in the footnotes

INDEX